THE
SOLITARY
SPY

THE SOLITARY SPY

A POLITICAL PRISONER IN COLD WAR BERLIN

DOUGLAS BOYD

The History Press

ALSO BY DOUGLAS BOYD:

Histories:

April Queen, Eleanor of Aquitaine

Voices from the Dark Years

The French Foreign Legion

The Kremlin Conspiracy: 1,000 years of Russian Expansionism

Normandy in the Time of Darkness: Life and Death in the Channel Ports 1940–45

Blood in the Snow, Blood on the Grass: Treachery and Massacre, France 1944

De Gaulle: The Man Who Defied Six US Presidents

Lionheart: The True Story of England's Crusader King

The Other First World War: The Blood-Soaked Russian Fronts 1914–22

Daughters of the KGB: Moscow's Cold War Spies, Sleepers and Assassins

Agente – Female Spies in World Wars, Cold Wars and Civil Wars

Novels:

The Eagle and the Snake

The Honour and the Glory

The Truth and the Lies

The Virgin and the Fool

The Fiddler and the Ferret

The Spirit and the Flesh

This book is dedicated to the memory of all the political prisoners detained in the Stasi's Lindenstrasse Interrogation Prison in Potsdam, and to our predecessors who suffered there under the KGB from 1945 to 1952 and under the Gestapo from 1933 to 1945.

Cover Illustrations: *Front*: Old prison wall in Siberia (locrifa/Shutterstock); *Rear*: 'Unity Bridge' during the Cold War (Author).

First published 2017

The History Press
The Mill, Brimscombe Port
Stroud, Gloucestershire, GL5 2QG
www.thehistorypress.co.uk

© Douglas Boyd, 2017

British Library Cataloguing in Publication Data.
A catalogue record for this book is available from the British Library.

ISBN 978 0 7509 6978 9

Typesetting and origination by The History Press
Printed in Great Britain by TJ International Ltd. Padstow

ACKNOWLEDGEMENTS

Like most writers, I have a retentive memory, but there would have been gaps in this narrative without the assistance received from several former comrades-in-arms of JSSL Intake 35.

John Fuller gave me a copy of his unpublished memoir and kindly allowed me to quote from it. John Anderson climbed several times into the loft – an activity not recommended at our age – to consult letters he had written home during National Service. Similarly, Alan Bamber perused many letters to his then girlfriend, whom he later married, and sent me digests. Duncan Brewer, Harvey May, John Toothill, Colin Priston, Brian Howe and Gerry Williams also racked their brains to check my recollection of specific events, while John Griffin displayed impressive powers of instant recall on the telephone. Ron Sharp suffered most, being awoken many times to be grilled before his breakfast over details of which I was less than 100 per cent sure – a technique I had picked up in the Lindenstrasse Prison.

My neighbour, former Coder Special Gareth Mulloy, has been a tower of strength, lending material and plundering his own and other coders' memories. The staff of the Bundesbeauftragte der Unterlagen des Staatssicherheitsdienstes der ehemahligen Deutschen Demokratischen Republik in Berlin were not just helpful, but extremely sympathetic, as was Gabriele Schnell at the former interrogation prison on Lindenstrasse in Potsdam, who gave me access to her archives of personal accounts of the Stasi's victims.

In Berlin, Dave Manley's widow Ingrid was a great help, digging back into her tangled past and arranging a visit to the former RAF Gatow, now the Luftwaffe Museum with its impressive collection of military aircraft, where the last German commandant was our guide and a fund of information.

It would be ungrateful indeed not to thank also my predecessors at JSSL, Geoffrey Elliott, Harold Shukman and Leslie Woodhead, whose fascinating books about times and places where I was not have been a precious resource.

In the production of this book, I have once again been immensely helped by the great tolerance of my wife, Atarah Ben-Tovim, living with a historian who is mostly 'somewhere and sometime else'. Jennifer Weller has again been a great support, not least for the maps. At The History Press, I thank commissioning editor Mark Beynon, who first suggested that I write this book, editors Lauren Newby and Vanessa Le, and marketing executive Rebecca Barrett.

CONTENTS

LIST OF ILLUSTRATIONS

LIST OF ABBREVIATIONS

AC1   Aircraftman First Class
AC2   Aircraftman Second Class
AFN   American Forces' Network broadcasting organisation
A level   Advanced (higher) level of General Certificate of Education
AMP   Air Member for Personnel
AMT   American Military Train
BAFV   British Armed Forces Voucher (forces currency)
BMT   British Military Train
BRIXMISS   British Military Mission
BStU   Bundesbeauftragte der Unterlagen des Staatssicherheitsministerium
                der ehemaligen Deutschen Demokratischen Republik (Stasi archives)
CND   Capaign for Nuclear Disarmament
CO   Commanding Officer
CPGB   Communist Party of Great Britain
DDR   Deutsche Demokratische Republik (Stalinist East German state)
DF   Direction Finding
DI   drill instructor
EOKA   Ethniki Organosis Kiprion Agoniston (Anti-British Greek Cypriot
                underground fighters)
GCHQ   Government Communications Headquarters
GDR   German Democratic Republic
GRU   Glavnoye Razvedatelnoye Upraveleniye – Soviet military intel-
                ligence organisation
HUMINT   Human Intelligence, i.e. spies
HVA   Hauptverwaltung Aufklärung – External espionage arm of the Stasi
ICBM   intercontinental ballistic missile
IED   improvised explosive device
IM   inoffizieller Mitarbeiter (Stasi informer)
IRA   Irish Republican Army
JSSL   Joint Services School for Linguists
J/T   Junior Technician (rank)
KGB   Komityet Gosudarstvennoi Bezopasnosti – Soviet Committee of
                State Security
LAC   Leading Aircraftman (rank)
MfS   Ministerium für Staatssicherheit – Ministry of State Security of GDR

MO	Medical Officer
MP	Military Police
MT	Motor Transport (Section)
NAAFI	Navy Army and Air Force Institutes (cash canteen and shop on military premises)
NATO	North Atlantic Treaty Organisation
NCO	non-commissioned officer
NKVD	Narodny Komisariat Vnuktrennikh Dyel – Soviet State Security organisation pre-KGB
NSA	National Security Agency
NVA	Nazionale Volksarmee
OHMS	On His/Her Majesty's Service
OKW	Oberkommando der Wehrmacht – German Army High Command
O level	Ordinary (lower) level of General Certificate of Education
POW	Prisoner of War
PTI	Physical Training Instructor
RAF	Royal Air Force
RIAS	Rundfunk im Amerikanischem Sektor – Radio in the American Sector of Berlin
RN	Royal Navy
RTO	Railway Traffic Office(r)
RTU	Returned to Unit
SAC	Senior Aircraftman (rank)
SAS	Special Air Service
SED	Sozialistische Einheitspartei Deutschlands – Socialist Unity Party of GDR
SIGINT	Signals Interception
SOE	Special Operations Executive
SOXMISS	Soviet Military Mission
SSEES	London University School of Slavonic and East European Studies
Stasi	Staatssicherheitsministerium – Ministry of State Security of GDR
TICOM	Target Intelligence Committee Missions
USSR	Union of Soviet Socialist Republics
VHF	very high frequency
Wop	wireless operator
WRNS	Women's Royal Naval Service

FOREWORD

On 7 June 2014 Ben Farmer, defence correspondent of the *Daily Telegraph*, reported that the Ukrainian crisis had exposed a critical shortage of Russian-speakers in Her Majesty's forces, so that senior intelligence staff had been trawling veterans' groups to find retired linguists prepared to don headphones again and help fill in as interceptors, of which the Commons Defence Select Committee reckoned there was a shortfall of 700 posts. There was, therefore, little possibility of real-time SIGINT (signals interception) if Downing Street's barbs aimed at President Putin finally provoked a reaction in the bullring of realpolitik. The reason was that, for the past two decades, language training in the forces had apparently concentrated all its resources on Arabic, Farsi and Pushtu.

In May 2016 Douglas Chapman, MP for Dunfermline, stated in Parliament, 'There are now only fifteen members of Her Majesty's armed forces who can speak Russian to a reasonable level'.[1] That news would have come as a shock to retired National Service Russian linguists like the author and also to the 'regular' linguists who replaced us when National Service was abolished. However, intelligence gathering has changed massively since we snooped in real time on Soviet Air Force traffic in Gatow and elsewhere. Among the 5,000-plus operators at GCHQ in Cheltenham, one would hope that there are more than fifteen men and women who speak and understand the language of President Putin.

One would similarly assume that the armed forces of the Russian Federation have trained thousands of competent English-speakers. And yet, on the day after the shooting down of Malayan Airlines flight MA17 over Ukraine on 17 July 2014, a senior Russian Air Force general showed radar plots of its flight route, which indicated that the aircraft had been diverted by Kiev Air Traffic Control from the 'safe corridor' used by all civilian flights and that the missile had come from Ukrainian Government forces. His commentary in this important broadcast was translated with great difficulty by a female officer, whose command of English was less than fluent.

Of course, SIGINT has changed. The British Government's Intercept Modernisation Programme was announced in 2009 to 'allow communications data capabilities for the prevention and detection of crime and protection of national security to keep up with changing technology'. In this time of data mining, instead of pencils and log pads, black boxes entitled 'deep packet sniffers' are used to suck in and sort out every Internet connection, text message, phone call and credit card use of everyone on the planet via snooper satellites, so that when an ISIL terrorist in Iraq calls his mum in the UK an alarm bell rings in Cheltenham. So, that's all right, then.

Or maybe not – algorithms, not human operators, now decide what is important traffic and what is not. Yet, even the massive computers at the National Security Agency (NSA) in Fort Meade, Maryland, can crash, like the time in 2003 when they were all offline for three whole days. Was the hacker responsible one of the team traced to IP addresses in China that hacked into the Pentagon several times in 2007? Nobody talks about it.

But it is worth wondering whether the fate of the world will one day hang on the use of the last-resort hotline connecting the Oval Office in the White House and Putin's bunker beneath the Moscow Kremlin. It would be sad if neither president could find anyone on his staff linguistically equipped to talk to the guy at the other end of the line.

Douglas Boyd
South-West France, 2017

INTRODUCTION

On the evening of 1 October 2008 a heterogeneous group of tourists assembled in the private dining room of a beer cellar in the centre of Berlin, literally a stone's throw from the Kaiser Wilhelm Gedächtniskirche, a landmark at the eastern end of the fashionable Kurfürstendamm. Built by Kaiser Wilhelm II in the 1890s, this large church was substantially remodelled by British bombs on the night of 23 November 1943. With only the spire and part of the entrance left standing, it was afterwards dubbed with typical Berliner wit '*der hohle Zahn*' – 'the hollow tooth'. Originally due to be demolished at the end of the Second World War, it was left standing instead as a memorial – to what exactly is uncertain.

The eight men in the group assembling in the beer cellar had all served in Britain's Royal Air Force, but were not responsible for the damage, being ex-National Servicemen who had been conscripted during the Cold War and served on the ground in Berlin, then known as 'the divided city' because it was split into French, British, American and Russian sectors, the whole surrounded by the bleak, no-go vastness of the self-styled German Democratic Republic – the least democratic and most repressive Stalinist state in Eastern Europe (see map, p. 24).

Five of the six women present were wives of the men. The sixth was the widow of one of their comrades. Ingrid Manley was a Berliner, born and bred, whose groundwork had done much to make the visit a success, but she was not the reason why this reunion was being held in Berlin, which since 1990 was once again the capital of a united Germany. That decision had been taken at the previous year's reunion dinner, as the most fitting way to mark the fiftieth anniversary of the men's arrival in Berlin on 23 July 1958. That it was being held two months late was due to the quirkiness of reunion ritual: the date having been graven in stone as conveniently near the end of the summer vacation, back when most of the attendees were at university in the years following their demobilisation from the RAF half a century earlier.

At the top of the table, John Anderson had been a head teacher in the Midlands and was still an active Methodist preacher. Next to him, Alan Bamber was a retired IT specialist from the West Country. Dave Bruce was older than the others, his call-up having been deferred while he qualified as an accountant in Aberdeen. John Fuller was a Church of England priest. Brian Howe, a retired teacher from Bristol, was the British organiser of the 2008 event. Colin Priston, the tallest, literally by a head, was a former Hong Kong civil servant. Still with the accent of his native Bradford, John Toothill had for many years been the warden of the Lake District National Park. Douglas Boyd, author of this work, had been a BBC Television producer and impresario before becoming a novelist and going straight as a historian for the past twenty years.

There were five men missing from the group assembled in the beer cellar. Retired company director Ron Sharp was at home in London, where his wife had not long to live. Harvey May was in parts unknown – fittingly for a man with a long career in British Airways behind him. Sometime Jesuit novice Gerry Williams was not well enough to travel. Retired head teacher John Griffin was otherwise committed. Of the others, there was some dispute over which held the record for non-attendance at the reunions. It was the only ex-regular in our intake, Duncan Brewer, who had certainly never been to a single one. Two men from the group had died: Nottingham solicitor Dick Moffat and globe-trotting Dave Manley, whose last years had been spent working for the European Union in Kazakhstan.

Other diners looking in might well have wondered what bonds of personal chemistry could have brought together those eight men at what was, for most of them, an annual reunion, for which the venue changed each year. The answer is: their shared experience as spies, snooping on the massive armed forces of the Soviet Union and other member states of the Warsaw Pact during the long period after the Second World War when the world was poised on the brink of nuclear war (of which the acronym was MAD – standing for Mutually Assured Destruction). They were, in short, survivors of Intake 35 of Britain's top-secret Joint Services School for Linguists (JSSL).

The programme of other activities arranged by Ingrid included a tour of central Berlin and a visit to the former RAF airbase at Gatow, where the men had served. Some were going on afterwards to visit other places of interest in Germany before heading home. The author's itinerary included a railway station where he had been arrested by men with loaded guns and the former political prison in Potsdam where he had subsequently been held incommunicado in solitary confinement under interrogation by the Staatssicherheitsdienst – the secret police of a government that had no diplomatic relations with Great Britain – and, even more terrifyingly, by officers of the KGB.

PART 1

2.3 MILLION MEN

1

THE REASON WHY

Lenin's foundation of the Communist International, or Comintern, in March 1919 launched a clandestine struggle to destroy the Western democracies from within by industrial sabotage, infiltration of their trade unions, and subsidising armed rebellion, especially in colonial countries.[1] However, the Soviet Union ended the Second World War against the Axis powers with huge, well-equipped armies and air forces that had advanced into Europe and occupied territory many hundreds of miles to the west of the former Soviet borders, giving supremo Josef Stalin the military power to continue the expansion of the Russian Empire by less subtle means. The political pressure on the British Prime Minister and the US President to 'bring the boys home' had no counterpart in the USSR, ruled by the General Secretary of the Communist Party of the USSR, whose vague title masked Stalin's total power over 170 million Russians, other Slavs, Balts, Caucasians and Asian races in the Soviet Union.

At the Potsdam Summit Conference in July 1945 – only two months after the final German surrender – the new US President Harry Truman and the new British Prime Minister Clement Attlee realised that Stalin intended to 'adjust' the southern frontier of the USSR, shared with Russia's traditional enemy Turkey, as though it had been an enemy belligerent in the Second World War, during which it was neutral. Iran being known to have substantial reserves of oil, Stalin also intended to keep significant Soviet forces in that country, through which massive amounts of Western materiel had been delivered to the Soviets during the war.

The agreed date for withdrawal of Western and Soviet forces from Iran was 2 March 1946, on which day British forces in central and southern Iran began to withdraw, but Soviet troops stayed put in the north of the country, not leaving until May 1946 – and then only because Iran was the first country to use the UN Security Council to resolve the deadlock. This was a shot across Stalin's bows, proving the observation a century earlier by British Foreign Minister and Prime Minister Lord Palmerston:

It has always been the policy and practice of the Russian Government to expand its frontiers as rapidly as the apathy or timidity of neighbouring states would permit, but usually to halt and frequently to recoil when confronted by determined opposition; then to await the next favourable opportunity to spring upon its intended victim.[2]

Keeping a wary eye on the US Sixth Fleet deployed in the eastern Mediterranean, Stalin did just that, reluctantly complying with the UN resolution.

On 5 March 1946 Britain's wartime premier Winston Churchill, who had failed to be re-elected in the 1945 General Election, made a speech at Fulton, Missouri, in which he contrasted the realities of life in the Soviet Union with the Anglo-Saxon tradition of civil freedoms epitomised in Magna Carta, the Bill of Rights, the principle of habeas corpus, trial by jury, English common law and the American Declaration of Independence. He went on to say:

A shadow has fallen upon the scenes so lately lit by the Allied victory. Nobody knows what Soviet Russia and its Communist International organisation intend to do in the immediate future, or what are the limits, if any, to their expansive and proselytising tendencies. I have a strong admiration and regard for the valiant Russian people and for my wartime comrade, Marshal Stalin. There is deep sympathy and goodwill in Britain – and, I doubt not, here also – towards the peoples of all the Russias and a resolve to persevere through many differences and rebuffs in establishing lasting friendships. We understand the Russians need to be secure on her [sic] western frontiers by the removal of all possibility of German aggression. We welcome Russia to her rightful place among the leading nations of the world. We welcome her flag upon the seas. Above all, we welcome – or should welcome – constant, frequent and growing contacts between the Russian people and our own people on both sides of the Atlantic.

It is my duty however – for I am sure you would wish me to state the facts as I see them to you – to place before you certain facts about the present position in Europe. *From Stettin in the Baltic to Trieste in the Adriatic an iron curtain has descended across the Continent.*[3] Behind that line lie all the capitals of the ancient states of Central and Eastern Europe. Warsaw, Berlin, Prague, Vienna, Budapest, Belgrade, Bucharest and Sofia, all these famous cities and the populations around them lie in what I must call the Soviet sphere, and all are subject in one form or another, not only to Soviet influence but to a very high and, in some cases, increasing measure of control from Moscow.[4]

Churchill's oratory was such that the nineteenth-century metaphor 'Iron Curtain' was thought by many to be his own creation on the spur of the moment, so graphically did it describe the fate of the Central and Eastern European countries occupied by Soviet troops. Russia's Central Asian and Caucasian possessions had historically enjoyed few links with the West, but the Baltic States, Czechoslovakia, Hungary and Poland had been part of Europe geographically, politically and culturally – as had been Eastern Germany and Austria, Bulgaria, Romania and Yugoslavia. Now, they were like a fast vanishing mirage: geographically still of the Continent but politically distant as their puppet governments imposed by Moscow punished brutally all dissent and any unofficial contact with the West brought severe sanctions.

During a US Congressional debate on 16 April 1947 the American financier and presidential adviser Bernard Baruch labelled the stand-off between the Soviet bloc and the Western democracies for the first time as 'the Cold War'. Political commentator Walter Lippmann picked up the apt expression and used it as the title of a book. By September, it was in use worldwide because it exactly described the increasingly dangerous tension between the two power blocs, in which the temperature was kept below flashpoint for half a century thanks to nuclear weapons, ensuring that this new kind of war was waged on political, economic and propaganda fronts by the major 'belligerents' and would turn hot only on the periphery of their spheres of influence in the form of proxy wars, notably in Korea, Malaya, Vietnam and Africa – and in the Cyprus emergency 1955–59 and the Suez invasion of 1956.

The complete Sovietisation of Central and Eastern Europe began in Russian-occupied Germany and Austria, plus Poland, with Czechoslovakia losing its democratic freedoms in February 1948 and Hungary after the elections of May 1949. The essential technique used was the same everywhere. As recounted by Wolfgang Leonard, one of Walther Ulbricht's team of puppet leaders in the Soviet zone of occupied Germany, they were told by him not to appoint Communists as head of any public authority except the police. The population was deliberately misled about the Soviet takeover by the selection of respected bourgeois figureheads from other parties, who could be controlled behind the scenes by their deputies, all of whom *were* Communists. Thus, there was an appearance of democracy in local and national governments, but control lay firmly with the Moscow-dominated Communist Party in each country.

The West's response to this was the North Atlantic Treaty Organisation (NATO), founded on 4 April 1949 and numbering among its member states Belgium, Canada, Denmark, France, Iceland, Italy, Luxembourg, the Netherlands, Norway, Portugal, the United Kingdom and the United States. Greece, Turkey, West Germany and Spain joined later.

As preparation for NATO, Britain's Socialist Government led by Clement Attlee brought in the National Service Act of 1948, which introduced for the first time in Britain universal peacetime conscription for all physically fit men aged 18 or over. Being protected from invasion by sea in all directions, the United Kingdom had traditionally relied upon the Royal Navy to police the seaways, and kept a far smaller standing army than most European countries, which had extensive land frontiers to defend. The passing of the Act put 2.3 million young British men in uniform, at first for eighteen months, then from 1950 to 1960 for two years of their lives, followed by three years on the Reserve, liable to recall should the Cold War suddenly heat up. The last conscripts were finally demobilised only in 1963. Of these young men, almost 2 million served in khaki, with 433,000 in RAF blue-grey and a mere handful in the Royal Navy's bell-bottoms and Jack Tar caps. For the majority of conscripts, especially during endless months of fatigue duties in the army, the enemy was boredom, summed up in the maxim, 'If it doesn't move, paint it white. If it does move, salute it.'

Tens of thousands of conscripts did, however, see active service abroad, many of them with the British Army of the Rhine occupying the British zone of occupied Germany. By 1951 British and Commonwealth forces were also engaged in the Korean War (1950–53) alongside predominantly US and South Korean forces and contingents from many other countries, in a war whose grim monochrome images in magazines like *Picture Post* were far from the genial, jokey world of the TV series *MASH*. Certainly for 13-year-old boys like the author, aware that they too would be in uniform in just five years' time, they were scary.

Because the USSR was a member of the United Nations Organisation, US pilots flying Lockheed F-84 and Republic F-80 jets who got into close-quarters dogfights with MiG-15 jets painted in North Korean or Chinese colours, were warned not to speak about the white Caucasian pilots flying them,[5] who were Second World War Soviet fighter aces sent by Stalin with the 3,000-plus men of his 64th Fighter Corps. Although wearing Chinese uniforms and ordered to use only their basic Korean on the radio, the Russian pilots occasionally resorted to swearing in their own tongue when in a tight corner – which was a bit of a give-away when the transmissions were intercepted. And intercepted they were, as when one pilot announced in March 1953 to a comrade, *'Stalin umer'* – 'Stalin has died'.

During that war the Royal Navy kept at least one aircraft carrier on station, as did the Royal Australian Navy. Other Commonwealth countries also sent warships. A National Serviceman named Bill Tidy – later to become a famous cartoonist – found himself detailed off to control the loading and unloading of merchant shipping at one important Korean port. Placed in charge of 2,000 Japanese dockers, he rose to the occasion but, wearing only a corporal's stripes, was surprised at first by the excessive traditional Japanese respect shown by his work force to their two-stripe 'general'.[6]

Less fortunate young Britons found themselves fighting in the hostile winter climate of the Korean mountains against human waves of North Korean and Red Chinese soldiers, most famously at the vehicular ford across the Injin River, a traditional invasion route targeting the South Korean capital, Seoul. On 22 April 1951, 650 men of the Gloucestershire Regiment found themselves attacked from all sides by a complete division of 10,000 Red Chinese soldiers. Equipped with no radios, the Chinese commanders transmitted orders by bugle call, causing a British bugler to be ordered to sound various British Army calls in the hope of confusing the enemy.

They certainly confused his own side. Just forty of the 'Glorious Glosters' escaped back to their own lines, leaving over 600 men dead, wounded or force-marched as prisoners of war (POWs) to death camps and brainwashing sessions on starvation rations in the north.

A contributory factor in the disaster was said to be a British commander back at headquarters telling his American opposite number, 'Things are getting a bit sticky at the ford'. The typical tight-lipped British understatement was misinterpreted as meaning that massive US artillery support was unnecessary when it might have given the besieged men a chance to break out.

Soviet expansion into Central and Eastern Europe post-1945.

In 1953 Soviet infantry and tanks were used on the streets of Germany's divided capital to suppress the 17 June uprising against Moscow's puppet government of the so-called German Democratic Republic (GDR). Western forces watched across the Potsdamer Platz, but did not intervene. Although direct conflict between the two superpowers was generally avoided, French forces in the colonies of Indochina fought their own war against the Communist Viet Minh from 1946 to 1954, when Washington's refusal to actively support the government in Paris saw that war fizzle out after the massive French defeat at Dien Bien Phu in May 1954. Having allowed the

French colonial and Foreign Legion forces to bleed to death in Indochina, Washington then sent more than half a million American troops to Vietnam after France signed a peace treaty with Ho Chi Minh, thus prolonging the agony of the Vietnamese people by nearly two decades of increasingly industrial-scale destruction and killing, in which millions died, but open conflict between the superpowers was again avoided.

The United Kingdom's parallel 'hot war' was in Malaya (1948–60), where the British-trained Malayan People's Anti-Japanese Army of guerrilla fighters had been disbanded in December 1945. Despite various incentives to hand in their weapons, some 4,000 mainly Chinese fighters controlled by the Malayan Communist Party went underground – actually under the trees of the jungle – fighting an anti-colonial war to drive out the returning British authorities. The conflict was never officially dubbed a war because London insurance companies would not have compensated the British owners of tin mines and rubber plantations that were sabotaged and destroyed. So it was quietly agreed that this was to be called 'the Emergency'. It became more than an emergency when the defoliant Agent Orange was sprayed from the air as a weapon of war onto jungle sheltering the insurgents and onto civilians' crop fields – provoking genetic damage which is still blighting a third generation of sufferers – and in the process providing President Kennedy with a precedent for using Agent Orange in Vietnam with even worse effects.

Commonwealth troops from as far away as Fiji and Rhodesia were drafted into Malaya where, despite an amnesty offered to the guerrillas in the jungle in September 1955, the war that dared not say its name continued.

On the other side of the globe in Hungary, virtually an entire nation rose up against Soviet oppression and the Soviet-controlled secret police in October and November of 1956 in a rebellion that cost 2,500 Hungarian lives and countless injured. Nearly a quarter of a million Hungarians grabbed the moment when the frontier was unguarded to flee into Western Europe and claim political asylum.[7] It was at this point in the sometimes hot Cold War that the author and his coevals entered the lists, although not as combatants.

In a turf battle between the British external intelligence organisation known as the Secret Intelligence Service (SIS) and the domestic counter-intelligence service designated MI5, the latter won the job of carrying out counter-intelligence in Malaya. (Knowledge of this curious arrangement would later enable the author to identify an MI5 watcher at JSSL Crail.)

After the Malayan Emergency ended officially on 31 July 1960, Britain's National Servicemen who were unfortunate enough to become involved in this dirty war were reborn as the unlikely heroes of the light-hearted 1969 film *The Virgin Soldiers*.

National Servicemen also risked being killed and had to kill others in Kenya during the Mau Mau uprising (1952–60) and in the Franco-British-Israeli Suez Invasion (October–December 1956). Although Prime Minister Sir Anthony Eden famously told the House of Commons that the invasion was not a war but just 'a state of armed hostilities', young Britons died, were wounded or suffered post-traumatic stress there. A 19-year-old Liverpudlian friend of the author, while on night sentry duty in a British camp near Suez, saw an intruder crawl under the perimeter wire, challenged him, received no reply and fired one shot, killing the Egyptian dead. Sixty years later, he is still traumatised by the memory of that night.

2

THE JOINT SERVICES SCHOOLS FOR LINGUISTS

When the Cold War began – or, in historical perspective, recommenced in 1945 after the end of the Western Allies' uneasy alliance with the USSR against Nazi Germany[1] – Britain's three armed services had very few commissioned officers and hardly any other ranks who could speak the language of the new enemy. Some tuition in Russian had been previously conducted in the forces, including an intensive course for regular army officers at King's College London, completed by a four-month total immersion spell with Russian émigré families in Paris or elsewhere in Western Europe. Although the millions of refugees, then dubbed 'displaced persons', in Europe could furnish plenty of interpreters, the urgent need for forces personnel who could themselves speak Russian led to the first large-scale training scheme to produce Russian-speakers: in 1945–46 Anglo-Russian academic Professor Elizaveta Hill planned and ran a six-month course in Cambridge for about 200 Russian-language interpreters, required to serve in liaison capacities on the staff of the Allied Control Commission in occupied Germany. At the University of London's School of Slavonic and East European Studies (SSEES) twenty servicemen and four women also attended a course that continued to supply small numbers of service personnel competent in Russian and other East European languages.

In 1949, when the continuing need for large numbers of Russian-speakers was obvious, the Ministry of Defence began to study ways of setting up courses to train National Service conscripts. After the outbreak of the Korean War in June 1950, the duration of compulsory military service for men aged

18 and over was extended from eighteen months to two years, giving sufficient time for in-depth Russian language training followed by a period of service in the field as 'war translators' and a longer course for 'interpreters', who would then be available for recall during their time on the Reserve after their full-time service had ended. An eventual figure of 4,000-plus National Service Russian-speakers was thought adequate. In addition, the Air Ministry laid on four twelve-month courses for up to forty regular officers and other ranks, mainly from the RAF.

In 1949 the first language school in the series later designated Joint Services Schools for Linguists opened in Kidbrooke, south-east London, transferring to Coulsdon, near Croydon, two years later, where it continued until 1954.[2] In October 1951, after much committee toing and froing, courses commenced for the two levels of student at JSSL Bodmin in Cornwall. When this camp closed, JSSL Crail in Scotland functioned until 1960, also supplying small numbers of Polish and Czech linguists. Perhaps because students were drawn from all three services, the total number trained in the several JSSLs is surprisingly not known. The most reliable estimates vary between 4,182 and 4,270. The higher-level 'interpreter' courses run at London and Cambridge universities were fed by the highest scorers in a major test sat by all students after six to eight weeks at JSSL.

Civilians often scorn the military way of doing things, when usually the problem lies with the politicians in charge. However, for once, the urgency of the situation and the inadequacy of the existing language training facilities impelled an efficient approach on both planes, Prime Minister Attlee and his Socialist Cabinet giving the go-ahead for one of the most impressive training schemes of any armed forces anywhere. It was thought that the brunt of a future Soviet attack would be by air, with the major burden of response falling on the RAF, which would need more trained Russian-speakers than the army, with the Royal Navy requiring only a few linguists, designated Coders Special, to serve aboard warships confronting the Soviet Navy. In the RAF, Russian graduates of JSSL were designated Linguist A, but there was also tuition at RAF Tangmere, near Chichester, where small numbers of Mandarin-, Cantonese-, Polish-, Czech- and later Hungarian-speaking linguists were produced, designated Linguists B for Cantonese, C for Mandarin, D for German, and so on.

However, the majority of the armed forces' language students were studying Russian. Being an inflected language, it is far more difficult for English-speakers to acquire than French or Spanish. Even German and Latin, inflected languages commonly taught in British schools at the time, use the same alphabet as English, whereas Russian is written in a modified Greek alphabet, has many grammatical peculiarities that do not come easily to Western Europeans and verbs with perfective and imperfective 'moods' that often do not resemble each other – e.g. *idti* and *khodit*, both of which mean 'to go', as do a confusion of other verbs, depending on whether one is walking, travelling in a vehicle, once or several times, etc., etc.

That there are no definite or indefinite articles also takes some getting used to, and the converse is also true, one female Russian instructor asking the colonel in the mess at JSSL, 'Would you please pass water'. *Odyin*, meaning the number one, takes the nominative case of its noun, which seems logical, but *dva*, *tri* and *chetyrye*, meaning two, three and four, take the genitive singular; and subsequent numbers use the sometimes baffling genitive plural.

Just when the student has got to grips with that, he learns there are alternative numerals, starting *yedinitsa*, *dvoika*, *troika* for one, two, three, and so on. Since the student linguists were mostly being trained for interception of SIGINT traffic, where critically important encoded messages were usually expressed in five-number groups, Russian numerals had to become – as the modern cliché has it – part of each student's DNA.[3]

With almost all the National Service recruits lacking even basic knowledge of any Slavonic language, let alone of an eastern Slavonic tongue written in Cyrillic script, there could be no equivalent of a three-month brushing up of school-learned A level French or German for service use. Quite logically, the training scheme of what were initially referred to as 'war interpreters' was divided at the outset into an advanced interpreter's course and an academically lower-level linguists' course. The interpreters' courses, on which the students wore civilian clothes, were conducted in small groups in association with London and Cambridge universities and lasted the full two years of National Service. Being designed to produce Reserve officers fluent in Russian to the point of being capable of liaison duties, administration of occupied territory or taking command of thousands of POWs in the event of a shooting war, they were intensive to the extent that most alumni considered the work far harder than their subsequent university courses. The lower-level linguists' course lasted seven and a half months and produced SIGINT operators with better than A level command of Russian grammar, pronunciation and comprehension, including a fair vocabulary of words like *mashinostro'itelny zavod* (machine-tool factory) and *nizhny krai oblachnosti* (cloud base) which one would not need for reading Tolstoy or Dostoyevsky.

In addition, the students needed specialist technical training to intercept and log in real time, during their second year of service, clipped Soviet military radio transmissions frequently larded with obscenities – which also had to be learned – and partially inaudible due to bad reception. At each of the two levels, the JSSL method was extremely well thought out and effected with the minimum of 'bull' and discipline from 1951 to 1960.

The vast majority of the students on JSSL courses were not wearing uniform by choice, but any natural resentment at their forcible conscription was tempered by the awareness that their service lives were among the best that could be enjoyed by National Servicemen, although mentally very demanding. Weekly tests were built into the schedule and failure on more than one due to lack of application or the intellectual inability to keep up was automatically punished by the dreaded initials RTU, standing for Returned To Unit – i.e. the world of 'blanco and bull' – for the rest of one's service. For many students, in addition to learning Russian, JSSL acted as a finishing school in which they mixed daily with other young men from all social backgrounds, who went on to become ambassadors, actors, writers, barristers, journalists, poets, painters, university professors of many disciplines, a Governor of the Bank of England, a BBC Controller of Music, MI5 and SIS officers, the director of the National Theatre Sir Peter Hall, and a director and deputy director of Government Communications Headquarters (GCHQ). Traitors George Blake and convicted paedophile Geoffrey Prime, the latter uncovered due to his sexual crimes, were also graduates of JSSL.

Of the four alumni who became nationally famous playwrights, neither Michael Frayn nor Alan Bennett found material to use in their plays in the fourteen-hour days they had spent studying on the interpreter course. Yet Jack Rosenthal wrote the successful 1992 TV film, *Bye Bye, Baby*, based on his time as a Coder Special.

Dennis Potter turned his experience of several months as a linguist working in the War Office for MI3(D) deciphering soiled Soviet 'toilet paper' into the script of the 1993 television series *Lipstick on your Collar*.[4] Among the attributes of modern life with which the cash-strapped Soviet armed forces did not provide for their millions of men was toilet roll, so soldiers relieving themselves on exercises were in the habit of tearing up recently outdated code books and other documents for use as 'bumf'. Potter confessed that he and his comrades wondered how the soiled sheets of paper arrived so fast in Whitehall.

The answer lies in Operation Tamarisk, in which the officers assigned to BRIXMISS – the British Mission permitted (with some harassment) to travel around the Soviet zones of occupied Germany and Austria as observers – stopped at open-air latrines that had been used on Warsaw Pact exercises and scooped up the sheets which, presumably after being sanitised, were flattened out on the desk of Potter and his comrades to reveal who-knows-what dirty secrets.

The quid pro quo for BRIXMISS was SOXMISS, composed of Soviet officers similarly allowed to travel more or less freely in the Western zones of the two occupied former belligerent states. Other trained army linguists posted to MI10 yawned their way through Russian newspapers and magazines in the soporific search for they were not quite sure what. Although the author's comrades in RAF uniform did not complain of this, apparently many army linguists had to interrupt their shifts in the set rooms to 'clean the bogs' – surely one of the greatest wastes of money in military history.

Finding Russian-language instructors for JSSL was not, at the time, too difficult. A few were British officers who had acquired Russian before or during the war. In time, some were themselves the product of JSSL; but the majority of teaching staff were fluent Russian-speakers of Slav, Baltic or other Eastern European origin. They were an odd bunch of refugees in two generations. The younger ones were fugitives from post-war Soviet 'justice' who had managed to make it to Paris or Britain without being handed back to Stalin's murder squads in Central Europe,[5] plus some more recent defectors who had successfully made a home run. The older generation were educated men and women of bourgeois or noble origin who had escaped to the West during or just after the October Revolution. Among the more colourful were an ancient, moustached cavalry colonel, who limped with a wooden leg in place of his own, lost while fighting the Reds in the Russian Civil War, and a countess who always dressed in black because she was in lifelong mourning for Tsar Nikolai II and his family, murdered at Ekaterinburg in July 1918.

As to premises for a hush-hush school for spies, Britain was littered with unused military camps, abandoned since the war. The first choice was Kidbrooke in south-east London, where the RAF set up a modest Russian language school for regular officers and NCOs as early as 1946. Commanded by Flight Lieutenant Wood, it aimed to produce thirty trained linguists a year in a twelve-month programme, but this output was soon proven manifestly insufficient for eventual Cold War conditions.

By 1950 a Ministry of Defence Working Party on Russian linguists approved a two-tier approach. It was thought that Cambridge University could host as many as 300 student interpreters, with a further 150 being trained at London University, but the main priority was to train many hundreds of men for SIGINT, the interception and logging in real time of the radio traffic of Soviet and other Warsaw Pact armed forces. Whereas the interpreter courses occupied virtually all the obligatory two years' service, it was vital for the linguist students to complete their training much faster, so that they could put in several months of SIGINT work before they were demobbed.

There were, of course, many Russian-speakers in Western Europe who could have performed these tasks but, for security reasons, it was not considered a good idea to have foreigners in such top-secret activity, particularly if they had relatives living in the target countries and could thus be pressured into betraying details of their work. The JSSL tutors of foreign origin might also be subject to pressure but, since they were involved only in instructing in Russian language, history and culture and were not supposed to know what specialist technical training their students received after leaving JSSL, nor the work they did after posting to Berlin-Gatow, Butzweilerhof near Cologne, Cyprus, Hong Kong or the many other listening posts on secure services premises across the world and afloat on the Baltic and other seas, there were few secrets the tutors could betray.

This was a time of austerity in Britain – food rationing did not end until 4 July 1954 – so the cost of setting up tuition facilities and staffing them was under close scrutiny. The Treasury's allocation of £200,000 to get the project off the ground made this far-sighted plan the equivalent of a multi-million pound initiative in today's money. In 1951 Clement Attlee's Socialist Government sponsored the Festival of Britain to mark the centenary of Prince Albert's 1851 Grand Exhibition as a way of declaring that the United Kingdom had recovered from the devastation and cost of the Second World War. There was also talk of it heralding 'a new Elizabethan age' because HRH Princess Elizabeth, who would become head of state at her coronation in June 1953, was already frequently making public appearances instead of her increasingly ailing father, King George VI.

In September of that year the first two JSSLs were installed in camps at Bodmin in Cornwall and Coulsdon, near Croydon. The Coulsdon contingent was accommodated in huts that dated back to the First World War, belonging to the Brigade of Guards Depot, and stayed in use until 1954. As alumni have commented rather smugly, the mostly bespectacled and untidy JSSL students were a bizarre contrast with the 'shaved-scalp, razor-creased and shiny-booted neighbours' on the other side of the camp.[6] But the intellectual stimulation of the course did not generate body warmth, and the makeshift huts were so unbearably cold in winter that students used to glean reusable lumps of clinker from the pathways of the Guards Depot in the hope of getting some heat out of the ancient cylindrical stoves. JSSL Coulsdon closed in February 1954 after a final parade had been inspected by no less a person than the Director of Military Intelligence – surely rather a give-away, since no staff member or student was supposed to know the point of the training.

3

BODMIN

The Coulsdon students transferred to Bodmin, a market town in Cornwall with population of 6,000 at the time, lying halfway between Exeter and Land's End, where not much had happened in the millennium and a half since St Petroc (Patrick) founded a monastery there. Flight Lieutenant Wood came from Coulsdon to serve as deputy commanding officer of the Bodmin JSSL under a Royal Navy commander who had been a wartime interpreter in Japanese, doubtless considered by their lordships of the Admiralty to qualify him for the job.

Accommodation for the students was in barracks known as Walker Lines, a collection of wooden huts erected at the start of the Second World War just off the A38 main road. It had been used to accommodate men returning from the disaster at Dunkirk in 1940 and also as a holding tank for US troops in the build-up to D-Day in 1943–44. More recently, it had been the headquarters of the Army Education Corps. It is now the site of an industrial estate.

For the five years of its existence, JSSL Bodmin was almost universally detested by students and instructors for its lack of comfort, even by service standards, and for its isolation and the bitter winter weather with blizzards howling in from the eponymous moor that must have reminded some instructors of Siberia. Heating of the draughty wooden huts, each accommodating fourteen men, was by Cannon No. 20 pot-belly stoves left behind by the Americans, with so voracious an appetite for fuel that students were driven to make nocturnal raids on the coal pile outside the sergeants' mess. The water heating arrangements being even more inadequate, water for shaving after reveille at 0630hrs often had to be warmed in each man's enamel mug on the stoves, if they were still alight. In one winter when the pipes were frozen solid for several days on end, designer stubble was accidentally invented because nobody could shave, electric shavers then only being seen in a few Hollywood films.

Body heat also suffered, the quality of the food having been a source of discontent at several JSSLs, in many cases because the catering staff were augmenting their pay by selling supplies on the black market and feeding the students dishes like macaroni cheese several times a week instead. On one memorable occasion, a sentry stopped a motorbike leaving Walker Lines and discovered that the sidecar was well named: the 'sleeping soldier' slumped in it was a whole side of bacon camouflaged in a battledress jacket.

In terms of recreation, Bodmin was the pits, its main claim to fame being thirteen pubs, which no student ever managed to drink his way through in one evening, although several tried valiantly. The ironically termed Palace Cinema showed few films to tempt the young intellectuals temporarily foisted on the town and films shown in the camp theatre tended to be uniformly boring Soviet propaganda. The 'camp' attraction, in the other sense of the word, was provided by the gay bar of the St Petroc's Club, whose host was the boyfriend of ultra-masculine film star Eric Portman. His choice of background music was limited to the louche and suggestive replaying of the song from the musical *Kismet*, 'Take my hand, I'm a stranger in paradise …'. There was a local dance hall, the Tremarrow Palais de Danse, where an intrepid Russian-language student might hope decorously to hold a girl for the duration of a dance, but the atmosphere was described by one student thus:

> As we stride in, a quartet of apple-cheeked natives approaches us and we are forced to drink a quart of cider each … We discuss the local chapels and we perform the heart-wringing West Cornwall Schottische. Then we are beaten up and thrown out [while] down on the beach the local men huddle around their beacons and wait for the pleasure-steamers to pile up on the rocks.[1]

In short, Bodmin was not much fun.

The teaching staff comprised eight service officers, eight British civilians, twenty-two of Russian or Soviet origin, fifteen Poles, six Latvians, two Ukrainians, one Estonian, one Lithuanian, one Czech and one listed as 'stateless' – with only three women in all.[2] Scheduling the teaching activities of this heterogeneous bunch to cover the overlapping, incoming and outgoing intakes would have been a headache for experienced academic administrators, let alone Flight Lieutenant Wood and his boss. In addition, no less than 120 other essential staff under the adjutant furnished cooking, cleaning, clerking and all the other paper-pushing activities of a military establishment. That the camp administration was in army hands while the students belonged to all three services, was an additional complication.

Inevitably, some instructors were less charismatic than others, and were rated by their more critical pupils in units based on the Russian for 'boredom' – which is *skuka* – on a scale going through multiple 'skuks' to 'megaskuks' and finally 'killerskuks', of which the last was reputed to be potentially fatal.[3] One Bodmin alumnus recalled the slightly crazy atmosphere of this vintage of Russian language training being epitomised by an early lecture delivered by a seedy old Slav, who took the assembled students on a verbal tour of the city of Moscow, during which they had to parrot each of his sentences. After he proclaimed, 'You are in park. *V parkye*. In bloody Moscow. You see woman with big breasts – *s bol'shimi grudinkami*',[4] 200 solemn youthful voices repeated, '*s bol'shimi grudinkami*', as 200 brains stored *grudinki* (breasts), singular *grudinka*, in the right notional pigeonhole alongside *golova* (a head), *noga* (a foot or leg – yes, really) and other body parts.

Each year's four intakes – at first called Translator Entries – arrived in February, May, August and November. Although initially it had been planned to juggle which students were sent to Bodmin and which to Coulsdon, this proved an unnecessary extra complication on top of the movement orders, pay and kitting-out arrangements, rationing requisitions and accommodation of the students. The differences in the disciplinary methods of the three services – the army being strictest and the navy most relaxed – were eventually ironed out because study was paramount.

So loose were the reins of service discipline that the pressure which drove the students to swat up in their spare time was largely self-generated, against the background threat of being returned to their parent units as the penalty for unsatisfactory progress. As to the level of linguistic proficiency achieved, it was generally reckoned by those monitoring the students' progress that the linguist courses raised knowledge of Russian from zero to between A level and university entry standard in less than eight months, while the interpreter courses in London and Cambridge, lasting a year longer, took their students to the level expected after a three-year university course.

Tensions based on politics, generation and nationality between the various factions among the instructors regularly provoked feuds – which makes it all the more commendable that the staff were somehow welded into an efficient teaching force by the camp administration. Instructors being only human, some clicked with their students and some became objects of mockery for their eccentricities. Most eccentric was Mr Koshevnikoff, who claimed to have been auditioned by Diaghilev for the Ballets Russes. He was prone to lying on the floor during lessons or leaving the classroom altogether to smoke outside, cigarette held between thumb and index finger in the Russian manner, while conducting the lesson through an open window.

Taken prisoner in the interventionist wars that followed the October Revolution and held in a POW camp for several years, Mr Dudariv had afterwards been held at a German POW camp, then a British camp for displaced persons in Germany. This was followed by a spell as an agricultural labourer in Britain before somehow being hoovered up to teach at JSSL. Sympathy or pity being in short supply among his students, he was reduced to pleading, 'If you fail your examinations, they will send me back to the fields and factories'. Another instructor burst out one day with, 'You don't know what slavery is until you have lived in the Soviet Union!'[5]

The least likely instructor to find in a military camp was Dmitri Makaroff, a White Russian born in Shanghai, who had grown up in Australia before bestowing himself on Europe. A man of undoubted creativity, Dmitri's great love was the theatre, where he had many professional friends. In an ambiance of typically Russian chaos, he co-wrote and directed with Koshevnikoff a production of *Boris Godunov*, enhanced by costumes that Dmitri had borrowed from a friend at Covent Garden. That was in 1953. In 1954, with the advent of the Coulsdon contingent, the two thespians produced a modern-dress version of *Hamlet* in Russian. Not content with that, Dmitri also produced *Othello*, in which the part of Desdemona was a feminine tour de force by a future British ambassador. Since all these plays were in Russian, the military side of the camp could only approve and politely applaud.

In the last offering to a few unappreciative locals and some dozing students, Dmitri – later to become an Orthodox monk – stole the limelight by taking the part of Bodmin's saint in *The Vespers of Petroc*, staged in the parish church with permission from the Bishop of Truro amid a choking cloud of incense fumes from several walk-ons enthusiastically swinging their censers, while Koshevnikoff was the backroom boy who translated everything into Russian and wrote the play.

This was probably the apogee of JSSL's creativity, with the Last Post sounded shortly afterwards by a steam locomotive pulling a specially chartered train out of Bodmin's station in 1956, transporting the 700-strong personnel, including students, instructors and administrative staff, plus all the paraphernalia of classroom teaching, to an almost equally inhospitable home nearly 600 miles to the north. Their departure was a severe blow to the local economy of central Cornwall, estimated as a loss of £100,000 a year in 1956 values.[6]

The destination of the special train was Crail in the East Neuk, or corner, of the so-called Kingdom of Fife that juts out into the North Sea between the Forth of Tay to the north and the Firth of Forth to the south. It was described by King James VI of Scotland as 'a beggar's mantle fringed wi' goud' – the golden fringe being the sea coast with several harbours, once packed with herring boats so numerous that one could cross from side to side by stepping from one boat onto the next and so on. By the time of JSSL's arrival, the North Sea herring shoals had been overfished to extinction and the medieval trade with the Low Countries in wool and salt was evidenced only by Dutch tiles brought back as ballast, to be seen on the roofs of the older cottages.

It was rumoured that the new location – formerly a Fleet Air Arm shore establishment named HMS *Jackdaw* and an underage boys' training school named HMS *Bruce* in the late 1940s – had been chosen to place the secret school in close proximity to Scotland's secret bunker, an enormous underground complex of accommodation and control rooms constructed as a Regional Seat of Government at the height of the Cold War in 1951, just a few miles distant, its entrance concealed from any Soviet bomber overhead beneath a fake Scottish farmhouse.[7]

On visiting a salt mine at Winsford in Cheshire, the author learned that the government had also allocated it as a safe hideaway for 'important people' in the event of nuclear attack. The plan was foiled by the men working the mine giving an ultimatum: they would not let the bigwigs go down the mine unless they and their families could also enjoy the same protection from the hazards of nuclear warfare. It seems the Scottish workers excavating and constructing the bunker near Crail were more malleable. As to its proximity to the spy school – was the intent to have a reservoir of linguists able to mediate between the 'important people' in the bunker and successfully invading Soviet troops? It seemed more likely at the time, to those who bothered to think about it, that the isolated site at Crail was chosen because it simplified the watch for illicit snoopers, although who was in charge of the very low-profile security of the camp was a mystery to the students.

Isolated JSSL Crail certainly was, being situated astride the narrow road from Crail village to the shoreline at Balcomie. The barrack huts can still be seen north of the road, halfway between the village and the coast. The school closed after the end of conscription in 1960, leaving the three services to make their own separate provisions for future language training, as they had prior to the opening of the JSSLs and, to some extent, during their existence. The Fleet Air Arm runway between the road and the shore has become a drag-racing venue – to the annoyance of Crail folk, whose peaceful Sunday afternoons are disturbed by hundreds of spectators' cars driving through their streets. The buildings of yesterday's linguists in the upper camp may still be seen clearly on Google Earth™, but are now inhabited by tomorrow's bacon, for HMS *Jackdaw*, aka HMS *Bruce*, aka JSSL Crail, is now a pig farm.

4

BASIC TRAINING

My own National Service obligations began some time before my 18th birthday in August 1956 with a summons in an unstamped envelope bearing the magical formula 'OHMS' to a medical examination in Chatham. Like most young men at the time, I had no desire to don Her Majesty's uniform, being a 'bolshie' youth – the epithet then not necessarily connoting Bolshevik sympathies, but simply bloody-mindedness. In my first years at the grammar school in Canterbury I had been flogged three times with a bamboo cane by the headmaster but, by the time I reached the first year of the sixth form he had grown tired and ill, stumbling short-sightedly towards retirement. I exploited the resulting decline in discipline by refusing to do games or physical education and regularly cut classes to read French and Spanish books and debate their content with a like-minded classmate, seated in the cloisters of the famous cathedral.

My generation had lived through the Second World War, some of my coevals had fathers who had been starved to death in Japanese POW camps, shot down over Germany, drowned by Admiral Dönitz's U-boats in the Atlantic, blown to pieces after treading on a mine in the North African deserts or just shot by the chance of war. However, a current joke was the fake advertising slogan, 'Join the Army, travel to distant lands, meet interesting people – and kill them'. Believing that any future war would be worse than the one I had known, it seemed to me that the price of peace was eternal vigilance, although I did not wish to be one of the vigilantes.

It being unlikely that I could claim conscientious objector status, since I did not conceal my atheism and thus had no clergyman or Nonconformist minister likely to plead in my favour, I arrived in Chatham on the due date, to join a couple of hundred other young men, clad only in underpants, who stood shivering in a long queue that shuffled along towards a seated man in white coat over army khaki. He was checking us for hernias by yelling, 'Drop 'em!' and grabbing each man's testicles quite hard, then shouting, 'Cough! Next! Drop 'em!', until he reached the last man in line. Another man in white coat over a khaki uniform shone a torch into the men's ears and a third white-coated man slapped a stethoscope very briefly against each man's bare chest. My father being in a tuberculosis sanatorium, I had a vague hope that the stethoscope would reveal a blip on my lungs, but it proved to be neutral.

Once dressed again, all those who were not obviously unfit, mentally subnormal or physically handicapped sat a simple aptitude test – something, if I recall correctly, to do with spanners and hammers, and which I refused to fill in. The bored conducting officer, an RAF flight lieutenant, said, 'You have to do the test. It's obligatory.'

I whispered back, 'Not for me. I've been preselected for the Russian course.'

To get rid of me, he wrote 'Preselected for Russian course' on my otherwise pristine paper. Already bilingual with French, and speaking fluent Spanish and reasonable German and Italian, plus O level Latin, I was determined to be one of the 4,000 young intellectuals who had the amazing good fortune to spend half their compulsory military service in intensive Russian language training at the JSSL, about which I had learned from older alumni revisiting the Simon Langton Grammar School for Boys in Canterbury during my last year there. Of what the second year of National Service might bring, I had no idea.

After a deferment of my call-up to enable me to sit the exams of the Institute of Bankers, in which I failed to pass the requisite three subjects at each attempt – fortunately, for this was long before bankers awarded themselves enormous bonuses for mediocre performance – I was duly called up in May 1957 and sent a railway warrant to travel to Cardington in Bedfordshire. A youthful ambition to join the Royal Corps of Naval Constructors – in those days, the Royal Navy designed its own ships and supervised their construction in British shipyards – had incited me to join the Sea Cadets, a youth organisation run by RNR and RNVR officers with the help of retired chief petty officers, petty officers and seamen. With the cadets I had enjoyed free visits to Chatham Dockyard, one unpaid trip across the Channel and even spent some all-expenses-paid holidays in naval barracks.

RAF Cardington was similar, except that its landmark feature was a pair of enormous hangars built to accommodate airships in the 1920s. After the tragic crash of the Cardington-based R101 near Beauvais in the early hours of 5 October 1930, killing forty-eight of the fifty-four passengers and crew in the explosion and fire fuelled by the enormous volume of hydrogen filling the main body of the dirigible, Britain abandoned lighter-than-air craft and the hangars were used for testing and repairing barrage balloons and training their handlers throughout the Second World War. The hangars were so monstrously big that – so we were told – clouds sometimes formed inside them and rain fell in there when it was fine outside.

Recruits who had been at boarding schools were able to take this introduction to military life in their stride, but some who had never left home before were very disturbed by the lack of privacy in barrack huts, each sleeping twenty or so men, during the week at Cardington. Another shock was to be deprived of all civilian clothes, which had to be parcelled up and sent home, symbolising loss of individual identity. We were kitted out with uniforms and all the trivia required for two years' service: a battledress uniform and beret for everyday wear, our 'best blues' with peaked cap for ceremonial wear, greatcoat, shirts, a tie, socks, underwear, hobnailed boots and cleaning materials. There was even what Queen Victoria's Tommy Atkins had called his 'hussif', or housewife – a cloth roll of pouches containing needles of various thicknesses, spools of thread, a hank of wool for darning holes in our socks, a thimble, safety pins and other miscellaneous items for minor repairs during our service.

Men's hair was not worn long in those days before young people had 'attitude', but in a style known as 'short back and sides'. Even this was not short enough for the RAF, so each man got a two-minute 'haircut' with a pair of electric clippers, leaving us with no hair showing below the rim of the beret. Lastly, we learned that we were no longer, for example, a person called Douglas Boyd, but '5044577 AC2 Boyd, sir!' AC2, standing for 'aircraftman, second class', was the lowest rank in the RAF. We were also known as 'sprogs'.[1]

The service number became so ingrained that half a century later, when proving my identity to a very pleasant National Insurance man in order to substantiate my claim for a state pension, I was asked, 'Do you recall your RAF service number?' Obviously, I had not used it for decades, but it tripped immediately off my tongue.

I asked, 'Isn't that strange, that I still remember it?'

He replied, 'Almost everyone does.'

In confirmation of our new identities, we received the all-important Form 1250, a photographic identity card to be carried at all times and handed in on demobilisation at the end of our two years' service – although mine was then embarrassingly in enemy hands.

By the end of the week, the more robust recruits were thinking that service life was not too bad, but the real stuff lay just ahead. From Cardington, we entrained for Wilmslow in Cheshire, a leafy and affluent suburb of Manchester, which then contained in its heart a hell officially known as No. 4 School of Recruit Training, into which we would be locked for most of a six-week period of basic training. On emerging from Wilmslow's railway station we were assailed by a pack of corporal drill instructors (DIs), yelling orders at us. Kitbags were slung aboard a convoy of grey RAF 3-ton trucks but we, wearing greatcoats in the middle of May, were marshalled into ranks and marched at the double – i.e. running in a muck sweat – what seemed like a mile or more to the camp, with the DIs screaming orders at us all the way until we were brought to a shuddering halt in a drill shed where the kitbags had been dumped on the concrete floor. After more screaming, sometimes with the screamer's face inches away from the victim's, we were harried 'at the double' in squads of twenty-one – making seven ranks of three men abreast – across the camp to our billets, kitbags bumping up and down on our left shoulders. No sooner had we collapsed on our beds than the DI entered to give us our first lesson in service etiquette: when he entered the room, the first man to see him must shout, 'corporal present!' Immediately, all must stand to attention at the end of their beds, silent and staring straight ahead, because he was, for the next six weeks, God.

God sauntered along both sides of the room, looking at each of the twenty-one recruits as though a dog had left it on the pavement. 'What have I done,' he yelled, 'to get a load of shit like you dumped on me?' He stopped in front of an older man, a qualified engineer from Glasgow, whose call-up had been deferred while he sat the Higher National Certificate examinations. We were callow and frightened youths, but the Glaswegian was taller and solidly built, and did not look afraid.

'You are the Senior Man,' the DI announced. 'Understood? When I am not present, you are responsible for this rabble.'

'Excuse me, Corporal,' someone said. 'I need to go to the lavatory.'

There was an incredulous pause, followed by a scream of, 'Do it in your pants, and don't EVER address me again unless I tell you to. And the rest of you, do NOT turn and look at shitty-pants. In my presence, you face the front until I order you to face some other way.' His voice became more nearly normal. 'Now, my last squad were quite good when I'd finished with them. They left this place tidy, but you lot have walked all over the lino in your boots. Scratches everywhere!' He stamped his studded boots with each step, deliberately gouging more scratches in the waxed linoleum of the floor. 'You men NEVER walk on this floor, or you'll spend every night polishing it until I can see my face in it.' He pointed at piles of oblong pieces of wax-impregnated felt carpet underlay by the doors. 'You take two of those, one under each foot, and shuffle – so that you polish the floor with every step. Got it?'

The harangue continued with a demonstration of how to make our five blankets and two sheets into a bed pack, assisted by a public school man who had been in his school cadet force – and a few more DOs and DON'Ts, (mostly DON'Ts) until the DI suddenly lost interest. 'Senior Man! March these filthy pigs to the trough for their tea. After that, they will all take a shower and wash their hair and clean their teeth before pressing their uniforms and polishing the floor like a mirror. Got that?'

'Yes, Corporal!' yelled Senior Man.

The food in the canteen, noisy with a couple of hundred men eating, was fine by me, but other recruits must have had mothers who were better cooks than mine. In reply to the orderly officer's shout of 'Any complaints?' a few tentatively raised their hands. 'Good,' he beamed, 'Cook needed some volunteers to scrub the greasy tables outside the back of the cookhouse. At the double, move!'

Senior Man was wiser, murmuring quietly, 'What is this shit, anyway?'

I could see the cans behind the counter labelled *Pomodori spelati*, so I translated, 'Peeled tomatoes from Italy, Senior Man.'

He chuckled, 'You must be our resident intellectual. There's one in every barrack room, I'm told.' I would have found Italian easier to understand than his Glaswegian accent, but that's what I understood him to say.

The lights went out at what we already called 2200hrs, by which time we thought we had done a good job re-polishing the floor. I padded through the darkness in my socks, holding my boots, boot polish and brushes to get to work in the showers, where the lights stayed on all night. The others were also there, polishing cap badges and boots, with the exception of the public school man, who had finished, and Senior Man, who had paid someone else to polish his boots.

In my ignorance, I had thought a bit of polish and a vigorous brushing would suffice. I found most of the others grouped around an old sweat who had re-enlisted. Heating the handle of his spoon over a cigarette lighter flame, he melted polish and forced it into the dimpled toecap of each boot, rubbing and adding more polish and generous gobbets of spit for half an hour until the dimpled leather was as smooth and shiny as patent leather. I had not previously understood the expression 'spit and polish', which was a remnant of Tommy Atkins' Victorian English. The old sweat was paid in cigarettes by men who watched his demonstration. With one in the corner of his mouth, from time to time he muttered words of advice. One was that he should really be Senior Man, 'not that great Scottish oaf'. Another was that we did not know what was going to hit us, next morning on the parade ground.

An hour later I thought my boots looked good, although his perfect shine eluded me. The DI had warned us he wanted every man and the billet spick and span at 0630hrs. It was well after midnight when I crawled into bed, leaving several men still in the showers, pressing their trousers on the one ironing board while one or two were still fighting their toecaps, which I thought not as good as mine. Somewhere in the back of my mind, I wondered whether that thought was really worthy of the intellectual I believed myself to be. Had I capitulated already?

After breakfast on day two at Wilmslow – more Italian peeled tomatoes with soggy bacon, sausage and greasy fried bread – we stood rigidly at attention beside our beds, only one of which passed muster. From somewhere the public school man in the next bed to mine had procured pieces of cardboard and secreted them in his bedding to give sharp edges to his 'biscuit' of immaculately folded sheets and blankets, with all his kit laid out as shown in a large poster at the end of the billet. The DI looked disappointed, but managed to find fault with the hussif turned the wrong way round. There were about 500 faults with my bed pack, which ended up on the floor, necessitating each blanket and sheet to be refolded in the approved manner. Other men had an even worse time, with every item of kit hurled about, making it hard to recover the right ones. Although nobody was struck, the violence and anger of the DI inculcated a feeling of fear that did not leave us until the end of basic training.

Kit inspection over, we were taught to march in formation by the DI wielding a pace-stick to regulate each step of the tallest and smallest to the

Queen's favourite length of 30in. On the parade ground twenty or more squads were going through the same manoeuvres, the shouted instructions of their DIs merging into a cacophony of 'BY THE RIGHT … AS YOU WERE … THAT MAN … DID I SAY RIGHT ABOUT TURN? … SHOWER OF SHIT! … ARE YOU BLOODY DEAF OR JUST STUPID?' Without making the mistake of turning our heads, the other corporal DIs, who appeared to have been cloned, came and went in our peripheral vision. Few were tall, but all wore their immaculate best blue uniforms with shining boots, and had 'slashed' their caps to bring the peak down over the forehead, forcing them to hold their heads back and appear to be looking down their noses even at men much taller than they were with an expression of constant disdain.

About ten o'clock – sorry, 1000hrs – several squads were dismissed for a 'Naafi' break.[2] Not having earned that privilege, we were kept at it in the grey drizzle until midday, when we nearly missed lunch (called dinner), because the billet had to be tidied first for that afternoon's inspection. After doubling to the canteen under Senior Man's orders, with our mugs and 'irons' held in the left hand behind the small of the back – leaving the right hand free for saluting, of course – we just made it before the doors were closed, and queued for shepherd's pie with boiled cabbage and the inevitable peeled Italian tomatoes, followed by rhubarb crumble and custard. This time, no one complained.

As it was still raining, we stayed in the billet until the DI appeared, some men fingering the two rows of rifles chained to a rack in the centre of the billet and speculating when we would get to fire them. The answer was never: they were just for drill, and polishing inside and out, as we later learned. At the double, we were marched across the camp to a drill shed where, defying the rain, we marched and counter-marched, ears straining for our DI's commands against the echoes of all the others' orders bouncing off the walls. The boots hurt my feet. With a blister growing on one heel, I was wondering how long this could go on. One by one, the other squads were dismissed, but each time we executed a manoeuvre, somebody got it wrong, so we had to do it again. The culprit was often the same man, a gangly youth with spectacles who had been at a Steiner school and seemed unable to co-ordinate his limbs normally. For the first time in my young life, I appreciated how a group could come to hate one member and turn on him. Finally, long after all the other squads had left, the DI halted us and walked up and down the ranks, shaking his head. He did not even bother to do that with Steiner Man, but walked straight past him.

'Senior Man,' he said, 'do you know how long I've been a drill instructor?'

'No, Corporal.'

'Three bloody years, during which I have turned several hundred useless fucking idiots into airmen, but in all that time I have NEVER SEEN SUCH A USELESS PILE OF SHIT AS YOU LOT. What are you?'

Nobody spoke.

'WHAT ARE YOU?'

A few voices answered uncertainly, 'A useless pile of shit, Corporal.'

'WHAT ARE YOU?'

At the top of our voices, we all shouted, 'A USELESS PILE OF SHIT, CORPORAL!'

'Good,' he said. 'So you've learned one thing today. Now, out of the goodness of my heart, I let you off easy this morning. Tomorrow's room inspection will not be so generous, so don't lie in your pits wanking all night, get that floor like glass before you go to bed, understood?'

'YES, CORPORAL!'

Shaking his head in mock despair – or maybe it was real – the DI said, 'Senior Man, march this pile of shit back to the billet at the double and then double them to the canteen. You may just make it in time for tea, if you're lucky.'

The tea itself, stewed for hours in huge canteen urns, had a taste somewhere between mushrooms and mothballs. For this reason, it was generally considered that it had been liberally dosed with bromide, to inhibit sexual desire. Yet, never had peeled tomatoes and stewed tea tasted so good, and the noise of a couple of hundred men talking and eating seemed almost peaceful after the din of the drill shed. The smell of wet uniforms drying on our bodies reminded me of the family dog after a walk in the rain, and for once I felt nostalgic.

And so the first week passed. After church parade, Sunday was a free day, on which Senior Man privileged us with a sight of pictures of what he said was his girlfriend. They were probably taken on a Box Brownie camera: rather fuzzy black-and-white photos of a curly-haired, skinny girl with a nervous smile and her legs wide apart, taken from all angles. Back in the pre-Internet age, we had cheesecake pictures of film stars on the cover of the weekend tabloid newspaper *Reveille* and topless girls in *Razzle* magazine, but even there the girls had their legs together or their knickers on. *Health and Efficiency* – a magazine that justified quasi-nudity by claiming to be for naturists – had photographs showing the joy of open-air table tennis and other jolly romps in the nude. The women had bare breasts, but the crotch area of both men and women was carefully airbrushed out, to produce a species of sexless angels. Like most of the others, I suspect, I had never seen pornography and thought this girl's rampant bush of dark pubic hair unattractive, although other men affected, or maybe felt, excitement. One or two took Senior Man up on his offer to borrow a picture for ten minutes in the toilets against payment of five cigarettes. I did not know what to make of this, but saw the other side of Senior Man when an aggressive little Cockney punched Steiner Man several times in the showers for all the grief he caused us, and was hauled off him and slammed against the wall with the warning in just-intelligible Glaswegian, 'Do that again, laddie, and I'll really hurt you. Leave the stupid cunt alone.' In fact, nobody else talked to Steiner Man, so that brief assault was the only contact he had had since we arrived in Wilmslow.

On Day One of Week Two some men were already crossing days off on their demob calendars, which I found too depressing for words, with twenty-three and a half months to go. That morning, the DI had to run his moistened finger along the top of a door to find some dust there because everything else in the billet was clean and the floor like glass. Steiner Man still got an earful on parade, but the two men whose beds were on either side of his had taken to making his bed pack and laying out his kit for morning inspection because it was easier than having the DI furious to start with. Someone even pressed his uniform a couple of times, to save him looking like a total scarecrow.

The corporal took a key from a uniform pocket and unlocked the chain on the gun rack, tossing one Lee–Enfield .303 rifle to each man. I just caught mine. Having avoided sports and PE at school by a series of forged sick notes, I had not built up the same muscles as some of the others and the rifle was far heavier than I had guessed. A couple, including inevitably Steiner Man, missed theirs entirely, which clattered to the floor.

'More floor polishing tonight,' was the corporal's only comment. 'The rest of you are going to love those men.'

Taking the last Lee–Enfield for himself, he ordered us to stand easy, the rifles against our right legs, butts tight against the right boot.

'Now then,' he said, 'anyone here like poetry?'

I adored French and Spanish poetry, but knew that was weird. And anyway, I had rapidly learned never to volunteer.

'I have a little poem for those of you as likes poems,' he continued. 'This is my rifle.' He patted it. 'And this is my gun.' He patted his crotch. 'One is for shooting and the other's for fun.' A couple of men sniggered, but he did not seem to have been expecting much reaction. Although made as weapons, for us the Lee–Enfields were for polishing, inside and out – and woe betide the man who went on parade with a speck of dust or fluff from the pull-through[3] visible to the DI's eagle eye when he squinted down the barrel with the breech open.

That first day with the rifles was warm and sunny, so we were in shirtsleeve order, sleeves neatly rolled up above the elbow. After half an hour's drill, our left collar bones were bruised and sore from the slamming of the rifles against them. I had seen many photographs of men in the Second World War shooting, drilling and marching with the same rifles. Whatever the Lee–Enfield was like on the battlefield, as a drill accessory it was punishing. Each time it slammed against my left shoulder I was in pain, but if any man tried to soften the blow, it made him late and the whole squad had to do the same drill again. Steiner Man excelled himself, dropping his Lee–Enfield a dozen times before having it taken away by the corporal and being ordered to stand at the edge of the parade ground. He was still there when we were dismissed and all except him doubled away to the Naafi in the hope of reaching the head of the queue before it was time to be back on the parade ground. When we returned to the billet at midday, Steiner Man's bed was bare, his kit gone and another recruit was sitting there. Later, much later, in the six weeks of pain and polish when we had 'got enough time in' and could occasionally talk to the corporal man-to-man, someone did ask him what had happened to our tame idiot. 'I 'ad him shot,' he said, deadpan. 'My squad has to win the drill competition, see? And that little shit was a sabbatewer. That cunt over there …', he nodded at another DI, '… put him on my list deliberate.'

Occasionally there were relaxed moments, like the afternoon when the corporal had us fall out on a stretch of grass for instruction in the parts of a rifle. His voice was like a terrier's bark, but in my imagination I heard the deeper voice of the regular sergeant in Henry Reed's evocative poem *The Naming of Parts* taking his recruits in 1942 through the same rigmarole, 'This is the upper sling swivel … and this is the piling swivel, which in your case, you have not got'. But there was no japonica in the neighbouring gardens, because none were in sight. As far as the eye could see, all was grey asphalt, blue-grey uniforms, grey buildings – apart from the grass on which we lay. It was a world of masculine monochrome, where the flash of colour from a dress or the sound of a woman's voice would have been as intrusive as a lightning strike.

Payday came at last. Even this was done by numbers: stepping smartly up to the table behind which a corporal and an officer sat, announcing one's number and name, placing one's beret on the table and seeing the money placed in it before executing a smart right turn, to make space for the next man. It all made sense, but seemed like a frozen moment from the Crimean War.

In the world outside RAF Wilmslow, May of 1957 saw two important political developments. On 23 May the British, American and French zones of occupied Germany fused together, becoming the Federal German Republic and a member of the North Atlantic Treaty Organisation (NATO), with an obligation to maintain military forces. In protest at the imminent militarisation of the new German state, on 15 May the USSR and the countries it occupied in Central and Eastern Europe united themselves in the Warsaw Pact, a military coalition designed to confront NATO. By the end of May, the two antagonistic power blocs were established, confronting each other for the rest of the Cold War, but this momentous moment went completely unnoticed by those of us being terrified daily on the square at School of Recruit Training No. 4.

I was looking forward to actually firing a rifle on the range as a way of validating all the bruising from the drill rifles on the square, but first we were lectured by the range sergeant on giving fire directions in the style 'eleven o'clock, bushy-topped tree, two men in ditch just to the right' and calculating 'aiming off' to allow for crosswinds deflecting the bullet from its intended path. It astonished me that mere wind could push a bullet off course. While appreciating the theory of ballistics, I discovered I was no marksman, my eyesight not being good enough. Given ten rounds, I hit the target card only twice, but nowhere near the bull, and bruised my right collar bone with the recoil. Handing me my card, the range sergeant said, 'This Cold War … if it ever turns to a shooting war, my advice is to shoot yourself. You might just manage that, if the wind is in the right direction.'

Unknown to me, sweating it out on the parade ground at Wilmslow in increasingly hot weather, other future linguists were enduring similar basic training at RAF West Kirby, designated No. 5 School of Recruit Training, and at RAF Bridgnorth, designated No. 7 School of Recruit Training. Presumably, the missing numbers 1, 2, 3 and 6 related to other out-stations of the Royal Air Force version of hell that had closed before our time.

Two of my future comrades suffered at West Kirby, where the poor eyesight of Dick Moffat, a qualified solicitor, was somehow responsible for a stray bullet passing very close to the range sergeant. Somewhat dyspraxic, Dick also set his uniform on fire while on parade by dint of stuffing his lit pipe into his pocket. He also failed to shine on fire drills, where he became entangled in the hose. There too, Colin Priston, who was the tallest member of our fraternity, found that if he stood straight his rifle did not touch the ground, for which he was bawled out by the DI. He could make it touch the ground by leaning sideways, but was then bawled out, 'Stand straight, that man!' His worst memory was of being set to trim the grass between the huts with scissors for an inspection by the Air Officer Commanding. Whether this was fully compensated by a passing-out outing arranged to Southport, where Priston and his fellow recruits danced and socialised with the girls from Littlewoods Pools, is unknown.

As the day of our drill competition at Wilmslow approached, there were – to my horror – moments when the simultaneous *crash!* of twenty-one pairs of boots – the origin of the expression 'square bashing' – the single slap of twenty-one palms against the magazines of the rifles at the 'present arms' and the crisp *crunch!* as the whole squad right- or left-turned at exactly the same split second, made me hold my breath. Confusingly, I felt ashamed that I took pride in us all 'getting good' after a short sample of the way whole armies had been made to work and fight as one man in pharaohs' Egypt, Nebuchadnezzar's Babylon, the Roman legions and all the goose-stepping Soviet and Nazi troops reviewed by Stalin and Hitler in the cinema newsreels.

Of course, we did not win the drill competition, that distinction went to another squad who doubled everywhere chanting what sounded like US Marines' marching songs. Senior Man, who knew the ways of the world, organised a whip-round for our DI during the last afternoon Naafi break. It amazed me that he got enough for a bottle of whisky. After dismissing us for the final time and with the rifles all chained up in the rack, the DI grinned, 'You're still shit. But you'll pass, lads.'

Strangely, the worst moment of those weeks was not the rifle drill, although collar bones stayed bruised and sore for a fortnight afterwards. On one hot sunny June afternoon towards the end of the basic training weeks, the wind blew in strands of gossamer transporting thousands of tiny spiders which crawled all over our faces and bare arms. It being forbidden to move on the square, even to brush off the torturous little arachnids, I counted the seconds, and suddenly realised – it sounds so trite when written down – that nothing lasts, and nor would this. It was a strange epiphany, but I never forgot that lesson, even when in jail.

Another bad moment was the gas chamber. On a different hot afternoon we were marched to a brick-built bunker on the edge of the camp, overlooking the London–Manchester mainline. Passengers rubber-necked at the windows of a passing train as the squad ahead of us emerged, eyes streaming, choking, gagging, and with two men vomiting onto the grass. When it was our turn, we put on the gas masks and entered the bunker, as ordered. The gas was turned on as we solemnly marched round and round. After a couple of minutes, the DI ordered us to remove the masks. I suppose we all tried to hold our breath, but it was impossible. And anyway, in that confined space, the gas hit our eyes first before burning its way into our lungs. Repeating in my head my new mantra that nothing lasts, it nevertheless seemed an age until the DI, still masked, opened the door and we stumbled out, bent double, half-blinded, eyes streaming, choking and racked with coughing that felt like vomiting and, for several, was. 'That,' said the DI, removing his mask and holding it up, 'is just to prove to you that these things do work.' Nobody disagreed.

But I forgave the system – Clement Attlee for introducing National Service and even the DI for all his bullying and screaming – after the three wonderful days when we were driven in trucks to the Derbyshire Peak District to live under canvas, sleep on groundsheets laid over springy heather and swing on a rope over muddy pools, clamber over obstacles and spend a day in small groups, navigating with map and compass across the roadless waste. The mosquitoes bit, the sunburn hurt, the muddy pools were wet and smelly and the cross-country march with blisters on both feet was exhausting, but the scenery had me spellbound. Being a southerner who had never seen the majestic untamed hills and moors of England's glorious north country, I had what I suppose a believer would call a religious experience: a sense of oneness with nature, the miracle of life and the great fortune of being young, fitter than I had even been before, and healthy. Did anyone else feel that? I've no idea. It wasn't the sort of thing men talked about, but for me it more than cancelled out everything else.

At the end of basic training and a week's home leave, I returned to RAF Wilmslow to find that the next Russian language course did not begin for several weeks, which I was to spend in the Pool Flight, where all sorts of odds-and-sods – in service parlance – killed time before their next posting. We no longer marched everywhere, but strolled, feeling very superior to the new intakes going through hell on the square and doubling to and from the canteen. A long-suffering flight sergeant known as Chiefy Lumm, who must have been near retirement, was theoretically in charge of Pool Flight. After he dismissed us at the end of a cursory inspection following breakfast each morning, we took the advice of another old sweat who had re-enlisted, to disappear in the direction of the fatigues allocated for that day. Once out of Chiefy Lumm's sight, we crawled under one of the huts – in this section of the camp they were built on piles – where we smoked and chatted the morning away, dropping our voices each time the wheels of Chiefy Lumm's bicycle and his desperately pedalling legs came into view on his perpetual search for his missing charges.

Others in the Pool Flight actually did the chores, as it was less boring than killing time. One man was given a pot of paint and a brush and ordered to paint some dried-out grass a vivid green – this for an inspection of the camp by a very senior officer. Another man, whom we got to know later at Crail, was Dave Bruce, a qualified Scottish accountant, who spent his weeks in Pool Flight putting some order into the accounts of the Officers' Mess, protesting, 'Their bookkeeping is simply abominable. It's a scandal!' When he had finished this chore, for the first time it was possible for the Mess President to see exactly who owed how much to the mess funds.

Dave was one of three other men awaiting the next Russian course at JSSL in the Pool Flight. The first one I met tricked me on the day of my arrival into taking his place on the fire piquet. He had the assurance of a man with one week's more service than me, so I innocently believed him when told it was my turn. At 2200hrs we were divided into teams of two men armed with pick handles, who patrolled the camp all night to give the alarm in the event of fire – or to attack an intruder with the pick handles, we supposed. Even in the Peak District I had never witnessed the dawn, and watching the sun come up over the hills of the High Peak next morning as the night fled west was another revelation, which did not stop me asking the trickster why he had put me on fire piquet.

'You told me you live miles away in Kent,' he grinned. 'It was my turn really, but I go home each night at the weekends because I only live 7 miles away. So you took my place.'

I had to admit it was neatly done, and played the same trick myself on newcomers, because I went home with him each weekend from then on, hitching our way back to camp at dawn on Monday in time for the morning parade. Sixty years later, he is still my closest male friend, although we should never have met in any other situation. As Field Marshal Slim said, 'National Service was good for the youth of the country, but it nearly destroyed the armed services'.

PART 2

SCHOOL FOR SPIES

5

RABOTA REALLY DOES MEAN WORK

Like Bodmin, Crail was well away from the bright lights of civilisation, the last leg of the long northward train journey being on the nineteenth-century Anstruther and St Andrews East Coast Line. It is presumably different for regular servicemen, but being a conscript in uniform numbs the brain. No journey planning is involved: the traveller is handed a travel warrant; this transforms into a ticket and, since one has not chosen to make the journey, little interest is taken in the scenery. After travelling all day, the author and forty-plus RAF fellow students for JSSL alighted at Crail Station like zombies awaiting the arrival of Doctor Samedi.

Not all arrived without problems en route. The men coming from No. 7 School of Recruit Training at Bridgnorth had only been given rail warrants for Leuchars Junction because Crail, being administered by the army, was 'not an RAF destination'. After the Admin staff at RAF Leuchars solved the problem – not for the first time – eventually all of us newcomers clambered aboard soft-topped military trucks, to be deposited at the end of a ten-minute drive in what would be our home for the following seven and a half months.

Although JSSL Crail was administered by the army, accommodation was in single-storey wooden barracks still named after admirals of the Royal Navy – Anson, Benbow, Collingwood, Drake and Frobisher. Whether one row of huts began with E, nobody can remember. Leslie Woodhead, who arrived there the previous autumn, described his first impression thus:

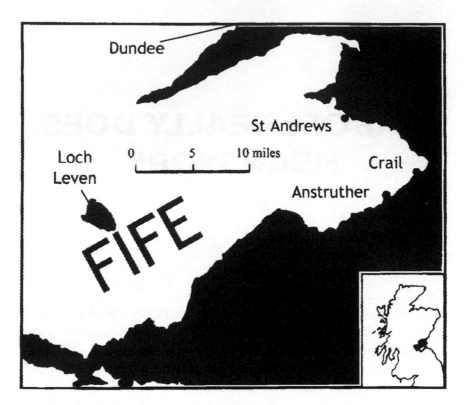

The Kingdom of Fife.

A pewter sea lined the horizon. A dank grey mist rolled to meet us, and the cold seeped through our stiff greatcoats. Then, like a black-and-white photo emerging from the developing dish, low huts began to take shape behind a barbed-wire fence. 'I suppose that's it,' someone said. 'Looks a bit like Stalag Luft 11.'[1]

Later, we too would come to know the winter face of Crail, with gales of rain, ice storms and blizzards sweeping in from the North Sea. On the evening of our arrival, we were dimly aware of men in the uniforms of all three services wandering about in the dusk. After breakfast on the following morning, we paraded at 0830hrs, army and RAF men wearing battledress and beret, with the much smaller navy contingent in bell-bottoms, jerseys, Nelsonian collars and flat, peakless caps. Army students still sported the distinguishing insignia of their various regiments and corps: a rainbow of shoulder flashes and berets in all colours and cap badges different for each regiment or corps, to which they still belonged administratively. We RAF students were in the majority, assembled for inspection by a Czech wing commander named Kaczmarczek, who was inevitably nicknamed 'Wingco Cash-My-Cheque'. He had flown with the RAF during the Second World War, and was presumably working out his time to pensionable age in this considerably less exciting job. The senior naval officer was named, unforgettably, Commander David Maitland Makgill Crichton and had achieved distinction not only on Second World War arctic convoys to Murmansk, but also by getting a First in the notoriously difficult Civil Service Russian Interpreter exam. Legend had it that all the permanent staff had been posted to Crail as punishment for some military misdemeanour, and the rumour was that the triple-barrelled commander had managed to ram his ship against either a dock wall in the Far East or another of HM ships somewhere on the seven seas.

Cash-My-Cheque then handed us over to an RAF sergeant named Hoey, who did not conceal his low opinion of our appearance and marching ability, perhaps comparing us with the army contingent, all creases and shiny boots, being bellowed at by a large guardsman, a veteran of the Korean War who wore a red sash. This was Corporal of Horse Charnley, who was addressed at all times as 'Horse'. The Horse bellowed his orders, Hoey echoed them and the petty officer in charge of the naval coders seemed to be making polite requests to his chaps.

The khaki ones stamped their feet a lot, as though they were still in Catterick. Those of us in blue-grey marched casually but tidily – apart from one man who swung his left arm with his left foot and his right arm with his right foot, and who was later concealed each morning in the middle file, to avoid enraging any watching NCO or officer. It seemed that the Royal Navy does not rate marching very highly because stamping hobnailed boots at each step would not have been good for wooden decks in the 'hearts of oak' days, nor is there space to practise aboard modern warships. So the trainee coders moved in an easy stroll, as though on sea-legs, having just lately come ashore from a liberty boat. Army and RAF students had canvas haversacks, looking like war surplus leftovers, but the coders upstaged everyone else with smart briefcases.

Past the armoury and down the hill this heterogeneous band was marched in its various ways, as it would be on five days a week for the next seven and a half months. Past the camp theatre, also used as a gymnasium, we came to the main gate, notionally protected by the guard house. Across the Crail–Balcomie road lay the lower camp, where, outside the first building, two regimental policemen sneered impotently at us. In tribute to their less than impressive physique, they were universally referred to as Wiry Twerp and Japanese Joe. The hangars and the space between them were still a dump for what at first were thought to be torpedoes, but turned out to be paravanes for mine-sweeping, left behind by the Fleet Air Arm. The last real soldiers to serve there were Scots who had been shipped off to Korea, many of whom never saw the heather-clad hills of home again. There was a runway and taxiways, still in remarkably good condition, plus an area of hardstanding, which we learned was called in Russian, *stoyanka*.

In the shadow of a complex of disused aircraft hangars lay the brick-built Admin building and a confusion of temporary single-storey buildings used as classrooms. The military profile was very low key. There were, somewhere, but never seen by the author, a small number of interpreters dressed as officer cadets and midshipmen while they worked out the last few weeks of their National Service, a small number of Norwegian SIGINT personnel and a brigadier named Meadmore – himself a graduate of the pre-war Russian course run by the London University SSEES – who had overall responsibility for all activities on the camp.

The 'boss' on that first morning was Norval Lunan, a deceptively mild academic who ran the course with his staff of tutors. From him, the students learned that they were Intake 35. Some service officers must have conducted what was called 'indoctrination', but this had nothing to with politics or brainwashing and was concerned with getting all students to sign a copy of the Official Secrets Act, the infringing of which by talking to unauthorised persons about the course, the camp or just about anything else was a criminal offence. Neither then, nor ever at Crail, was any attempt made to suggest we were going to be deployed literally on NATO's front line, and locked in intellectual combat with the Soviet hordes. We learned that, as students on a course, we were *ucheniki* (singular form *uchenik*). Basic learning tools handed out that morning included a *Russian Grammar* by Anna H. Semyonova, a pocket book of vocabulary lists and various other books, including Elizaveta Fen's *Obyknovenniye Lyudi* – meaning 'ordinary people', who turned out to be boringly so. With satchels thus filled, everyone departed for the classrooms, which were comfortable enough in late August.

Even in our spare time, there was little fraternisation between RAF, army and navy. From the first day of language tuition, the services were separated, either for reasons of differing vocabulary or for security on the recently introduced principle of need to know. The trainee coders learned more nautical terms; the RAF men were stuffed with Russian terms for parts of aircraft – not that we knew where they were or what functions they fulfilled – and air and weather conditions; the khaki types mugged up tanks, tanks and more tanks. Most classes were, of course, composed of RAF students. Within each contingent, men formed small groups, usually based on the other men who shared their billet. The twenty or so men in any one billet were broken down still further into groups of twelve or so for lessons, so that each student received an adequate amount of individual attention.

In the RAF ranks of Intake 35 there were a couple of men who would have found it hard to keep up on a cookery or gardening course and soon disappeared into the mysterious realm of RTU, unmourned by their erstwhile comrades. Yet, by and large, the selection process did not waste much public money. The army contingent was, as always, different and had a number of patently unsuitable characters. The most outstanding was a witless regular corporal named Rogers[2] who was still mastering English at nursery level. It baffled the other contingents why he had been sent on an intellectually demanding language course, until they learned that totally useless soldiers were traditionally sent on training courses, one after another, as a way of getting them out of the regimental depot for a few months each time.

But the khaki lot also included a number of rather aristocratic types – public school men with double-barrelled names, who had joined such-and-such regiment because an uncle once played polo with distinction when serving with it in India or a grandfather had 'fallen gloriously' as its colonel in some colonial battle or other. The navy needed so few National Service ratings that family connections were even more important there and one coder told us that they had all been psychologically screened by Wren officers, to weed out the ones who might go bonkers if posted to submarines, although these were unlikely vessels for Russian linguists to serve in.

In the RAF contingent, only two men were unable to keep up the pace. One was the regular who had trouble co-ordinating his legs and arms, and was nicknamed Jingle Bollocks. He had been posted to JSSL Crail because he had done an O level Russian course at school. In his kitbag was a pair of knee-length boots in soft leather – the type in which Cossacks do their knee-dancing. Of these he was immensely proud, until the day when a man who shall be nameless dropped a cream bun into each boot just before Jingle Bollocks arrived in the billet to put them on. It was cruel humour, and perhaps more humiliating than his eventual rejection from the course after the First Major Test, when JB disappeared into the limbo of RTU.

Although planning documents for JSSL contained the instruction that 'the idea should be consistently conveyed [to the students] that the learning of Russian is not as difficult as it appears to be',[3] the author's group of twelve students first heard the language of the tsars when a large, pallid, shaven-headed Estonian man named Mandre-Methusalem entered the classroom and said, '*Ya svobodny chelovyek i ya zhivu vo svobodnoi stranye*'. Pointing to himself, he repeated the sentence, which left no one any the wiser, except that *ya* seemed to mean 'I' or 'me'. He picked up a pencil and stated, '*Eto karandash*'. Pointing to the window, he announced, '*Eto okno*'. Parroting the words, we had learned the Russian for pencil and window – and *eto* had to mean 'this'. What was not clear initially was that, since the present tense of 'to be' was not used, it also meant 'this is'. Next, we learned to say our first sentence, '*Ya lyotchik i uchenik.*' Literally, 'I am an airman and student'.

An exponent of what the Victorians called 'an object lesson', M-M decorated the walls of his classroom with pictures from magazines, in order to illustrate short stories by pointing at each noun in turn: '*CHELOVYEK imeyet NOVY AFTOMOBYL*' – 'The MAN has a NEW CAR' – and so on. *Uchenik* Peter Crowther recalled M-M's many pictures of Italian film star Gina Lollobrigida and the embarrassing moment when a vacuum cleaner – *pylesos* in Russian – was delivered to the camp, all the way from Edinburgh, after M-M had thought he was asking the shop for a brochure from which to tear a picture to illustrate the sentence '*GINA LOLLOBRIGIDA nosila PYLESOS*' – 'GINA LOLLOBRIGIDA was carrying a VACUUM CLEANER' – as film stars do.

In instalments over the coming weeks, it came out that Mandre-Methusalem had been the top divorce lawyer in Estonia before the Second World War, during which he had been arrested by the NKVD and later imprisoned by the Gestapo. In the final desperate fighting of 1945, he had embarked – voluntarily or not, no one was ever clear – on one of the last German ships to leave Tallinn Harbour before the Red Army executed *Tallinskaya nastupatel'naya operatsia* – the Tallinn Offensive – in September 1944. Shortly after putting to sea, M-M's ship was bombed and sunk by a *shturmovik* – a low-flying Soviet fighter-bomber – leaving him to swim 2 miles to shore, his ability to do which saved him from joining the tens of thousands of troops and civilian refugees who ended up at the bottom of the Baltic in those terrible months. At some moment in this harrowing experience, he received a grazing wound from a Soviet bullet, which left a long and deep scar across his bald scalp. How he travelled from Soviet-occupied

Estonia to Crail after that remained a mystery. Most of the instructors had similar histories, in which their students, with the callousness of youth, took little or no interest and with which we certainly showed no sympathy. And yet, more than half a century later, these men and women who had been 'to hell and back', as the saying was, stand out among 'those we have known'.

Another Balt was Ernie Sternbergs from Riga, the capital of Latvia. He was a diminutive, plump little man, who owed his life to his small stature: all his classmates had been commissioned as officers and were shot by the Soviets, but he had been rejected as too short to serve as an officer. This ex-SS dynamo of a man who – so unsubstantiated rumour held – had been an interpreter at Treblinka Death Camp, certainly burned with ardent hatred of everything Soviet, having lost several teeth during the Russian occupation of his country, whether from scurvy or a Russian fist was unclear. In a letter home, *uchenik* Alan Bamber described him well:

> He is only about 5' 3" and he stands on a large orange box to reach the blackboard. He stands there waving his arms madly and shouting louder and louder until he becomes a frightening mass of sound. Then he'll suddenly break off and say something slowly and softly. He succeeds in driving his points over remarkably well in this way. He also … speaks fluent Russian and other Slavonic languages, plus English, Latvian, Latin, Greek and French.[4]

Sternberg's jokes embodied unspeakable pathos: 'Which is the largest country in the world? The answer is Latvia because all the land is by the Baltic but most of the population is in Siberia'.

But the young students soon grew bored with their instructors' past suffering. RAF *uchenik* Tony Tindall recalled Polish Count Tyszkiewiecz, habitually clad in a green cloak and wide-brimmed hat, asking his class for help when unable to recall the English for *podvodkaya lodka* (submarine). 'Shitty underpants!' someone shouted helpfully from the back of the class. 'Ah, thank you,' said Tish, 'I remember now.'[5]

At the opposite end of the linguistic spectrum from Sternberg, Bloody Boris was the nickname for an instructor whose slender grasp of English vocabulary obliged him to substitute 'bloody' for all the missing words, e.g., 'You bloody boys are here to learn bloody Russian and I'm your bloody instructor'. In contrast, the wraithlike, sometime seminarist, Anatol Scobiej still seemed shattered by his deportation to Siberia in a cattle truck many years before. A Pole named Melechowicz had lost one eye and both forearms in the war, yet was able to balance a glass of vodka on his single remaining elbow and down shot after shot. Oleg Kravchenko – Ukrainian in name if not ethnicity – admitted having fought in German uniform because only Hitler's army was fighting the Soviets in Europe in 1942. Yevgeniy Galko only reached JSSL because he hid in some mountainous region of Austria in the spring of 1945 while British forces were hunting down and driving tens of thousands of his fellow Cossacks, who had fought on the *Wehrmacht* side, across the demarcation line to be slaughtered by Stalin's firing squads.

A Crail staff list from 1956 – and there is no reason to think things were different in 1957 – listed the instructors thus:

> The ratio of British to foreign personnel was almost exactly as envisaged by the authorities five years earlier. Listed as 'civilian language instructors', fifty-three men and four women were cited, along with their ages, starting dates and whether their work was principally training interpreters or translators. Nearly half were stated to be Russian, of whom thirteen were specifically designated 'ex-Soviet' and one stateless. Eight were from the Baltic States of Estonia, Latvia and Lithuania and two from the Ukraine – all four countries then in Moscow's inflexible grip, just as they had been before the Bolshevik Revolution. Eight were British and there was a solitary Czech.[6]

Only three instructors were under 30; thirteen were in their 60s; and the average age was 50. The largest subgroup, after the Russians, were the fifteen Poles, of which the most flamboyant was Jozef Godlewski, a formidably moustached former colonel who had fought in the Polish Legion during the interventionist war that ravaged Russia after the October Revolution, and later became a Polish senator. Single instructors lived on camp in the officers' quarters and took their meals in the Officers' Mess. A protest led by Godlewski in 1954 at their low pay of £400 per annum had apparently elicited only the information that they were not entitled to pay rises negotiated by the National Union of Teachers because they were civil servants, but not entitled to civil service rates either, although the minimal salaries they earned were presumably better than what they would have received as taxi drivers/hotel doormen/dressmakers in Paris. Godlewski's campaign for a fair salary bore fruit in September 1959 when the Institute of Professional Civil

Servants wrote to advise him that he and his colleagues were entitled to a scale of between £940 and £1,135 per annum.

Prior to this, instructors who had families sought low-rent accommodation in Crail or the neighbouring village of Anstruther, in which to eke out a frugal existence, some preferring to use candles rather than electric light because they were cheaper. Their precarious financial situation and the treadmill existence of producing intake after intake of competent translators in a language that many of them hated made their exile in Scotland bad enough, without the nightmares that some suffered, believing that they would, when the Cold War hotted up, inevitably fall into Stalin's clutches. Our student pay, of course, was laughable, even at the time: £1 2s 6d, or in modern terms £1.12 per week.

Lunan explained in that first briefing that the adult brain could only concentrate fully for forty-five minutes without a break, so tuition was divided into forty-five-minute periods, taking up eight hours a day on five days a week, with regular after-hours 'homework' – largely the memorising of daily vocabulary lists of thirty words each. At the end of each week a test would determine those who passed and would stay on the course and those who would be returned to their units, wherever they were. The First Major Test was to sort the sheep from the goats: the top six students would disappear to London or Cambridge for the higher-level course while the rest of us laboured on in Crail.

A typical daily timetable consisted of two periods of grammar, a period of reading aloud and practising pronunciation, a mid-morning Naafi-type break followed by translation from English into Russian orally or in writing and then translation from Russian into English, rendered more difficult by covering subjects like piezo-electric particles, of which no student had heard, even in English. Paramount was *diktovka*, with the speed of dictation gradually increasing throughout the course until delivery was at the speed of normal speech. Why this was so important the students then had no idea and the instructors were not supposed to know, either. A nastier variant was called 'written interpretership' in which an instructor read out a text in Russian without interruption and the students had to write down in real time an accurate English translation. From the beginning of the course, most Russian texts used were 'real', being transcriptions of BBC Russian Service broadcasts. Typical was one beginning, '*Sevodnya vo frantsuzkom kabinyete president Faure zayavil chto* …' – 'Today in the French Cabinet, President Faure declared that …'.

After straggling most unlike the Duke of York's men back up the hill for lunch in the canteen and down again for the afternoon lessons, the immediate problem was fighting off the siesta syndrome, daydreaming in the warm sunlight coming through the classroom windows and watching dust motes in the sunbeams, while the instructor's voice droned on in initially incomprehensible Russian. Many men came to hate John Peters, a principal character in *Obeknovennye Lyudi*, of which the first sentence was '*Dzhon Piters i yevo zhena Meri zhivut v nyebolshom domye nyedaleko ot Londona …*' – 'John Peters and his wife Mary live in a not-big house not far from London …'. There was also a book produced, in the innocence of the Second World War, about the adventures in an unrecognisably friendly Russia of two British servicemen, Jack and Bill – immortalised as *Dzhek i Bil v Rossii*. Nearly seven decades later, ex-linguists who meet up at reunions can still recite whole chunks to each other:

'*Vot nash aftobus!*'

'*Kak vy znaete chto eto nash aftobus?*'

'*Potomy chto ya zametil vchera chto aftobus nomer chetyrye idyot v gorod.*'

'That's our bus.'

'How do you know that's our bus?'

'Because I noticed yesterday that bus No. 4 goes into the town.'

And so on, in soporific stupor.

Alas, those innocent times of Soviet–Allied friendship had never existed because all the Western personnel posted to the USSR for whatever reason during what Russians call the Great Patriotic War were harassed and spied on by the NKVD and GRU, but the books were still there in the JSSL library as testimony to forlorn wartime hopes. If it was boring for the students, what must have been going on in the instructors' minds after so many courses had already explored downtown Moscow with Jack and Bill?

There was also *Boevyie Budny* – a collection of military tales vaunting the prowess of the Soviet military, of which a typical example was a pilot who shot down three German aircraft before returning to base for breakfast with a healthy appetite, doubtless reporting to his commanding officer, '*Zadanie vypolnyl, tovarish kommandant!*' – 'I have completed the mission, sir!' In case the students were in any doubt about the prowess of *our* enemy, one former Red Army officer among the tutors used to warn his charges, 'If ever it becomes a shooting war, you will have no chance against the Red Army. They are the best soldiers in the world.'

The day ended with a vocabulary list of thirty words, to be learned by next morning – and another thirty the next evening, and the next. It does not sound like hard work, but was made harder by the apparently random choice of words, which had nothing to do with each other. Few students managed to recall all thirty words each morning, in addition to all the others they had learned, even with the weekly test looming at the end of the week under the shadow of RTU.

After the First Major Test, the six men with the highest marks, including Eddie George – later Governor of the Bank of England – were indeed selected for the interpreter course in London or Cambridge. Not all such top scorers actually got there, some power in the snobbish upper echelons of the armed services apparently deciding that certain very proficient trainee linguists were 'just not officer material'.

In Intake 35, one man saw little attraction in going off to spend the rest of his two years' service studying, since he was subsequently going to spend three more years as an undergraduate at Oxford or Cambridge. Future British diplomat Dave Johnson turned down his place, considering that the life of a translator, with overseas service built in, would almost certainly be more interesting than two years stuck in classrooms studying Russian to interpreter level.

Perhaps to combat the students' boredom at Crail with the same face and voice, each class had two main instructors: one for grammar and the other for conversation and dictation. A complete contrast with M–M was a diminutive 52-year-old lady going by the bastardised name of Anna Nikolayevna Nicholas-Eve. Occasionally, instructors would go off track and recount their experiences, so to give ourselves a break we became quite good at switching the points so that their trains of thought were diverted into the realms of reminiscence. Anna Nikolayevna needed no prompting, and gave us her personal odyssey on first encounter. After her father, the governor of the vast Amur region in the Far East, was shot by his own soldiers in the October Revolution, together with his favourite borzoi dogs, Anna and her sister – two teenage girls – walked several hundred miles through lawlessness and turmoil to reach Vladivostok, where they took ship for Shanghai. She gave all her students many useful tips, in case they should ever find themselves in the same situation: to take with one a hard soap that will not go rotten; never to ask a rich person for food, because he will give you none – peasants know hunger and will share what they have with hungry travellers; not to pack a bottle of ink, which may leak and ruin your changes of underwear, but take ink powder and mix it up as and when required. Although interesting, this information fortunately proved superfluous for us.

Gareth Mulloy, a trainee coder who arrived at Crail in November 1956, recorded this of his 51-year-old Russian instructor, N. Komarov:

[He] told us of being handcuffed with barbed wire [by his Soviet captors]. His description was so vivid that I still remember the Russian for it – *provolochnoye zagrazhdyeniye*. All [the instructors] were forced exiles from their native countries. Many had left families behind. None could ever contemplate returning whilst the Soviets remained in power. They had thrown their lot in with the West, and were considered as traitors by the Soviet Union.[7]

As in many other expat communities, there was constant in-fighting between the instructors, especially between the older ones, who had escaped before, during or after the Revolution and had been hating each other ever since, and the younger ones, whom their elders considered tainted by the Communism they had known and rejected. Occasionally students became embroiled. The first I knew of this was when Lieutenant Garrett, the National Service Medical Officer, skidded to a halt on his bicycle and whispered to me that Anna Nikolayevna was conducting a whispering campaign against me in the Officers' Mess and had told Lunan, 'that young man Boyd' should be RTU'd. Since 'that young man's' marks in the weekly tests were adequate, if not the best, she eventually lost interest, presumably picking on another victim. One supposes that whispering campaigns of this sort were part of the usual background noise in the Officers' Mess.

A large and lugubrious Ukrainian instructor named Nikolai Ivanovich Kravchenko confided that, after Soviet Central Planning starved to death 3 million of his people living on the most fertile soil in Europe in the 1930s, many Ukrainians had regarded the German advance in Hitler's Operation Barbarossa in 1941–42 as a liberation from Russian oppression. He did not actually say he himself had put on German uniform, but tens of thousands of Ukrainian men did so, and one could understand why.

Like schoolchildren, we students exploited any weakness of an instructor to make life easier. In Kravchenko's case, it was singing. He never grasped that British soldiers, and still less British airmen, had never had to march thousands of miles to battle, but were transported across the globe when necessary by the Royal Navy. Both Russian Imperial forces and the Soviet armies marched to fight. Even as late as the First World War, railheads were often several hundred miles distant from the fighting fronts. They therefore needed marching songs, as did their German and Austrian enemies, to keep in step and to keep their spirits up. So Nikolai Ivanovich led his impromptu classroom choirs in the 'Volga Boatmen's Song', with its chorus '*Ei ukhnyem, yeshcho razik, yeshcho da raz*' – roughly translated as 'Yo, heave-ho, one more time, just one more time' – after which he explained that those boatmen were not jolly tars like the classy coders in the next classroom, but starving human wrecks, clad in rags, whose brief and painful lives in the days before steam power were spent bent double on the banks of the mighty Volga, hauling barges upstream against the current, much as horses were used on tow paths in Britain.

Alcohol has always been a problem in Russia. One Victorian music hall song that Nikolai Ivanovich taught us had the refrain '*Levaya, pravaya, gdye storona?*', purportedly in the mouth of a Moscow drunk so inebriated that he cannot find the sides of the street, either to left or right, and accuses the street of being drunk, '*Ulitsa, ulitsa, ty brat pyana!*' There was '*Kalinka*', of which our singing of the rousing *accelerando* chorus brought protesting bangs on the wall from the instructor next door but, rather than overdose on grammar, even we non-singers joined in enthusiastically to keep Nikolai Ivanovich on the music track.

Some songs, it is true, gave historical insights. '*Pozhar Moskovski*' was the story of the Great Fire of Moscow in 1812, when its citizens burned down all their wooden houses to deny shelter to Napoleon's ill-fated Grande Armée during the approaching winter. There was a hint of romance in '*Ochi Chorny*' – 'Dark Eyes' – later recorded by the Red Army choirs under the title 'Moscow Nights' and turned into the 1961 British pop hit by the group Kenny Ball and his Jazzmen as 'Midnight in Moscow'.

More history came in the shape of the lullaby '*Spi mladenyetz, moi prekrasny*', which a Cossack mother sang to her 'beautiful boy-child' near the River Terek, which was a nineteenth-century Wild West-type Caucasian frontier. It begins like most lullabies with '*tikho smotrit mesyatz yasny v kolibel tvoyu*' – 'the moon shines peacefully down on your cradle' – but swiftly turns into a warning that the evil Muslim Chechen is climbing up the river bank and sharpening his dagger to slit the Christian baby's throat. One day, she sings, her baby will become a battle-hardened warrior and ride off to kill the Chechens in the on–off war that still continues today. More history still came in the plaintive folk song 'Stenka Razin', about the Volga pirate of that name who fell in love with a beautiful Persian princess captured during a raid on a Black Sea port. When taunted by his men, '*tolko noch' s'nei provozilsya, sam na utro baboi stal'* – 'that after one night with her he had become as soft as a woman himself' – Stenka proves his manhood Russian-style by chucking her overboard to drown in the Volga.

For reading practice, there was Pushkin's '*Pikovaya Dama*' – 'Queen of Spades' – which the composer Pyotr Ilich Tchaikovsky and his gay librettist brother, Modest Ilich, turned into an opera. Also by Pushkin, the book *Kapitanskaya Dochka – The Captain's Daughter* – featured the invalid Don Cossack officer named Yemelyan Pugachoff, who claimed to be the assassinated Emperor Peter III and led the greatest uprising Russia was to see before 1917, culminating in the capture of the city of Kazan, a mere 450 miles from Moscow. By June 1774, Pugachoff's troops were preparing to march on Moscow, when the current war with Turkey – one of many – ended in a Russian victory and Catherine the Great was able to divert troops to crush the rebels by savage and bloody reprisals. On 14 September 1774, betrayed by his own Cossacks as Stenka Razin had eventually been, Pugachoff was confined in a metal cage for transport to Moscow and public execution there by beheading and quartering.

Reading these literary works after having enjoyed Constance Garnett's translations of Tolstoy, Dostoyevsky, Turgenev, Chekhov, *et al.* while at school, the author's respect for Ms Garnett grew by leaps and bounds.

Event by event, in this oblique fashion the students picked up a lot of Russian history. Summed up as an unwavering policy of kill-the-neighbours-before-they-kill-you, this came many years later to be the core material of the author's history of 1,000 years of Russian expansionism, entitled *The Kremlin Conspiracy.*[8] Yet, there was never any overt anti-Soviet teaching at JSSL because the course was designed by intellects wise enough to understand that the bloody-mindedness of youth would have reacted in the direction opposite to that intended, so that it was best to leave us students to come to our own conclusions.

For those who could face more Russian in print, JSSL's library reading room had current Soviet newspapers and magazines. With the two main all-Union newspapers, entitled by Lenin *Pravda* (truth) and *Izvestiya* (information), the instructors joked, '*Nyet pravdy v Izvestiya, nyet izvestii v Pravde*' – 'There's no truth in *Izvestiya* and no information in *Pravda*'. Both these Soviet dailies were excruciatingly boring, with entire speeches of Politburo members reported verbatim, transparently mendacious statistics of successful collective farms and accounts of Stakhanovite miners who happily exceeded their daily quotas of coal by 270 per cent, while most of their comrades lived and worked by the motto 'They pretend to pay us, so we pretend to work'.

A great surprise, however, when reading *Krokodil*, *Ogonyok* and other Soviet magazines, which were still in their airmail wrappers, was to find that they had been posted from the publishers in Moscow direct to 'The Library, JSSL, Crail' – a top-secret establishment about which we students were not supposed to speak to our own families.

The other great nonsense was 'Bull' – a faint echo of what we had endured in basic training, but still pointless and irritating. The linoleum floor of the billet had to be 'bumpered' to a high gloss, bed packs made each morning and boots polished for the 0830hrs parade. Bull was reduced to a tolerable level after someone in our intake discovered that Sergeant Hoey was an ardent Glasgow Rangers fan. The game was on: those who knew anything about football lost no opportunity to praise his heroes and talk tactics and match statistics, reducing the parade-ground tyrant to a lifetime footie mate. Or maybe his conversion dated from the day Hoey tore John Griffin's bed pack to pieces and chucked it on the floor. He had chosen the wrong victim, for Griffin immediately marched – metaphorically – in high dudgeon down to the guardroom to report Hoey's action, for which the sergeant was reprimanded. Probably, both events coincided.

After the epiphany, Hoey was a changed man, although from time to time he could not stop himself checking the length of our hair by some ingrained reflex of the long-serving NCO. Our haircuts were not 'RAF-issue' because *uchenik* Gerry Williams had been a novice in a Jesuit monastery, where his duties included the occasional function of *tintinabulator tertius* – ringing the third bell of the day to signal the commencement of the day's chores, cleaning the toilets, polishing the corridor floors, peeling potatoes and cutting the brothers' hair. Perhaps his skill with the scissors had more to do with creating a tonsure on the crown of monkish heads than the no-hair-below-the-beret RAF style. On one occasion, Hoey yelled at someone on morning parade, 'Oo cut yor 'air? That bloody moonk?' After his conversion, our born-again sergeant left us pretty much to our own devices, devoting himself to a long-running feud against the Horse, of whom he said, 'I wish he'd fall off his bloody 'orse'.

In November 1957, flying visits to Crail were paid by a major general and a vice admiral; senior RAF officers did not appear to be interested in us. It was presumably on the occasion of one of the above inspections that I and a much older man called Phil Cooper were tasked as 'room orderlies', to ensure that hut Benbow 3 was clean and reasonably tidy. Cooper was an odd type, being around 35 – nearly twice our average age – and with results in the tests that should have seen him RTU'd. He had obviously been in the forces before: one big give-away was the way he created a perfect bed pack on day one and never undid it. Instead, he slept on the floor under his bed, wrapped in a single blanket, summer and winter. To kill time until the visiting officer's inspection, I asked Cooper a few questions and he became positively garrulous, chatting away about his time in Malaya during the 'emergency' when he had been driven up and down 'the road' in tanks, although not himself a tanker. The only recent history that fitted his account was of MI5's counter-intelligence role in Malaya, so it seems highly likely that he was a 'snooper', keeping an eye on us.

For those wishing to identify with JSSL, somebody invented a 'regimental tie' which could be purchased in St Andrews for the exorbitant price of 11 shillings and ninepence, approximately equivalent to 58p, or half a week's pay. There was also a 'school magazine' entitled *CAMOBAP* – that is 'samovar' written in Cyrillic characters which can be found on an English keyboard – which had been started as an excuse to avoid Wednesday afternoon sports activities. Michael Frayn, when he was *CAMOBAP*'s editor at Bodmin, had changed the title from the original name *Teapot and Samovar* on the grounds that teapots are for brewing tea, whereas samovars only heat the water. Whatever, each issue was half in Russian and half in English, the Russian half having to be laboriously hammered out on Banda stencils, using a mechanical typewriter with Cyrillic keyboard. The content, all by students, ranged from serious essays to spoofs, poetry, short stories and criticism. There were also notes by secretaries of the hockey, golf, music and ski clubs, as well as various societies – the Philosophical Society was reputed to be very philosophical about the fact that few people ever turned up at its meetings. With two or three issues per year, *CAMOBAP* was priced at 1 shilling and sixpence per issue – or 7.5p – the production costs being partly defrayed by advertisements paid for by local traders, who cannot have recouped very much in custom. Some willing volunteers who presumably enjoyed singing with Nikolai Ivanovich or other instructors, also produced for the price of one shilling the *CAMOBAP* songbook with the words of fifty-nine songs – a copy of which reposes in the author's library.

6

SVOBODNOYE VREMYA – WHICH SHOULD HAVE MEANT FREE TIME

With no classes on Wednesday afternoons, we *ucheniki* considered them free time, although the first one was devoted to a tour of the camp's amenities by Sergeant Hoey. Shown the armoury bunker, in which firearms and ammunition were stored, we were not allowed in. The highlight of the tour was another bunker near the perimeter fence almost entirely filled by the largest diesel engine any of us had ever seen. This was supposed to generate electricity, should the IRA ever cut the camp's power lines from the National Grid. We were instructed by Hoey how to start it up in that event: 'You close that switch an' press that button, then pump this one – or is it the other way round?' The information was irrelevant because we were also informed that the bunker was impossible to break into and, for security reasons, we were not allowed to know where the key was kept.

Contact with officers of any branch of the armed forces was minimal, but an army captain named Goss must have been lurking somewhere on camp to pick his moment for reminding everyone that our 'free afternoon' was intended to develop our pretty non-existent martial spirit. With this in mind, he devised an 'exercise' on the flat waste ground of the lower camp between the road and the runway. At the armoury, I was allocated a Bren gun – a light machine gun with its own folding bipod which is fired in the prone position. The description 'light' refers to the calibre of the .303 ammunition – when one has to run over rough country with it, it is a *heavy* machine gun. Cleverer men placed themselves in the armoury queue so as to get off lightly as 'servers', carrying just a couple of magazines of blank ammunition.

The day was warm and wet. On arrival at the scene of the exercise, Goss gave us our briefing. There was no point in him doing the service method of indicating a target with the rigmarole 'eleven o'clock, bushy-topped tree', etc., because the only feature in the flat Scottish-Siberian landscape was a small brick shed. Pointing to it, he ordered some men in the squad to outflank it and cause a diversion from the rear while I was to make a frontal assault with Ron Sharp. Between us and 'the target', there were several drainage ditches, which some of the more athletic might have been able to jump. We fell into them, getting wetter each time, our boots soon full of muddy water. When it started to rain heavily, reducing visibility for Goss with his field glasses, we loosed off all the ammunition and walked back to shelter and dry clothes.

We had failed to take the measure of Goss, who was not vanquished yet. Whether in revenge, or not, for the fiasco on the airfield, a few weeks later he devised another exercise from which his victims could not so easily escape. Transported in canvas-covered 3-ton trucks to a bracken- and heather-strewn hillside miles away from the camp, we were woken up by him slamming down the tailboard of the truck and yelling, 'When I give the order, I want you out of there like hot shit off a shovel.' Some brave spirit in the darkness of the truck – it sounded like Gerry the Monk – commented that hot shit would surely stick to a shovel. Goss' face went purple before he decided to ignore that. He shouted the command and all clambered down to be given the full 'eleven o'clock, bushy-topped tree' routine. From somewhere he had borrowed a few squads of real soldiers from the Black Watch, who were dug in on the opposite hillside. More than half of us wore glasses, but when someone remarked that he could not see the Black Watch, Goss hissed, 'That's because they're well dug in!' Although there were some entrenching tools in the truck, no one on our side volunteered to dig a trench.

Deployed with a Bren and Ron as my server, I dozed off in the autumn sunlight while Goss departed to deploy the rest of his unenthusiastic force. When the whistle was blown to indicate the start of the exercise, one or two of the fitter students went crashing through the bracken to be greeted by thunderflashes thrown by the Black Watch. Deafened by the explosions, they did not hear the umpire's shout that they had been shot and must lie down, but wandered about looking dazed, as they probably were. That was our cue. Without a word being spoken between gunner and server, the first magazine of blank ammunition was fixed on the Bren and emptied, *bang-bang-bang*! as was the second. With all the ammo gone, the Bren team declared itself shot in order to lie back in the shelter of the bracken to enjoy a smoke and test each other on that day's vocab list.

Another of Goss's follies was to make lifetime pacifist John Anderson kneel on frost-covered grass to dismantle a Bren and reassemble it. This was not quite the SAS trick of having to do it with one's head in a totally lightproof hood, but Anderson's protest was met with the tenuous argument that German paratroops had been able to take Crete in 1943 because the RAF personnel there were untrained in ground combat. Goss was out of time and out of place. Whether he had been sentenced to Crail because he was a bit nuts, or whether trying to instil moral fibre into such unsuitable material sent him insane, was unclear, but he seemed to disappear shortly after this.

The next incident in the students' perpetual skirmishing with the military involved the physical training instructor, a small and frighteningly fit man from the Royal Artillery, holding the rank of lance bombardier. Inevitably christened 'the Lance-Bomb', he took his job too seriously. On one occasion, angered by the physical inability of most *ucheniki* to haul themselves up a rope in the gym using just their arm muscles, he ordered the whole group to hang on the wall bars as punishment. One by one, they let go and dropped to the ground, which sent him into paroxysms of uncomprehending rage, screaming, 'It's a mootny!' Nothing happened.

Another low-level mutiny was over a 'Keep Off the Grass' notice. The men from one hut persistently took a short cut to the cookhouse across a stretch of grass. When this was re-seeded for an inspection and a rope stretched across to demarcate the no-go area, the miscreants moved the rope out of the way and continued treading across the re-seeded earth. A real sergeant major appeared, called all the students together and defused this silly situation by saying, 'Look, you lads have a very nice life, but don't push it. Right?' His approach won points for reasonableness and that mutiny was called off.

When a new and rather too keen CO named Colonel Askwith arrived fresh from serving in Berlin, speculation as to the nature of the grievous error that caused him to be posted to Crail was that he must have betrayed military secrets after some Russians got him drunk there. The rumours were probably unfounded. Askwith was given to striding around the perimeter with his dog, and making disapproving grunts each time he found a hole someone had cut in the wire to make a shortcut to the nearest pub.

On one occasion, *uchenik* Duncan Brewer, who regularly played trombone with Jimmy Spowart's Dance Band into the early hours, was wriggling back into camp underneath the perimeter fence at dawn after an unofficial three-day absence when he became entangled in the barbed wire. Out for an early morning walk, Askwith approached with his two liver-spotted retrievers. Duncan lay still while the dogs licked his face. Askwith came over to see what had attracted them, looked down at the man on the ground, said nothing, turned and walked off, the dogs following him back to the Officers' Mess. The NCOs being nearly innumerate, nobody had missed Duncan at roll call and the instructors had not squealed. He was the only member of our intake who voluntarily signed on for a third year's service, which made him a 'regular', paid at a higher rate than National Servicemen. He had even been prepared to sign on for nine years if accepted for aircrew training, but was not thought to have the necessary military characteristics.

Askwith rapidly came to the correct conclusion that the vast majority of the students were unfit, despite Goss's occasional *folies militaires*, and organised a cross-country run for the following Wednesday afternoon. The coders, always one step ahead, arrived on sports parade not in the service-issue singlets, shorts and plimsolls, but wearing jodhpurs and riding boots. Announcing grandly to the Horse that they had opted for an afternoon's equestrian exercise, courtesy of a titled lady who had several mounts in her stable nearby and was distantly related to one of them, they departed in style.

A handful of others paraded in civvies with bags of golf clubs, before strolling off in the direction of the Balcomie golf course, one of the three oldest in Scotland. Dave Bruce had explained to us that in Scotland golf was not a posh sport, but we did not know enough about that pastime of the rich in England to realise that his handicap of three made him close to professional standard.

One man, at least, betook himself to St Andrews to keep up his fencing with the university fencing club. Others disappeared to play rugby. Surprisingly, our intake included a full team of fifteen, who played the gentleman's game of Rugby Union against RAF Leuchars and the Black Watch. Largely due to playing on frozen-hard pitches that winter, many injuries occurred, one man going down with a damaged ankle and a neck injury in the same match. Another man received a kick in the head, which did not sound very gentlemanly to us non-players. To some extent, the team lost impetus after the corporal from the permanent staff who was its trainer was summarily posted away in January 1958 after being caught *in flagrante delicto* with a local girl in the gym when he was supposed to be on duty as guard commander.

Marched down to the camp gate on that first Wednesday afternoon of Askwith's tenure, the rump awaited their punishment for lack of imagination. A few of the fitter *ucheniki* clearly enjoyed romping through long grass, and raced off into the distance while the rest of us trotted round the first bend of the course and lay down on the grass – the near-perpetual rain must have eased off for a while – enjoying a smoke before taking a shortcut to arrive back at the camp having left a decent interval after the real runners finished the marked course. Several minutes later, around the bend trotted Askwith in singlet and shorts. He halted and surveyed the scene with unfeigned disappointment. 'Come on, chaps,' he murmured, 'That's not the spirit.' The smokers watched him sprint off into the distance with nobody following.

About this time, the most memorable of the tutors came to our rescue. Dmitri Makarov was a rotund dumpling of a man who spoke in a rather prissy St Petersburg accent where every vowel sounded like a short 'i'. He was frequently bitchy about the other young tutors, of whom he said, 'They do not know how to speak correct Russian'. Coder John Drummond recalled one of his instructors answering the question why another instructor pronounced a word differently. 'What do you expect from a Bulgarian peasant?' was the reply.¹ Sounds rather like Dmitri. *Uchenik* Bamber described him in an early letter home as 'a conceited snob'. Dmitri might have objected to 'conceited', but would have accepted 'snob' as fair description. He claimed to be a close relative of Prince Yussupov, one of the cabal of nobles who murdered the mad monk Rasputin very ineptly and messily in the run-up to the Revolution. Dressed in a duffle coat, with ivory cigarette holder jauntily at an angle, Dmitri wandered amiably enough through life, rarely actually looking at his social inferiors, which designation embraced all of us. His perpetual companion was a one-eyed pug dog he had christened Mamai after the last of the Tatar-Mongol emperors who ruled Russia from the twelfth to the fifteenth century after killing off half the population. During lessons, Mamai spent the time licking his private parts in the classroom.

The most blatantly unmilitary member of staff, Dmitri negotiated – with Lunan presumably – an alternative Wednesday afternoon 'exercise' in the form of amateur dramatics. It was a trump card because the plays produced by Dmitri were to be in Russian, starting with *Klop* – Russian for 'bed bug' – by the Futurist poet Vladimir Vladimirovich Mayakovsky, who shot himself in 1930 at the age of 36 in despair at what Lenin and Trotsky's revolution had evolved into under Stalin. Since *Klop* was in Russian, and we were there to learn Russian, Askwith could hardly object.

Perhaps the inspiration for *Sleeper*, the film by Woody Allen, who once referred to his family's Russian past as, 'When my grandmother was raping Cossacks in the pogroms', *Klop* is a satire on the 'new bourgeoisie' of the USSR. In it, Party activist Igor Prisipkin divorces his wife to marry the pretty daughter of a hairdresser. At the drunken wedding feast, someone knocks over the oil lamp that sets fire to the festive scene, killing everyone present except Prisipkin, who is so coated in ice from the firemen's hoses that he enters a cryogenic coma. Melted out and resuscitated 'after ten 5-Year Plans', the only creature to which he can relate is a resuscitated bed bug, trapped in his shirt collar, which was also preserved in the ice block.

Performances were given in the week of 5 January 1958 and featured Colin Jones as Prisipkin, with Brian Howe, Gerry Williams and Ron Sharp among the cast. The female parts were played by three coders, for whatever reason, the bride looking enticingly pretty as 'she' shot seductive glances at Prisipkin. The scenery was designed by trombone player Duncan Brewer, who used Dmitri's note 'A/C Brewer has permission to leave camp to buy paint' as a passport to freedom whenever he chose. The suave John Griffin acted as stage manager. Dmitri, as usual, was ubiquitous and it must be some credit to him that he later took the production to London's West End with professional actors. At Crail, his *Klop* validated itself by introducing us to words not in our vocab lists like *sukinsyn* – son-of-a-bitch.

Having a mother who was an actress, and who had dragged me to the theatre all too many times in my childhood, I had taken a vow never to tread the boards myself or even enter a theatre of my own free will, but some fellow *ucheniki* seemed to bounce from one production to the next. The panto *Spuderella* featured Alan Bamber as the pianist in the sketch 'Shooting the Pianist', with the novel twist that the piano player shot the singers. Never a generous critic of other people's productions, Makarov opined that the sketch was the least funny humorous turn he had ever seen.

Perhaps the most original JSSL production, described by coders Cash and Gerrard, was a 'sods' opera' at JSSL Coulsdon, where the actors spoke their lines in correct Russian. Every few minutes, they froze in silence and two stagehands carried on an inept translation into English written on a strip of paper, imitating the subtitling methods and quality of Soviet productions. The humour lay in the way that, when the speech was long, the translation was short and vice versa. '*Da*' (yes) was translated as 'On behalf of the Supreme Soviet, etc., and the Autonomous Republic of etc., I as the Chairman of the etc., agree'.[2] There were echoes of this linguist humour in Allen's film *Bananas*, where a State Department interpreter translates the official greeter's welcome to an English-speaking head of state thus:

Greeter: 'I would like to welcome you to the United States.'

Interpreter: 'He says he would like to welcome you to the United States.'

Head of State: 'Tell him I'm very pleased to be here.'

Interpreter: 'He says he's very pleased to be here.'

Dmitri being Russian in every fibre of his being, and perhaps because he had grown up thousands of miles distant from the USSR, the second 'Russian production' was Eugène Ionesco's recently written play, *The Picture*, which I volunteered to translate into English from the original French, using my highly prized portable typewriter to make Banda stencils – then the only way of producing many copies of a document. This was the time of Becket's *Waiting for Godot* and Ionesco's dialogue likewise did not make much sense in either language. For each Wednesday afternoon rehearsal, three times as many men as were required for the cast and backstage crew crowded into Dmitri's classroom, out of reach of the regimental police, who fumed impotently outside. My translation entitled me to be there with them. It was chaos, but Russians thrive on chaos so our saviour seemed delighted with the enthusiastic turnout.

There was also a Russian choir, formed and conducted by Scobiej. It was not quite the massed tenors and basses of the Red Army Choir accompanied with balalaikas and accordions that toured Western Europe in the 1960s and later, but it did capture something of the soulfulness of traditional Russian folksong. A few of the more serious singers joined the Crail Choir for a performance of Handel's *Messiah* in December 1957 and the Anstruther Operatic claimed several more. For those who preferred listening, the Music Circle gathered regularly to forget the realities of service life by sharing the enjoyment of classical recordings, which were then just approaching what one could call high fidelity.

On arrival at Crail in August 1958, the weather was mild and the Fife coastline beautiful, with crystal clear but very cold water, so tempting that I on one occasion stayed in too long, got excruciating cramp and had to be towed to shore by Ron, without whose gallant rescue this book would not have been written. At weekends, those of us who needed solitude in this intensely communal life went for long walks along the Fifeshire shore, finding deserted jetties and rotting carcases of boats that hinted at a larger, more self-sufficient population in the not-too-distant past.

Crail itself was still an active fishing port, with ancient cannons set in the harbour wall as bollards to which the boats were moored, but for most students the cultural highlight of the Crail experience was The Music Box, a coffee bar with a juke box. Students like me, who had never heard pop music before, were amazed that some fellow *ucheniki* knew many of the songs on the 'singles' in the machine and could sing along with them in a DIY forerunner of karaoke. Elvis Presley was belting out 'All Shook Up', Nat King Cole was crooning 'Send for Me', the Everley Brothers had 'Bye Bye Love' and Harry Belafonte brought the warm Caribbean breeze to freezing Fifeshire with 'Island in the Sun' and 'The Banana Boat Song'.

Those preferring alcohol without noise, to frothy coffee with it, patronised one of the three pubs in the village, two of which had the peculiarly Scottish licence permitting the serving of alcohol on Sundays to 'travellers' – defined as those who lived more than 3 miles away. The pub halfway between the village and the camp was a popular watering hole, where the quickest way to get sloshed was by drinking Drambuie-and-whisky on payday evenings. When one inebriated student fell over the side of a bridge after leaving the pub, none of his fellow tipplers noticed.

There was also the bleak darkness of Aird's Cinema, where one sat in the uncomfortable rear seats smelling strongly of tomcats' urine, for performances starting at 1815hrs on Monday, Wednesday and Friday. Priced at 1 shilling – equivalent to 5 new pence – they sufficed to watch commercial films like *Twelve Angry Men*, starring Henry Fonda, and *The Sheepman*, with Glenn Ford and Shirley MacLaine. There were also, in that time before every home had a television set, cinemas in Anstruther and Pittenweem, the latter being a conversion of a small Victorian theatre which had catered for Glaswegians who came in specially chartered trains in the early years of the twentieth century to spend their summer holidays on the sunnier east coast in Fife.

Weekend boredom was combated by taking the single-decker country bus into the ancient university town of St Andrews where a more modern cinema had widescreen projection. Yet the seventh art – which Lenin had considered the most important of them all – was better served during cultural evenings in the camp theatre/gym, when the film society screened some Soviet propaganda films, treated as comedy by the audience, plus D.W. Griffith's 1915 masterpiece *Birth of a Nation*, Max Ophüls' *La Ronde* in the original French version, Akira Kurosawa's eye-opening *Rashomon* and a hauntingly beautiful Russian ballet film titled *Utrennyaya Zvyozda – The Morning Star*. The silent 1925 Soviet black-and-white masterpiece, Sergei Eisenstein's *Bronenosetz Potyomkin* about the mutiny aboard the battleship *Potemkin* during the 1905 Revolution, with its iconic sequence of the pram, supposedly containing an infant whose mother had just been shot by the tsarist guards, bumping unattended down the Odessa steps leading from the city to the waterfront, was possibly included to justify the rest of the programme.

So JSSL enriched its students not just linguistically, but in many other ways too, changing the horizons and expectations of many. Exposure to these masterpieces of cinema was my first step in a career after National Service in the film and television industries, starting with courses at the British Film Institute, delightful evenings at the Everyman Cinema in Hampstead and eventually appointment as a staff producer/director in BBC Television.

Girls were in very short supply, although some *ucheniki* recall coachfuls of local maidens arriving at the camp for dances, a young Scottish lady with the name of Alvrena Grubb ensnaring one student's heart. Where are you now, Ms Grubb? John Griffin has never forgotten your name at least. In St Andrews, the repertory company of the sixty-seat Byre Theatre intro-duced Crail men with thespian tendencies to John Osborne's *Look Back in Anger* in daily performances. Alas, the ladies on stage being in an older age bracket than us is perhaps why Brian Howe joined the St Andrews Operatic Society, playing the tenor lead part of Nanky Poo in *The Mikado*, surrounded by admiring young ladies.

Kate's Bar in St Andrews was thought to be a KGB entrapment den, with bottles of vodka and slivovitz openly on display behind the bar – suspicious choices of liquor in the land of malt whisky, doubtless intended to loosen the tongues of the unwary. In the Students' Union and a ballroom above the Town Hall, local girls and some of the 600 female undergraduates of the third most ancient university in Britain – after Oxford and Cambridge – inflamed Crail students' lusts by demurely allowing themselves to be held closely for the duration of a dance in the fashion then normal for ballroom dancing partners. 'High tea' in the several tea rooms of St Andrews was a welcome change from camp food and, for those with a liking for history in three dimensions, the Bishops' Castle was worth a visit, with its infamous bottle dungeon hacked out of the bedrock where prisoners were dropped in through the only entrance – a small hole at the top – breaking their legs as part of the torture. With the floor hacked out concave, they could in any case not have stood up or laid down on it.

Such was the lure of the bright lights of St Andrews that several students, including the author, were overtaken there one Saturday night in February 1958 by a violent blizzard that prevented the last bus from returning to Crail. With insufficient money to rent a room, we presented ourselves at the police station, where a sympathetic sergeant allowed us to kip down in the cells, which had to be locked according to the regulations. After dozing on waterproof mattresses, designed for incontinent drunks and which smelled powerfully of urine and rubber, we were let out after the late Scottish dawn and literally fought our way through the snowdrifts, taking turns to 'break trail' for the several miles back to camp. Once there, it was to find no electricity because the lines were down for the whole day. Whoever had the vital key to the bunker housing the standby generator must have been on leave or drunk, for no current flowed that day, and the only available food was bread, butter and corned beef, which did not stop John Anderson from valiantly walking the 2 miles to Crail's twelfth-century church through the snow, to participate in its quarterly Holy Communion service. There he was greeted by the sight of the elders of the kirk attired in morning dress for the occasion. When snow continued into March, some aspiring ice sculptors created a decorous nude model of French film star Brigitte Bardot outside the cookhouse.

Like Napoleon's army 'marching on its stomach', even language students had to be fed. The JSSL cookhouse was run by the army, employing as cooks a number of cheery local men who had obviously exercised a different profession in civilian life, to judge by the food they turned out. The reason for their good cheer was apparent when the quartermaster and chief cook were dismissed for selling supplies, the theft of which accounted for our inadequate diet. Their penalty was prison. The tinned Italian tomatoes, however, stayed on the menu throughout – perhaps because no civilian would buy them.

The cooks' thick East Neuk accents were apparently decoded by some students, who listened with interest to their tales of fishing on the high seas. On one occasion when the orderly officer asked the usual, 'Any complaints?', Gerry the Monk spoke out in innocence, 'Yes, sir. There's a hair in my pudding.' Seeing that the orderly officer did not seem to think this worthy of reply, he added, 'But it's short and curly, sir.'

Pubic hair not being known for causing dysentery, it was probably just the normal standard of poor hygiene that caused Alan Bamber's attack. The 'treatment' prescribed by Lieutenant Garrett was for him to be locked into an empty billet on zero rations to clear the infection from his system. In response to his pitiful pleas of 'I'm hungry', he was fed through the window by sympathetic friends with food bought in the Naafi, which did not retard his recovery.

The more squeamish *ucheniki* who had funds could purchase haute cuisine like egg and chips, or even steak, in the Naafi. The Naafi also offered table tennis and snooker facilities. After previous postings to naval and other barracks, Coder Peter Duskin appreciated the Crail Naafi, which was, he said:

> … unique: there was no screaming and shouting, no juke box surrounded by jiving MT drivers, none of the things that had sometimes made the Naafi in other camps seem like a bad pub. Conversation was usually a quiet buzz, there were always people playing chess or bridge, and, if anyone was playing the piano, he was probably playing Brahms or Chopin. It was all highly civilised.[3]

The hard core of our bridge players – Anderson, Fuller, King and Bamber – were also sometimes joined by others, including Eddie George until his departure. The addicts customarily spent the weekends playing a long game that started on Friday evening and appeared to continue, with breaks for meals, until Sunday evening when they got some sleep before Monday's lessons.

Few of us knew there was a camp chapel, disguised as yet another hut in the lower camp. John Fuller and John Anderson – to become respectively a Church of England canon and a Nonconformist preacher – took charge there, Anderson delivering a sermon on the theme 'Love thy Neighbour', which earned a thunderous rebuke from the bishop – presumably His Grace of St Andrews – that no one should be allowed to preach in an Anglican church without a licence. It was not quite 'bell, book and candle', but with most *ucheniki* a heathen bunch, one would think the bishop should have been grateful for the initiative of the two Johns, instead of lambasting them with an episcopal bollocking.

Every so often we had to take turns playing soldiers for the night. Paraded outside the guardhouse with a few rifles and no ammunition, we pretended to go through the motions of guarding the main gate until dawn. Since all the permanent staff knew there were so many holes in the perimeter fence that the IRA would not need to use the gate, this was just one more piece of play-acting to remind us that we were in the armed services. The worst moment of guard duty was in winter when an overzealous orderly officer yelled, 'Turn out the guard!' and the guard commander had to waken all the men sleeping, fully dressed. We pulled on our boots and laced them up, shrugged into our greatcoats, grabbed our rifles and paraded outside in the dark and rain or snow.

There was also a fire piquet of men who passed the night wandering around the camp with pick handles, taking shelter from the elements whenever possible. When one man questioned the uselessness of the sentry guarding the gate with a rifle, but no bullets for it, the inspecting officer said that was to prevent us hurting ourselves! Another man realised the futility of our mounting guard when told that he must not obstruct the local single-decker bus from driving through the camp, ferrying the locally employed staff to work early in the morning.

One trick was to borrow the highly bulled boots belonging to a Yorkshire student named Barnfather and, on their merit, be selected as 'stickman' who did not have to stand his turn in the sentry box. This gave little shelter from the elements and no comfort, being designed to make it impossible to take the weight off one's feet by slouching against a batten. The consolation for the last man on sentry duty, until he was stood down at dawn, was to see again the purity of the sunrise in the clear Scottish sky, like a watercolour as the day slipped towards us across the North Sea from Scandinavia.

On one occasion, a group of trainee coders deliberately failed a test in protest against having to do night-time guard duty, which was hardly good preparation for eight hours of intense mental effort. The whisper was that they actually addressed a written protest to London – the War Office? The Admiralty? – but it seems more likely they would have taken their 'grip-chit', as it is known in naval parlance, to the triple-barrelled commander, whose responsibility they were.

Only one RAF student in Intake 35 had a driving licence. This was Dick Moffat, the popular, short-sighted and dyspraxic solicitor from Nottingham, who was older than most, having had his call-up repeatedly deferred in order to pass the Law Society exams. With a joint kitty of £16,

Dick managed to tour the Western Highlands in a rental car one weekend, transporting three like-minded souls, all of them sleeping in barns to save money – except on one night when they discovered an empty house. After settling down for the night, they discovered that the adjacent railway line was used every half an hour by fast and very noisy trains. It was even worse than being on guard duty.

For most of us, however, trains were the only affordable long-distance transport. By the time Intake 35 had settled in, the Edinburgh Festival was over, but culture-hound John Anderson made it, sleeping rough on a bench in Waverly Station for one night to eke out his miserable pittance as a National Service conscript. He recalls a woman student from St Andrews claiming asylum in his carriage on the return journey after fleeing her previous one because it was 'full of nauseating Crail types'. One imagines a chorus of, 'Oh, aren't they awful!' greeting this news.

On one memorable weekend, a group of less cultured *ucheniki* exploited a forty-eight-hour pass by taking the train on Saturday morning to Scotland's grand capital, there to stroll along Princes Street and sample the sights and delights of the city. Seeking cheap lodging that evening, we asked – as one did in those days – a patrolling pair of policemen for advice. After the older constable realised how low was our budget, he suggested 'Mr McKay's lodging'. The younger constable protested, 'You couldna send decent young lads to a doss-house like that'. But McKay's lodging turned out to be a foretaste of heaven.

Unfortunately, one or two men were ill during the night, having 'imbibed', as they say in Scotland. Next morning all were treated to a feast of porridge, oat cakes, bacon, sausages, fried bread, mushrooms, finnan haddie, coffee and tea. The price was 10 shillings each for bed and board. One honest soul, feeling guilty, confessed that the bedrooms were in rather a mess. The venerable McKay, speaking in the soft lilt of the Western Islands, said that he had been awakened by the noise of our carousing, yet refused any help in clearing up because 'Ye're young men. Go out and enjoy yourselves. That's what youth is for.' Alas, on later visits to Edinburgh, McKay's lodging was impossible to find, so that more than one student was left wondering whether, like Brigadoon, it only materialised from time to time when impecunious and hungry young men needed shelter for the night and a slap-up breakfast.

After Christmas, we southerners had a shock, having had no idea what the real winter would be like. Billets and classrooms both turned out to be ill-heated when the Scottish winter arrived with blizzards driving in on the east wind from Scandinavia and Siberia beyond. In conditions of white-out – or more accurately, grey-out – we marched each morning blindly to class, army and RAF students cowering inside our greatcoats as we skidded on the ice, occasionally falling over to our own amusement and the anger of the NCOs. It was so cold that most men kept their pyjamas on all day under their other clothes, to have an extra layer of cloth between body and elements. For once, we were one-up on the coders, who had to make do with their navy-issue Burberry raincoats with a very thin lining because they had not been issued foul-weather clothing on account of not being at sea.

The tension of the early months had gradually dissipated. Confident that we no longer risked being RTU'd after all the time invested in us, some less conscientious *ucheniki* reverted to skiving. One of my best ideas was to report sick, declaring to our very amenable MO that I had headaches caused by changing focus from the book on my desk to the blackboard 100 times a day. He obligingly wrote me a prescription for an eye test in Edinburgh, with travel warrant for the journey. Learning this, Ron Sharp also reported sick with eye trouble and Lieutenant Garrett said, 'There was a chap in yesterday with the same problem. Name of Boyd. Do you know him?'

'Don't think so,' Ron said.

'Well, you could travel down together.'

'Okay,' said Ron.

The eye tests revealed no problem, so we had the rest of the day to ourselves: a pub lunch and more than one drink afterwards. So it was that we boarded the last train of the day in Waverley Station to find that the window in our compartment was stuck in the down position. In trying to heave it up by the thick leather strap with alcoholic abandon, it suddenly leaped upward – and shattered, with glass all over the platform. We sauntered casually into another compartment, but the train did not leave until a man in uniform had accused us of damaging British Rail property, noting our names and home address at JSSL Crail. Nothing happened for a couple of weeks, until Wiry Twerp hauled me out of Mandre-Methusalem's classroom one morning and snarled maliciously, 'You're for it now, you are!' Ron had been collected from his classroom by Japanese Joe, with a similar comment. Marched to the police office, we were confronted by a short railway detective with a moustache and a quiet Edinburgh voice who went through the whole rigmarole – to boot that we had on such-and-such a date wilfully damaged the property of British Rail, etc. We let him finish with, 'What have you got to say for yourselves?' The two regimental police were thoroughly enjoying themselves, thinking that their moment had at last come.

'Actually,' Ron replied, 'I'm glad you came. That window was patently dangerous. It just fell apart. Suppose a child had been passing on the platform. It could have been seriously injured. We did think of writing to British Rail to complain, but our studies here leave us little time for that sort of thing.'

The detective's chin literally dropped on hearing an educated southern accent. 'Oh,' he said, 'that's not necessary. I'll fill in a report form for you. When they told me your address was at an army camp, I thought you must be hooligans from Glasgow, or Black Watch or something. I'm very sorry to have disturbed you two young gentlemen.'

Those were the days when a well-modulated 'educated voice' caused bobbies to salute one and reserve their more aggressive tendencies for the lower orders. We sauntered nonchalantly out of the police office, behind us Wiry Twerp and Japanese Joe exploding in indignation at the detective, 'You should have nicked them both!'

As the Scottish winter reluctantly gave way to spring, 469 miles to the south at Easter 1958 campaigners against Britain's possession of nuclear weapons organised the first of a series of protest marches. Some 3,000 supporters of the Campaign for Nuclear Disarmament (CND) marched for four days from London to demonstrate outside the Atomic Weapons Establishment near the small Berkshire village of Aldermaston, where they were joined by an estimated additional 9,000 protesters. Having no political affiliation, I thought the idea of unilateral disarmament proposed by the CND ill-advised, or worse, since it would place Britain – no longer the planet-spanning empire it had been before the Second World War – potentially at risk of aggression by another power that had not similarly disarmed. It seemed to many people that, however sincerely pacifist many members of CND might be, the *organisers* of the affiliated movements must be closet Communists working for Stalin's USSR, of the genre then known as 'fellow travellers', and that since Britain's main adversary in the Cold War had no intention of unilaterally disarming, the CND's policy, if adopted by the government, might well *provoke* another war.

In any case, somebody in JSSL expressed better than me what many of us vaguely felt: that somewhere in the vastness of the steppes there must be a mirror-image Crail. There were several, as it happened. We imagined a converted collective farm, far from even the nearest railhead and lashed by Siberian blizzards, where Western dissidents coached Moscow's future snoopers and deep-cover agents on the intricacies of estuarian English, with every vowel a diphthong. Was there indeed a counterpart of Dmitri, wandering in that seemingly aimless manner of his, to the horror of the smartly uniformed officers in charge, from a production of kitchen sink drama – John Osborne, say – to the next play by Oscar Wilde? Were the female instructors boarding school educated veterans of the CPGB whose poor Russian changed to impeccable Roedean accents when speaking English in the classrooms, enlisted to coax some slender tractor driver's son into corset and crinoline, to simper on stage as Gwendoline in a production of *The Importance of being Ernest*? And how did the languid *apparatchik*'s son playing Lady Bracknell manage that line, 'A *hand*bag?'

Well, as the course drew to its end in April nobody in Intake 35 was taking it as seriously as in the first weeks and months. But then, not a single *uchenik* knew that we would shortly be serving on the front lines of the Cold War.

7

FROM *UCHENIKI* TO *KURSANTY* – THE SHEEP FROM THE GOATS

As to how the students for the Russian language courses were selected, an early planning paper listed the desiderata as a will to learn, good concentration, memory, accuracy, good health, age not over 25, a knowledge of the parts of speech and their functions – acquired in the author's case from prep-school exercises in parsing whole chapters of authors like Sir Arthur Quiller Couch – and a GCE A level pass in Latin or another foreign language. A slight knowledge of French or German was thought to be irrelevant and certainly of less value than an A level in a science subject, which was presumed to have inculcated the habit of accurate working.

On the majority of courses, known in services' jargon as 'intakes', most students came from grammar schools and would eventually marry girls from the same stratum of society. Typically, they had already been accepted for a place at a good university on completion of their two years' National Service, with a smattering of rebels like the author who had already decided, for various reasons, that three years of academic life in an arts discipline like modern languages, was a waste of anyone's time.

Life for the half-dozen top scorers in the First Major Test at Crail was an abrupt transition. Heading for the higher-level interpreters' course in Cambridge or London, they doffed uniforms, subsequently needed only for pay parades, and were issued with grey flannel trousers and Harris tweed jackets – normal wear for university students in those days. In inclement weather they wore civilian raincoats and trilby hats, this gentlemanly attire sartorially distinguishing them as officer cadets, or *kursanty*, from the uniformed *ucheniki* left behind at Crail.

The Cambridge course was run by Professor Elizaveta Fyodorovna Hill, daughter of a Scottish-Russian couple in Moscow who fled to Britain after the Bolshevik Revolution destroyed the family fortunes. A personal friend of émigré tsarist General Yevgeny K. Miller, who had been kidnapped in Paris by Smersh, smuggled back into the USSR, tortured and murdered in Moscow during May 1939, Professor Hill understandably had a lifelong hatred of Communism, balanced with a deep love for the Russian language and its literature. Known affectionately among her students as Liza, she was never called this to her face. A petite woman of high intellect, she controlled her students and staff as a benevolent tyrant.

This formidable woman had played a central role in the planning, establishment, initial curriculum and development of JSSL. She began by recruiting tutors in the large immigrant community in and around Paris, to which older émigrés gravitated because French had been their second language before they were forced by war or revolution to leave their homelands and because France had traditionally been a *pays d'accueil* for political refugees ever since *the* Revolution in 1799. Few had fluent English, but this was considered of little importance, since instruction was to be virtually all in Russian. Although most of them had good reason to hate the Soviet governments that had impoverished them and killed members of their families and friends, their politics were unimportant, for there was never any anti-Soviet indoctrination at JSSL and, surprisingly, several known card-carrying members of the Communist Party of Great Britain (CPGB) were among the students.

One of her early ideas was that cadets on the higher-level course should spend their last months in total immersion, living with an émigré family in Paris that spoke only Russian, but this idyllic arrangement did not go down well with the War Office, where Colonel Blimp was fearful that young National Service officer cadets bound by the Official Secrets Act[1] would be seduced by ladies of the night controlled by Soviet agents known to be active there. Another problem was the chronic lack of foreign exchange in Britain at the time to pay for the students' accommodation. Yet, one alumnus of JSSL, the future historian Sir Martin Gilbert, apparently did manage by a fluke of administration to spend a two-week expenses paid spell in Paris.

Liza had run Russian language courses for the British armed services between the wars and during the Second World War. Attributing her unflagging energy and enthusiasm to having had a Caucasian wet nurse, she was described by a future university professor among her JSSL *kursanty* as '… one of those super-energetic, positive and dynamic characters that one meets only once or twice in a lifetime'.[2] Another considered that she could have functioned equally well as chief instructor on a self-assertiveness course. Yet all regarded her with respectful affection, recounting how she would enter the classroom and construct an English sentence full of linguistic traps and turn her enthusiastic smile on one shaking *kursant*, who would stumble straight into the first trap, choosing the wrong aspect of a verb or selecting the wrong verb from the wide choice in Russian. The smile would be turned off and redirected to another student, leaving the first in limbo.

After the uneasy alliance between the Western Allies and the USSR ended in acrimony after the Second World War, there had been a plan to recruit Ukrainian exiles in Canada to serve as Russian–English and English–Russian interpreters for the British Control Commission in Germany. Although the languages are similar, Liza would have none of this, and convinced the War Office that she and her yet to be recruited staff could turn small groups of bright young English servicemen into competent Russian-speakers in twenty-six weeks of intensive tuition. With the USSR and its satellite states closed to almost all foreigners, the usual HUMINT methods of returning émigrés and undercover diplomats and businessmen recruiting in-country sources were impracticable. Therefore, SIGINT electronic intelligence – in other words, snooping round the borders of the Soviet bloc, intercepting their communications to check on troop movements, state of preparedness, etc. – took on a new importance and required an expanded training scheme to provide the necessary several hundred 'war interpreters', as they were designated.

The London interpreters' course within London University's School of Slavonic and East European Studies (SEESS) was directed by Ronald Hingley, a brilliant Russian scholar who won a scholarship in Greek and Latin to Cambridge University's Corpus Christi College at the age of 16, and apparently went on to teach himself German by reading Freud and Hitler and Russian by reading Dostoyevsky. An academic workaholic, he expected both his staff and students to work no less hard, telling the former that studying Russian was to be regarded as a military task with failure not an option and the latter that, if they let him down, '*Ya vam ustroyu skandal!*' – a phrase loosely translated as 'You won't know what hit you!'[3] In addition to the undoubted problems of devising the entire course, including the regular examinations, and himself writing some of the instruction books, Hingley suffered constant second-guessing by the principal of SSEES, George Bolsover, and was greatly relieved when he managed to escape to Oxford University in 1955, handing over to his equally humourless and workaholic deputy, Brian Toms. Both typified the Anglo-Saxon restrained and unemotional approach to the job in hand, in contrast with Liza's tempestuous Slavonic emotional outbursts. Both also felt a deep rivalry with the methods and achievements of her Cambridge course, although they were personally fond of her.

Bolsover was a dour northerner, politely described as no-nonsense and penny-pinching – euphemisms for his extreme rudeness, insensitivity and meanness. He had grown up the child of impoverished millworkers in the depressed Lancashire textile/mining/nail-making town of Atherton, north-west of Manchester. Gaining an MA in Russian at Liverpool University, he became an adult education tutor for Birmingham University and lectured on European history at Manchester University 1938–43. After serving as first secretary at the British Embassy in Moscow 1943–47, where he edited and produced a propaganda sheet entitled *Britanskii Soyuznik – British Ally* – which was intended to correct the comrades' bias against Britain due to two decades of intense anglophobic indoctrination, he returned to Britain and was appointed director of SSEES. Politically, his main task at first was to counteract the pro-Moscow stance of temporary lecturer and Comintern functionary Andrew Rothstein, son of notorious Comintern bagman and anti-British activist Theodore Rothstein.

The atmosphere encountered by the London *kursanty* was very different from that created in Cambridge by Liza's Chekhovian extended family of émigrés. It was, in fact, a serious grind, with little emphasis on Russian literature. Whereas Cambridge *kursanty* lived in a succession of country houses, being bussed into Cambridge for lessons, the London ones were billeted in a former hotel in South Kensington, taken over by the Royal Navy and dubbed HMS *President*. In this 'stone frigate', where the bedrooms were referred to as 'cabins' and leaving the building was termed 'going ashore', the starboard side of the ship on entering was accommodation for WRNS officers employed on secret work in the Admiralty, the port side being reserved for *kursanty*. With fourteen hours of classes and homework each day, and dire penalties for any skimped work, dalliance with the ladies would have been hard to fit in, even had they shown the slightest interest in the young officer cadets, some of whom managed to find time for theatres, concerts and exhibitions, thinking themselves fortunate to be on the loose in London with some money in their pockets on a salary of £5 a week, all found – which was more than half of what some of their fathers earned for a hard week in a factory or on the land.

The overall inspector of all language tuition in the British armed forces and GCHQ was a mild-mannered civil servant named Nakdimon Doniach, usually referred to as Naky. His parents, both active in the Zionist movement, immigrated to Britain after the father was arrested and imprisoned in Russia by the anti-Semitic Okhrana tsarist secret police. Born in Britain, Naky as a child showed even greater linguistic talent than his father, a teacher at SSEES. At 16, Naky was already studying Latin, Greek and Hebrew at King's College, London, plus classical Hebrew and Arabic, also winning prizes for proficiency in Aramaic, Syriac and Sanskrit. His career as a specialist bookseller of rare Judaica and Orientalia ended early in the Second World War when a German bomb destroyed his shop and stock, after which his exceptional intellect and extensive linguistic knowledge saw him headhunted by the RAF, initially for work at Bletchley Park with the rank of squadron leader. Teaching himself Russian with help from his mother, after eleven years in the RAF he moved to GCHQ as a senior civil servant and Britain's top authority on Russian language tuition during the Cold War.

8

THE GROANS OF GRUESOME GOBLINS

On 26 April 1958 the survivors of Intake 35 received their certificates confirming that they had passed out of JSSL Crail as qualified 'service translators' after completing the seven and a half month course and passing the final exam in 'reading and translation, dictation, written interpretership, translation from Russian in [sic] English, translation from English in [sic] Russian and writing a Russian essay'. The entire intake was given a week's home leave after promotion to Aircraftman First Class (AC1). At the end of the leave, the RAF element of Intake 35 met again on a deserted railway platform somewhere in Somerset. There were no man-hugs in those days – at least not between Englishmen – just a nod and hallo at most. Thence we were trucked to Pucklechurch, a sleepy village of grey stone houses 8 miles north-east of Bristol. The root of the name was said to be *puca*, a Celtic word meaning a goblin or evil spirit.

Although once the site of a Saxon palace, where King Edmund of the West Saxons was murdered in 946 CE, the village was in 1958 a dozy little place surrounded by green fields, but boasted a decent pub selling mild ale for 1*s* 1*d* and bitter for 1*s* 3*d* – slightly more than 5 new pence. Cheaper still was the locally brewed scrumpy cider, three pints of which in the authentically rustic Star Inn were enough to see the tyro scrumpyman reel out of the door and collapse on the village green feeling slightly ill.

The site of RAF Pucklechurch is now divided into an industrial estate and a prison for 400-plus Category C male sex offenders, which was destroyed in a riot in 1990. When Intake 35 arrived, it was a conventional camp of classroom and accommodation huts with a proper parade ground, looming over which were the enormous hangars that had been used for barrage balloon training and repairs by predominantly female personnel during the war. On the plus side, the food was immensely better than at Crail, but gone was the easy-going truce between students and permanent staff which we had enjoyed there. Not only did we have to smarten up for top brass inspections several times in our brief stay at Pucklechurch, but we also suffered regular PE sessions – in a hangar, if wet – and weekly kit inspections of our twenty-man billets, all of which were irritating distractions from the intensive technical training.

The technical courses for Russian translator *ucheniki* had only been moved to Pucklechurch from Wythall in Worcestershire in 1957. Somewhere in our new home, the trainee coders who had been at Crail at the same time as us were being given their technical training, but I never saw one, even at a distance. Other activities on the camp were kept in watertight compartments because we did not need to know about them. The Second World War posters showing torpedoed ships with the warning 'Careless talk costs lives', and the cartoons of blonde female spies in glamorous ballgowns listening to officers chatting about their work, with the slogan 'Keep mum, she's not so dumb', had all been overtaken by the new mantra 'need to know'. Very simply, if someone did not need to know something in order to do his job, he would not be given that information. Nor were we allowed to talk about our work to anyone who was not a trained Russian linguist. In case we had any doubts what that meant, we were made to sign yet another copy of the Official Secrets Act, with the officer in charge warning that it was a criminal offence to disclose information useful to an enemy, for which the maximum sentence was fourteen years in prison. Disclosing *any* information about our service experience, he warned, could see us locked up for two years. As two imprudent coders were later to discover, he was not joking. Had 'need to know' been the rule earlier, the enormous leakage of British secrets picked up from chums wearing the same old-school ties or belonging to the same clubs by Philby, Burgess, Maclean and Co. would have been drastically reduced. It was a case of bolting the stable door after many of those thoroughbred horses were long gone to Stalin's stable.

RAF Pucklechurch included a secret radar station and a Chinese intercept training facility about which we were not supposed to know, although Duncan Brewer recalls Chinese instructors driving bubble cars with transparent Perspex domes, in which they looked like benign alien invaders. Someone else bumped into a trainee Chinese linguist, who confessed that his course was a frustrating nightmare. Whereas we had reached somewhere above A level standard in Russian, the Chinese student linguists, so he said, were not taught to speak Mandarin or Cantonese properly, and certainly could not take dictation at normal speed in these alphabet-less tonal languages. The aim of their training was simply to enable them to log phonetically sets of four numbers indicating Chinese characters in intercepts captured at Batty's Belvedere on the Peak of Hong Kong Island, then a British colony.

Once, at Pucklechurch, I caught sight of Nikolai Invanovich's adult daughter, Rada Nikolaevna. My group's instructor, Sergeant 'Mick' Mulvaney, dismissed her as 'the camp bicycle – everyone's had a ride'. It seemed an unfair way of describing an attractive young woman, but rather typical of the masculine attitude to a single female in an otherwise almost all-male camp. What intrigued me was, what was a non-Brit like her doing in this nest of secrets?

The RAF contingent was again split up into small groups, but this time under regular NCO instructors. Sergeant Mick was an amiable 30-something man, who took service realities like rank and discipline with a pinch of salt. Some other groups had ranting DI-type instructors, one of whom cut his wife's throat, but Mick's quiet voice was far more effective. Since we were officially going to be 'wireless operators' (abbreviated to Wops), he gave us a brief introduction to radio technology as it then was. The sets we should be using were large VHF super heterodyne military communications receivers with five bandwidths, which the operator could tune very precisely to a given frequency and lock on to it. Mick's instruction in their internal intricacies was superfluous, any technical problems in the field being sorted out by mechanics who knew which end of a screwdriver was which. If one of us had ever opened up one of these expensive machines, it would probably never have worked again. John Griffin recalls half a century later, '… tedious lessons on the science and history of radio technology. I could not understand why we needed to know about beat frequency oscillators, for example.' The answer is, we did not, but they were part of the Wop course.

After helpfully distinguishing between 'planes', which are flat surfaces and 'aircraft', which were the machines flown by the RAF, Mick also gave us an interesting potted theory of aeronautics, from which we were surprised to learn that aircraft were held up by a quasi-vacuum created by the inclined wing surfaces travelling through the air. We were also taught the essentials of direction finding – using a dipole aerial to take a compass bearing on the source of a transmission. Where the bearings of two, or more, widely separated dipoles receiving the same transmission were drawn on a map and converged, was the location of the transmitter.

Breaking for lunch on the first day, we had a glorious surprise. As though to compensate for the poor food at Crail, the fare in the canteen at Pucklechurch was amazing, and even included an excellent steak on one occasion. Yet later we heard that the chief cook had also been in trouble – in his case, for using non-mess funds to buy better quality raw materials. With lunch behind us, we started our real *work*, which was initially completely baffling. Seated at benches equipped with headphone sockets and wearing headphones, known as 'cans', we listened as Mick played us what sounded like the groans of gruesome goblins being tortured in hell. Again and again, the same piece of tape was played as we strained to listen in English, Russian and whatever other languages each man had. After thirty minutes, Mick cut short our agony with the advice, 'Filter out in your heads the orchestra playing Shostakovich and the English football commentary, and just listen to the poor bastard speaking Russian'. Trying to do so, we could just hear a distant voice like Donald Duck with a bad cold. This, apparently, was a recording made in Berlin of a Soviet pilot calling his ground station, '*Dozhd, ya dozhd tridsat' syem. Kak menya slyshitye?*' – 'Rain, this is Rain 37. How do you read me?'

That was the first time we had heard operational traffic. Even after Mick had told us the words the pilot uttered, it was hard to pick them out of the deliberate 'interference' that had been added to the tape, to simulate the bad reception to which we would grow accustomed in the field. Yet, before the end of the course at Pucklechurch, we could hear a faint whisper and know exactly what was said. It helped that the pilots did not chatter about what they had eaten for breakfast or ask how each other was feeling after the previous evening's booze-up. The choice of messages was limited to contacting the ground station, checking its reception and reporting position, cloud and other weather conditions, manoeuvres being executed, observation of other aircraft, results of bombing runs, and so on. We would almost never hear the ground controller's side of the conversation, since VHF transmissions did not bend with the curvature of the earth. After the defection in 1952 of a British civil servant involved in SIGINT and the 1965 arrival of arch-traitor George Blake in Berlin – if not before – 'they' knew we were listening in, so radio discipline kept each transmission to a minimum, with both ground stations and every aircraft frequently changing call-signs – and sometimes changing them again a day later. Our job was to write down every message we heard in real time. It was someone else's job to work out which unit was using which call-sign on a given day.

Even civilian pilots speak in brief clipped transmissions; military ones flying 'fast-movers' even more so. To write down this new and confusing *diktovka* in real time, we had to learn a sort of shorthand or, more exactly, Russian speedwriting, so that frequently repeated phrases like '*kak menya sly-shitye?*' for 'how do you read me?' became '*kms*' in Russian script, and '*zadacha zakonchena*', meaning 'mission accomplished' was written '*zad/a zak/a*' – each message ending with '*priyom*' for 'over'. Since our log sheets bearing our personal intercept identity numbers were going to be read by other trained linguists, it was not necessary to translate the traffic; all the laborious learning process at Crail was to enable us to take down this new dictation accurately and fast. But we did have to absorb new vocabulary lists – of words like *shassi* (undercarriage) and *agregat* (power unit). We needed to know the terms for parts of fixed-wing aircraft – *samolyoty* – and helicopters – *vertolyoty* – that were likely to cause problems needing to be reported to base, even though we still had not the slightest idea where on an aircraft they might be or what purpose they served.

We also needed to understand the manoeuvres that Soviet pilots executed. So Mick explained the Soviet Air Force's system of short-range radio beacons situated at the four corners of the airfield, so that '*Nad pervom*', meaning 'over the first [beacon]', told us that a pilot had commenced his approach to land. This would, barring a disaster, be followed by '*Nad ftorym*' and '*Nad tretyem*' as he lined up over the second and third beacons, turning 90 degrees left each time, and with '*Nad chetvyortom*' telling us that he was lined up on the runway. If he was practising 'circuits and bumps' – landing, opening the throttle to take off again, flying a circuit and landing again, etc. – we might spend a couple of hours trying to stay awake as we logged the repetitive short bursts of transmission. Yet it was, so Mick promised us, all grist to the mill and vitally important for the analysts back at base or in GCHQ at Cheltenham to know exactly how ready, or otherwise, the Soviet Air Force was to launch the third world war.

With 80 per cent of SIGINT being provided by RAF linguists, as against 10 per cent from each of the other services, on a busy frequency we had to slip the carbons between the log sheets in several books at the start of our shift so we could swap from one book to the next without wasting time. Suddenly, in the midst of all this, we would be hit with very fast reading of numbers in five-figure groups, which we had to write down in different log books, whose pages were divided into little boxes. These transmissions meant nothing at all to us, or anyone else lacking the day's code book, so mindless accuracy was of paramount importance, if the logs were to mean anything when subsequently analysed.

Also paramount was picking up and recording any inadvertent slips in the traffic. Since call-signs were changed at frequent intervals, a unit using '*konferentsia*' (conference) today might switch overnight to '*molnya*' (lightning) to throw our analysts off the scent. But, human nature being what it is, quite often a busy pilot would use the previous day's call-sign and then correct himself with the universal expletive '*yob tvoyu mat!*' Any monitor picking up a gem like this would get a 'signal from base' – the peacetime equivalent of a mention in despatches.

At first, it seemed unlikely that we would ever get the hang of these strange activities, vital to the daily updating of the Soviet Order of Battle, but Mick assured us that by the end of the Pucklechurch course we should be able to do it in our sleep. He was so right that the author still counts off his daily exercises in Russian.

Mick's laid-back attitude extended to telling us some things we were not supposed to know – for instance, that British and other Allied aircraft packed with electronic equipment frequently flew 'ferret' missions, deliberately straying off course along the Soviet borders, to be detected by the other side's radar and trigger the launch of interceptor fighters, who chased them back to the right side of the border. The object of this dangerous exercise was to analyse Soviet radar transmissions and check how long it took to intercept the British intruder. Much later, this was common knowledge, as was the practice of huge nuclear submarines, armed with sufficient ICBMs packing enough destructive power to obliterate several cities, playing chicken under the oceans of the world. But at the time most of us were alarmed to learn that the powers-that-be sanctioned these dangerous games, which had, on occasion, fatal results for the players. In these operations, the US lost some forty aircraft and 200 men. After the implosion of the USSR, President Yeltsin said that he had created a special commission to trace any of these men who were still alive, but predictably no trace of them was found.[1]

For whatever reason, 17 May was the day we were promoted again – to the rank of Senior Aircraftman (SAC), having skipped the intermediate rank of Leading Aircraftman (LAC). As another reward for his group, one morning Mick unlocked a darkened classroom into which we were not normally allowed, to give us a break from the slog of trying to decipher some scrambled tank traffic of a Russian senior sergeant repeatedly screaming at his entire squadron of incompetents, '*Yob tvoyu mat!*' – roughly the equivalent of the English 'motherfucker', a word none of us had heard in those innocent times. Inside was a communications receiver different from the ones on which we were being trained, which Mick tuned to a frequency where we heard a clear beep-beep-beep signal. We were listening in real time to the telemetry transmissions from the Soviet Sputnik 2 satellite orbiting overhead. The passenger – a mongrel dog named Laika, or 'Husky' in English – had died shortly after launch when the cabin temperature went out of control, and the satellite had only a few more days to go before it burned up on re-entry into the earth's atmosphere on 14 April 1958 after 162 days in orbit.

To remind us that we were back on duty after our holiday among the civilians at Crail, hut and kit inspections were far more onerous than they had been there, including a regular 'Bull night' each Friday and a parade every Wednesday morning. All this was in preparation for the visit of the Air Officer Commanding (AOC) in July. What exactly he commanded, we had no idea or wish to know. On the day of the AOC's inspection we were kept standing on the parade ground for a couple of hours in a steady downpour, waiting for the brass to arrive. Back in the classroom afterwards, someone asked Mick what he thought about standing there all that time, getting wetter and wetter in his best uniform. Instead of inventing an answer, he grinned, 'I think of all the money they're paying me for doing nothing. Now, back to work.'

Alan Bamber wrote to his girlfriend:

> … conditions were at times not far removed from basic training because the AOC's visit was causing panic. We had to scrub kit bags, clean boot brushes and do countless other stupid things. The AOC's visit passed peacefully enough, for which blessing we had the weather to thank. It pelted down with rain and the visiting celebrity decided to cut short some of the planned inspections, probably out of self-interest as much as pity for the sodden airmen on parade. He did however visit our billet while we were at our Russian classes. We were told later that he was very pleased with it. I doubt if we regarded this as the most treasured of life's accolades, but a contrary judgement on his part might have had unpleasant repercussions.

At the same time as this confusing jumble of activities, those who wished to take the London University A level Russian exam had to read three set books, one of which was Pushkin's *The Captain's Daughter*. We had been promised that Russian editions of the set books were available in Pucklechurch, but they were not. Copies were sent especially from Crail, and arrived late. Feeling somewhat brain-dead with all the SIGINT instruction we were absorbing, we cheated and bought English translations of the set books. Bamber, an honest man, confessed this to the author in 2016, but we were probably all equally guilty. His notes of the exam in the last week of June included, 'one of the poems from Russian to English was almost untranslatable' – as poetry often is.

The stress was that our last-minute cramming came at the same time as our final exam on the Wop course – about which we need not have worried, some of the instructors telling their students, 'There's an exam before you get your stripes, but, by the way, you've all passed'. With previous intakes of linguists out there in the field being demobbed at the end of their two years, we were needed to replace them without delay, so there was no interruption in logging all those clipped messages and groups of numbers. Therefore, no one who had lasted the course was ever known to have failed the exam.

Apart from the pub, the countryside and the church named after Henry II's 'troublesome priest' Thomas Becket, not far away was Bradford-upon-Avon Saxon church, one of the earliest stone churches in Britain. In Bristol, just a couple of bus rides distant, there was a range of entertainment. For music lovers, orchestral concerts at the Colston Hall complemented a Yehudi Menuhin concert at Bath Abbey and a packed performance of J.S. Bach's *Mass in B Minor* in Bristol Cathedral. The more energetic could cycle to tourist spots like Wookey Hole and Cheddar Gorge. For the more sporting, available activities included tennis, football, athletics and cricket against teams from other RAF camps. There was even a station sports day. Late night bridge continued to be an obsession for our addicts, having been joined by a newcomer who had done A level Russian at school and therefore been accelerated through Crail to join our intake. Brian Howe once again sniffed out the local talent by what he dubs, 'cavorting with charming students from a Fishponds teacher training college'. We all had our priorities.

The camp's geographical position meant that it was just possible for me to hitchhike back to Canterbury on some weekends to see my girlfriend. Hitchhiking was easy in those days for men in uniform. I learned to sleep on the hot, vibrating metal covers of noisy diesel truck engines and spent one Sunday night clinging to a leather-clad biker roaring through the darkness along the old A4 trunk road. Having received T.S. Eliot's *Four Quartets* as a poetry prize at school, it seemed to me that the bike and its unknown rider and I, clinging to him, were the still point of the turning world as sleeping villages and towns like Reading and Marlborough whizzed past us without a sign of life. Getting colder and colder in my best blue uniform, the hat secured by the strap tight under my chin, I hoped not to fall off, unconscious from hypothermia.

At last, the bike slowed down and stopped and a Cockney voice said, 'You ge' off 'ere, mate'. With muttered thanks, I manoeuvred my frozen left leg over the pillion seat and started jogging the last miles back to camp, to try and restart my circulation, arriving with just five minutes to change into battledress and try to stay awake in the classroom for the rest of the morning.

That was actually not the most alarming lift during the time at Pucklechurch, which happened in a red convertible of unknown model with white-wall tyres, driven by a lady of about 50 with flaming red-dyed hair, red leather jacket and red leather trousers. Somewhere on the Guildford bypass, her left hand gripped my right thigh rather intimately as she shouted over the wind-noise, 'Have you got a girlfriend, airman?'

'Yes,' I replied. 'I'm on my way to visit her.'

'Shit!' she said, turning to an army bloke sitting in the rear seat. 'What about you, soldier? Girlfriend?'

'Afraid not, ma'am.'

I was relieved when she turned back to face the way we were travelling – until she braked to a stop and ordered me to get out and the khaki job to get into the front passenger seat. I watched them drive away, wondering how the journey would end for him, and thumbed down a nice, safe, smelly diesel truck with a monosyllabic driver, cigarette permanently glued to his lower lip, for the next stage of that odyssey. There was also a weekend coach service from the camp direct to London at the bargain price of 18 shillings return, but if there were insufficient takers, the coach was cancelled at the last minute so I usually chose to hitch lifts.

On 19 July, at the end of the three-month course, we were promoted to the dizzy heights of junior technician, abbreviated to J/T, which would remain our rank for the rest of our service. Removing the SAC rank badge – a triple-bladed propeller – from our sleeves and stitching on the J/T's inverted single chevron, the title 'technician' seemed odd to young men who regarded themselves as civilian intellectuals merely wearing uniform for a couple of years, and using their brains, not spanners and screwdrivers, for the RAF. The logic was that we were trained wireless operators after having learned to operate those communications receivers in their large, grey-enamelled metal cabinets, and a man trained to operate a machine was *ipso facto* a technician. Any implied insult to our intellect pretensions was softened by an increase in salary to £4 7s 6d at each payday – riches indeed! A hidden advantage of the trade ranks of junior technician, senior technician and chief technician was that whereas corporals and sergeants had disciplinary duties in addition to their service trade, because we had to work shifts around the clock we had no such duties.

As we learned that day, most of us were posted to RAF Gatow in the British Sector of occupied Berlin. Our single 'regular', Duncan Brewer, was originally posted to the enormous RAF base at Habbaniya in Iraq, but the Iraqi Revolution that same month, in which King Faisal II, Prime Minister Nuri al-Said and other leaders were assassinated, ending the British-imposed Hashemite monarchy, saw his posting changed to sunny Cyprus. It was, at the time, far from a holiday destination, with Turks and Greeks enthusiastically killing each other. On arrival, Duncan and several other linguists were transported in a 3-ton truck, lying on a bed of sand bags, supposed to absorb the explosion of any EOKA IEDs planted on the road. His base was not within one of the two large British sovereign bases, but in a smaller camp at Pergamos, where servicemen were forbidden to go out in groups of less than six men in uniform, with at least two carrying loaded Stens. It did not, however, take him long to adjust the two-days-on and two-days-off shift system by paying other linguists to do two days for him, making an unofficial six-day leave, to put to sea crewing on a Turkish fishing boat.

Like the author in Berlin, Duncan exploited the low price of cigarettes in the Naafi to smuggle them out to a local bar, where the owner marked their black market value up as credit on Duncan's slate for eventual conversion into food and drink. Although he created a very congenial personal lifestyle, minimally constrained by RAF discipline, one chore he could not dodge was occasional night duty on the camp perimeter, where an over-keen RAF Police flight lieutenant tested the vigilance of the guard by creeping up on the sentries to steal their rifles.

A combination of ionospheric conditions enabled RAF, army and naval linguists plus civilian operators in Cyprus to monitor Russian long-wave traffic from missile test ranges in the southern USSR. Most of the traffic intercepted on Cyprus was numbers, numbers, numbers, being the encoded results of Soviet missile tests, occasional excitement being afforded when a missile malfunctioned, turned around and 'returned to base' unexpectedly. Irritated by an intrusive nocturnal supervisor, the linguists tuned one set to very painful 'white noise', so that when he snooped on that set he received a most unpleasant shock.

With the selfishness of youth, the rest of us heaved a sigh of relief that we were not being sent to an island where the natives were killing each other and any British servicemen who got in the way. Our one married man, Harvey May, was posted to Digby in Lincolnshire as a favour, to spend the rest of his service among the potato fields listening to long-wave Soviet transmissions of telemetry numbers, numbers, numbers, with the compensation that this posting enabled him to see his wife fairly frequently. Our Scottish accountant, Dave Bruce, was also mystifyingly to remain in Britain. As we later discovered, this was because his handicap of three had him earmarked to play golf for the RAF Technical Training Wing in inter-service matches! He reported to Somewhere-in-Lincolnshire, to play the numbers game and golf on a base with hundreds of service and civilian SIGINT operators, and was obliged to stay there until the end of October, when his repeated pleas to the station commander saw him posted to Berlin after three months of what he later recalled as the loneliest days of his life. The truth behind that remark was that everyone in Intake 35 had become, in some sense, family; we did not necessarily all like each other especially but after a year of intensive training together, 'the others' were part of the scenery for each of us – and poor Dave was lost in a foreign landscape, knowing no one at all.

PART 3

BERLIN DAYS

9

THE STORY SO FAR

There was, in 1958, nothing new about signals interception. More than forty years earlier, during the First World War's 'war of the trenches' in Flanders, both sides used a primitive system in which small 'listening patrols' slipped across no-man's-land between the lines at night to place metal induction plates underneath the other side's field telephone cables. From the plates, a concealed pair of wires led back to 'our' trench, where 'their' messages could sometimes be listened in to by an officer who spoke the right language. Where wireless technology was used over longer distances, all sides in the conflict were already intercepting and/or jamming each other's diplomatic radio traffic, but military SIGINT was in its infancy, although the Germans were sufficiently technically advanced for them to regularly decipher coded communications between the Western Allies in Flanders so efficiently that Marshal Joffre's Order of the Day for the Battle of the Marne in September 1914 was deciphered and read by the German High Command before it had reached the French front line.[1]

At the other end of Europe, in the East Prussian pincer campaign of August–September 1914 the two Russian commanding generals, Samsonov and von Rennenkampf – who each blamed the other for Russia's defeat in the 1905 war with Japan – refused to co-ordinate their moves or even to communicate directly with each other for any reason, and sent their transmissions via Northern Front HQ at Bialystok, which introduced delay. Since Russian military radio communications were transmitted *en clair* ('in clear' = not coded), they were easily intercepted by front-line

German signals intercept units and analysed instantly by Russian-speaking German officers.[2]

Following the Armistice in November 1918, the small ANZAC-British-Canadian interventionist force under British General Lionel Dunster set up an intercept unit in Northern Iran and the Caucasus, which monitored Soviet traffic for several years afterwards. Between the two major wars British Post Office operators who were trained in Morse code detected unlicensed transmitters in Britain used by Comintern agents to communicate with Moscow Centre and logged their encrypted Morse code transmissions.

During the Second World War, when the USSR was officially an ally, illicit traffic continued from agents in Britain – as it did throughout the Cold War. Although the Enigma decryption at Bletchley Park eventually stole the headlines, there would have been no raw SIGINT material for Turing and his brilliant colleagues at Bletchley to decode without the work of the Y Service – men and women in Britain and literally around the world logging or recording millions of encoded Axis signals on wax discs. At a holiday music course in 1999, the author met a former army SIGINT linguist who, at the end of January 1943 in North Africa, had intercepted a transmission 'in clear' to OKW in Berlin from General von Paulus' surrounded 6th Army at Stalingrad, 1,500 miles distant. It read simply, '*Besprechungen mit dem Feind angefangen*' – 'We have begun negotiations with the enemy'. This was the first indication that von Paulus was defying Hitler's 'No surrender' order, and that the Allies could remove the German 6th Army from the Nazi Order of Battle.

Ashore and afloat, Royal Navy linguists strained to pick up the brief transmissions from surfaced U-boats that might be DF'd to track them down and sink them before they attacked another transatlantic convoy. In tropical heat and monsoon downpour, Australian signals interceptors listened in to Japanese traffic, as did Nisei Japanese-Americans on Pacific islands and the West Coast of North America. German and Japanese signals intelligence units were also efficiently intercepting Soviet Army, Navy and Air Force transmissions, where mistakes by sloppy operators often gave them a key to break the codes being used. Significantly, German attempts to crack GRU and NKVD codes were less successful because of far tighter discipline in those organisations. When reports of the German intercepts were forwarded to Berlin in Enigma traffic, some of them were re-decoded at Bletchley Park. This, in turn, alerted Allied Target Intelligence Committee Missions (TICOM) in April 1945 to head into Germany, hard on the heels of the front-line units, and grab from Soviet-occupied territory a quantity of documents, manuals and other material and equipment relating to German intercepts of Soviet traffic that required three freight wagons to bring it all back to Western-occupied territory.[3]

However, the NKVD had agents among the US cryptanalysts using the material. These included Bill Weisband, a Ukrainian-born man serving in the Army Signals Service, who spilled the beans, resulting in 'Black Friday' on 29 October 1948, when many Soviet radio communications systems adopted new encryption systems and traffic in clear diminished, except in real-time transmissions, for example, between pilots and ground controllers. Interestingly, Weisband was never prosecuted – perhaps because the Soviets must have known what was going on from many other sources.

SIGINT was routinely practised internally before, during and after the Second World War. Post Office and other listeners in Britain scanned the airwaves to pick up transmissions from both Soviet and Nazi agents in the British Isles and Ireland. In occupied France, interception of Allied agents' transmissions was the most important tool for tracking down and rolling up the SOE and other networks, thousands of whose members ended up in concentration and death camps after torture, following arrest.[4]

When that war ended in the European theatre in May 1945 the Western governments woke up to the fact that they had allowed Stalin's armies to occupy most of Central and Eastern Europe. The Baltic States, Bulgaria, Romania, Yugoslavia, Albania, Czechoslovakia, Hungary, Poland and half of Germany and Austria were behind what came to be known as the Iron Curtain, where Stalin's repressive grip on the native populations through secret police organisations modelled on, and controlled by, the NKVD and its successor the KGB grew tighter yearly.[5]

There was, however, one technical advantage for the West in this Soviet expansion into Europe: with no buffer states, Stalin's occupation forces were nose-to-nose with Western armies all along the borders of Czechoslovakia and Yugoslavia and along the internal frontiers dividing the Soviet zones of Germany and Austria from the Western zones. Of these, the strategically most important frontier was the internal border stretching 866 miles from the shores of the Baltic all the way through Germany to the Czech frontier, because the most likely invasion route by which the Soviets might invade Western Europe cut straight across that frontier on the perfect tank country of the North German Plain or the Fulda Gap, aiming straight at the US forces' headquarters in Frankfurt. In addition, as agreed at Yalta, the former German capital Berlin was divided into four sectors: British, French,[6]

American and Russian. Although the Russian, or Eastern, sector was almost as large as the three Western ones, they did give Western SIGINT units ideal conditions in which to intercept Soviet traffic from the surrounding Russian-occupied territory. However, when the first RAF Regiment personnel arrived to secure the base at Gatow on 25 June 1945, they were held off at gunpoint by the Russian ground forces already there and found themselves surrounded by barbed wire entanglements in a shrinking perimeter. Dogged persistence and calm eventually reclaimed most of the airfield and barracks from the Soviets.

In June 1948 Stalin attempted to force the Western Allies out of the former German capital by reneging on the Four-Power Agreement guaranteeing access routes for Allied road, rail and canal traffic to the three Western sectors of Berlin. Various gung-ho local commanders argued that heavily armed military convoys should force a passage along the autobahn to Berlin, brushing aside by force of arms any resistance encountered. Fortunately, wiser heads saw that this might easily spark a third world war. By chance, General Albert Wedemeyer, US Army Chief of Plans and Operations, was in Europe on an inspection tour. Having commanded the American China–Burma–India theatre in the Second World War, Wedemeyer had first-hand experience of the American airlift from India over 'the Hump' of the Himalayas to the Nationalist forces fighting the Japanese in China. Based on that experience, his considered opinion was that a similar airlift to Berlin could work.

Backed by the very hands-on General Lucius Clay, US Commander in Berlin, all available aircraft immediately began flying into the beleaguered city everything from aspirins and penicillin to coal and cement. They were swiftly joined by aircraft de-mothballed in many countries, flying 24/7 along the agreed air corridors into Tempelhof Airport in the US sector, Tegel Airport in the French sector and Gatow Airfield in the British sector. On the return leg, some aircraft carried exports from West Berlin factories. That winter, West Berliners huddled near their stoves, for which there was precious little fuel, but somehow the city survived. As West Berlin's anti-Communist mayor Ernst Reuter had predicted, the population's morale was strengthened by this show of Western determination not to leave them at Stalin's mercy, which they had already experienced briefly in the immediate aftermath of the German surrender. During the Airlift, thanks to brilliant air traffic control round-the-clock managing the flights of hundreds of aircraft in every twenty-four-hour period, very few of them crashed, killing crews, passengers and civilians on the ground.

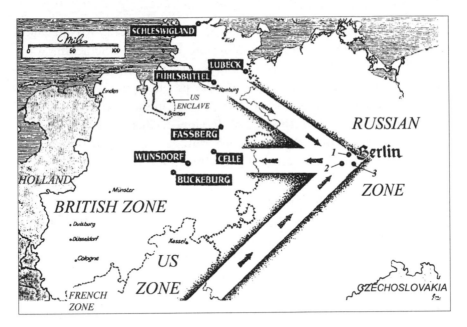

A contemporary map of the Airlift air corridors to Berlin.

Just once was there direct confrontation with the Soviet aircraft that flew alongside, watching all the Allied moves. On 5 April 1949 a Yak-3 pilot misjudged his distance while harassing a British European Airways Vickers Viscount and crashed into it, killing its ten civilian passengers and the crew. The Airlift continued until 12 May 1949, when the Russians backed down after eleven months, having failed to achieve anything. The barriers were opened on the Hanover–Berlin autobahn and surface traffic again flowed into Berlin, albeit sluggishly at first, with the Airlift continuing at a slower pace until 30 September. For a total cost of US$224 million it had delivered just over 1 ton of food, fuel, machinery and other supplies per inhabitant of the Western sectors – a total of 2,323,738 tons.

Under its Latin motto, *pons heri pons hodie* – a bridge yesterday, a bridge today – RAF Gatow continued as a British base for both army and air force units until 18 June 1994, when the airfield and base were handed over to the reunited German state's Luftwaffe. Although some training is carried out there and radomes hint at continuing signals activities, the main function now is as the Luftwaffe's museum, of which the outdoor exhibits included a splendid array of NATO and Warsaw Pact aircraft.

However, despite Berlin being technically the ideal place in 1945 in which to intercept Soviet radio traffic, opinions were divided on whether this was a good idea. On a battlefield, it was normal practice to obtain advance warning of impending attacks by digging in concealed listening posts near to the enemy's lines, with the 'acceptable' risk that the men in the listening posts were often the first casualties when an attack developed. Since a Soviet invasion of the Western sectors of Berlin would take from start to finish between a few hours to three days maximum, siting SIGINT units there could mean that the Western commanders would be blind and deaf once they had been overrun or wiped out. In the East German Nazionale Volksarmee invasion plans uncovered after German reunification, Grenzregiment 34 'Hanno Günther' was tasked with rolling straight across the airfield at Gatow, where the only resistance to this surprise move would have been provided by a detachment of the Royal Inniskilling Regiment executing a tactical withdrawal through the pine trees between the barrack blocks, armed with nothing heavier than rifles, Bren guns and maybe an anti-tank rifle or two. Without casting any aspersions, it may safely be assumed that the single RAF Junior Technician linguist on duty in the DF outpost actually on the airfield would have capitulated on hearing the first shout of '*Hände hoch!*', if not already blown to pieces by the first Communist tank shell.

The SIGINT operation in Gatow began on 31 March 1951, when a small contingent of linguist interceptors arrived there from 365 signals unit at RAF Uetersen, to find themselves on a ghost airfield, placed on care-and-maintenance after the 1948 Airlift and manned by no more than sixty RAF personnel. Officially, they were referred to as 3 Detachment of 365 signals unit under a CO with the comparatively modest rank of Flight Lieutenant, who was presumably regarded as disposable, should Gatow be invaded. The linguists were initially accommodated in offices within the station headquarters building adjoining the control tower until someone realised that if a second Soviet blockade necessitated another Airlift, they would have to be turfed out of there at exactly the moment when their snooping was most important. They were then re-housed in one of the original Luftwaffe blocks designated 'Hanbury', said to be 'at the junction of Trenchard and Halton roads', a description that baffles linguists of the author's generation, since the BAOR habit of giving English names to roads on British bases entirely escaped us.[7]

At the time, the RAF's main SIGINT base was sited in the comparative safety of the British zone at Hambühren, north of Hannover and

30-plus miles back from the inner-German frontier. It controlled eighteen out-stations, some of which were on wheels. Among the 220 personnel stationed at RAF Hambühren 1954-57 were thirty-six Russian linguists, plus German, Czech and Polish linguists as well as one or more analysts from Government Communications Headquarters. Another intercept base was the Gatow unit's parent base even further from the inner German border, at Uetersen in Schleswig-Holstein. British Army linguists in No 1 Special Wireless Regiment were based further back still, at Birgelen, almost on the Dutch frontier. Things changed after the Airlift and that regiment installed some of its personnel at RAF Gatow in 1953[8] – not that most linguists of Intake 35 ever saw any khaki-clad colleagues in Berlin, although some said they vaguely recalled playing rugby with them.

10

IN THE HEART OF HITLER'S REICH

After an end-of-course forty-eight-hour pass, Intake 35 reassembled at Pucklechurch to find that something had gone wrong on the logistics side. A new intake was occupying our billet, so we had to move lock, stock and barrel – with bedding and all our kit – to a transit billet for the night. It was thus in rather grumpy mood that we set off on 16 July for Berlin, first by train to London and then the boat train from Liverpool Street Station, to catch the Harwich ferry. Decanted on the dockside in the ferry terminal, we were herded by MPs aboard an ancient troopship and down into the ill-ventilated and stiflingly hot hold with little space between the two racks of bunks in eight-man cabins. Sweating in vest and pants, nobody had much sleep as the vessel lurched across the North Sea, the pessimists among us having worked out that, in the event of a disaster, there was no way we could fight our way back up to the deck, from where we might have a chance of being rescued.

Ferry ports look grim in the early morning, and the Hook of Holland was no exception. But just to be out of the troopship was wonderful, with the first breath of cool, fresh, Dutch air almost inebriating. A nice, clean, brown German train waited on the quayside to speed us onward towards the destination on our movement orders, but not all the way, since German trains could not traverse the Soviet zone, deep in the heart of which lay Berlin, 100 miles inside Soviet-occupied territory.

The next few days were more like a holiday than a tour of duty. For whatever reason of logistics, our onward travel to Berlin was leisurely. The first train took us to Dalheim in West Germany from where we were bussed to

RAF Wildenrath, to be processed as being on the strength of the RAF in occupied Germany. This was the first time we had stayed in a real RAF base with long runways, dispersal areas and aircraft taking off, day and night. On the next morning we set off by coach to München Gladbach, then train to Hamlin and another coach again to RAF Scharfoldendorf – a camp unlike any we had known in Britain. It was situated in a superb hilltop location among forests and mountains, which had been used for glider training of Goering's future aces in the years before Hitler could take his gamble of re-establishing, as the brand-new Luftwaffe, the Fliegertruppen of the First World War, which was forbidden under the 1919 Treaty of Versailles. It was, however, sobering to find the camp surrounded by a no-go area between double barbed-wire fences, where notices in German warned that Alsatian attack dogs roamed free at night.

There we spent three nights, the outdoor types enjoying tennis and sunbathing, while others made a trip to the legendary town of Hamlin, where they were surprised to find shops full of mice in china, glass, soap and edibles like chocolate, sweets, even bread rolls – but no celebration of the famous piper or the children who, according to the legend, vanished into the mountain.

Coached after this very enjoyable break to Hannover – a town then still largely devastated by British bombs except for ugly new concrete and glass buildings in what would later become the new city centre – we were warned not to leave the station because gangs of local youths sometimes attacked Allied servicemen in uniform to avenge the wartime destruction of their city. We duly boarded the British Military Train (BMT) for an all-night journey through the so-called German Democratic Republic (GDR). Warned to keep the blinds drawn and not peer out, and armed with our *putyovki* bilingual English/Russian travel documents, we settled down uncomfortably for the night. First stop was at Helmstedt's Checkpoint Able – checkpoints Baker and the more famous Charlie were in Berlin – for a last-minute check by British Military Police. Then came Marienborn, just across the border, where East German frontier guards came aboard the BMT to check the travel documents. Unknown to them – and us at the time – in a locked toilet compartment an army linguist was uncomfortably huddled with his comms receiver, tasked with monitoring any Russian military chatter he could pick up during the journey.[1]

Obviously the Deutsche Reichsbahn of the GDR did not rate us a priority train; the BMT stopped frequently at unlit stations or was parked in deserted sidings while other traffic thundered by, which is why the 175-mile journey took all night. At one of the many stops, John Griffin lifted a blind to peer out, and promptly dropped it on finding a Red Army soldier with rifle staring back at him a few paces away. In another grey dawn, we stepped down onto the platform of Berlin's Zoo Station under the zodiac sign of Leo, but feeling most unleonine, and blinked at the sun rising on Wednesday, 23 July 1958 – the first day of the rest of our lives.

In a sense, during training we had been rather carefree youths. Now, we were men, facing off several million other men, whose language we could speak, yet who were our very well-armed and battle-ready enemies. They were literally all around us. Like Custer at Little Big Horn, we were encircled by the enemy. It was a chilling thought. And there was also yesterday's enemy. The very name Berlin had, for so many of our formative years, been synonymous with Hitler; the Nazis; the Luftwaffe that dropped bombs on us; the scientists who designed, and the soldiers who fired, those terrifying V1s and V2s at London, the suburbs and targets as far north as Manchester and Liverpool in the months following the June 1944 Normandy Invasion; never mind the U-boats that killed some of our fathers and kept us short of food.

Yet the most terrible images of the German war machine were not these or the cities of half of Europe devastated by Allied bombing, but the newsreel images we had seen in the cinema of starving and dying prisoners in concentration and death camps apathetically watching bulldozers driven by Allied soldiers shovelling thousands of emaciated corpses into unmarked pits for disposal. The newsreel footage of the liberated camps was kept short by the censor, but was enough to terrify 8-year-old boys like us. All these negative impressions somehow survived the West's attempt to make the Berliners into heroes during the Airlift and afterwards.

From the warm compartments of the BMT we scrambled down with our kitbags, to find a military coach waiting to transport us to Gatow. The previous year, our predecessor Leslie Woodhead had recalled the strange sensation of being driven in a coach through the partly rebuilt city centre of Berlin after his arrival and then westwards along the Heerstrasse past Hitler's Olympic Stadium, setting of the infamous 1936 Olympics, where the Führer sulked after black American athlete Jesse Owens won four gold medals. The stadium, apparently undamaged – except for the giant reinforced concrete swastika which originally graced its roof, and which the Royal Engineers had blown to pieces in a spectacular explosion – was now used as the headquarters of the military administration of the British sector and also the offices of the MI6 outpost running its agents across Berlin.

With the American espionage services based on Clayallee in the US sector, the French Secret Service in the north-west at the Quartier Napoléon, the KGB embedded in the Soviet HQ in the eastern suburb of Karlshorst and the GDR's Hauptverwaltung Aufklärung having its headquarters in the massive Normannenstrasse HQ of the Ministerium für Staatssicherheit, there were *thousands* of Allied, Soviet and GDR agents, plus many freelancers scrabbling for titbits to sell to whichever side paid best. At the time it seemed that spying was the only growth industry in the former German capital, where the ultimate scoop was the CIA's tunnel into the Russian sector, through which the land lines to and from the Soviet HQ at Karlshorst were tapped to produce some 40,000 hours of recorded phone conversations and 6 million hours of telex messages.[2] But then the scoop turned on its creators when George Blake arrived in Berlin and spilled the espionage beans to Moscow, after which much of the traffic so assiduously collected was deliberately deceptive.

After the Olympic Stadium, we passed a road sign for Spandau, where the last four German war criminals were still held in prison under Four-Power guards, changed monthly. Suddenly we were in the countryside on a road paved with pre-war Kieselsteine cobbles, rolling between cottages and villas to arrive at the immaculate white pebble-dashed gatehouse of RAF Gatow.

In 1934, what had been a large stretch of open country between the Havel Lake and Gross-Glienecker Lake was cleared of vegetation for the construction of a major training airfield for Goering's Reichsluftfahrtministerium, or Air Ministry, by 4,000 labourers and skilled craftsmen who completed the major work in twelve months in defiance of the Versailles Treaty. In August 1935, when it was judged fit for purpose, flying training on the grass runways began, as did an air force academy, an air warfare school and a technical training wing. Hitler could not miss the chance of performing the opening ceremony, rightly confident that the victorious Allies of the First World War would do nothing about it. An English author who visited Gatow in 1936 wrote:

> Certainly, when the Luftwaffe came into being officially, it started to do itself well. At Gatow I was taken into a big mess with an attractive bar, a reading room and a silent room for writing, and I remarked that their officers were lucky to have such comfort. A Luftwaffe Staff Major who was with me said it was not the Officers' Mess, but the mess of the MT drivers.[3]

Flying training of pilots at Gatow lasted two years. After twelve months, flight crew were specialised for fighters or bombers, or became air gunners, navigators and radio operators. Only in the last desperate months of the Second World War, as Soviet armies neared Berlin, did combat aircraft land and take off from Gatow's grass runways. In one of the sillier stories of that war, on 23 April 1945 – two weeks before the final capitulation – Hitler despatched General der Flieger Karl Koller by air from Gatow to the Obersalzberg to inform Reichsmarschall Hermann Goering of his official appointment as Hitler's successor. By the time Koller arrived there, the Führer had changed his mind and Goering was arrested by the SS instead as a traitor.

Three days later, Gatow and its surroundings were occupied by Soviet troops. After the airfield was placed in the sector of Berlin awarded to the British at the Potsdam Conference in July–August 1945, from 1 August the base was officially renamed RAF Gatow and became home to 400 British servicemen, the Royal Engineers among them laying 1,450 yards of interlocking perforated steel strips to cover one of the grass runways so that heavier aircraft could land. On 9 December a ground-controlled approach system was installed and operational, making the airfield suitable to handle both RAF and British European Airways civilian traffic.

Possibly in far-sighted anticipation of the 1948 Soviet blockade of access to Berlin by road, rail and water, in March 1947 800 local workers were brought in to lay a modern concrete runway 2,000 yards long and, shortly thereafter, a second runway was laid. Originally dubbed 'Operation Knicker' for whatever reason, the Airlift was given the more suitable name 'Operation Carter Patterson'[4] after four days, and the following year saw Gatow's busiest time ever. The Gatow base is now known as General Steinhoff-Kaserne and is home to the Luftwaffe Museum, which is, as they used to say in the *Guide Michelin*, well worth the detour for anyone interested in aircraft and flying.

When Intake 35 arrived at Gatow, although the airfield had changed much since it was opened by the Führer with Goering twitching self-importantly two paces away, the barrack blocks were unchanged except that the carved swastikas had been chiselled off the exterior walls, leaving carved heroic heads of men in leather flying helmets and goggles peering down at us. These, we were told, were of famous German aces, and are still there. Indoors, there were impeccably clean parquet floors instead of the ubiquitous brown linoleum of British barracks, and hotel-quality, centrally heated, two-man bedrooms with double windows for insulation.

Compared with the spartan single-storey huts of Cardington, Wilmslow, Crail and Pucklechurch, the standard of accommodation at our new home was impressive. We were told that the solid, two- or three-storey brick-built blocks, designed by Albert Speer (still languishing in Spandau Prison), had been laid out in a fir forest to resemble a tuberculosis sanatorium or convalescent home when seen from the air but, since the nearby runways and control tower clearly gave away the function of the airfield, it seems more likely they were spread out to minimise blast damage if bombed. In November 1943 an RAF Mosquito did drop a few bombs, to show that we could, but without causing great damage.

We were allowed to choose with whom to share a room; I ended up with a rather crazy Bristolian whose martial arts training apparently required him to spend much time each morning narrow-eyed and grunting with concentration as he chopped away at the corners of our free-standing wooden wardrobes with bare hands, to toughen up their 'cutting edges' for lethal blows to the necks of opponents in the *dojo*.

Downstairs in the basement, we discovered enormous porcelain basins with stout chrome handles. These, we were informed, were 'honking sinks'. Apparently Goering's boys had to conform to Teutonic military etiquette by drinking their fill of beer in what was now our mess and then come down there to brace themselves with the handles while spewing up the beer already consumed and whatever food they had eaten too, so that they could go back and drink some more. This we learned from two rather strange German linguists who, with an eccentric Czech linguist, shared the accommodation block with us. Another identical block 200 yards away was the designated Signals Section, where they and we all worked. With a roof covered by an array of different aerials, it also contained a number of real technicians, who knew about screwdrivers, spanners and suchlike. One turned out to be a man who recognised me from basic training. His question, 'What are you doing in Gatow?' I batted away with, 'What are you doing here?' Neither of us could answer. He and his mates worked on the top floor of the Signals Section – which was a no-go area for us – detecting and analysing enemy radar transmissions, but we were not supposed to know that.

The perimeter wire of the camp enclosed several square miles of land, some of which was under concrete for use as runways and hard standing but much of it was forest or farmland, worked by an old man with horses instead of tractors, and who spoke a dialect I found hard to understand. Near the gate was a Naafi shop, a squash court, a tennis court and an Olympic-sized swimming pool, which only a handful of us ever used and where the lifeguard was perpetually drunk. A character who had strayed out of Carol Reed's film *The Third Man*, his main interest was trying to sell us expensive watches, a large selection of which he wore on each arm. Our sporting comrades, when off duty, enjoyed competitive squash and both football and rugby matches against other teams of British servicemen.

The physical security of the Signals Section – our place of work – was in the hands of a small number of RAF Police, who checked our ID cards in a barred cage each time we went on shift. Somewhere on the camp, there also lurked a few *Giftzwerge*, as the Germans called them, i.e. 'poison dwarfs', charged with defending us in the event of an attack from the GDR. These were infantrymen from the Royal Inniskilling Fusiliers, known as 'the Skins' – detached from their main barracks in neighbouring Kladow. On seeing them, one of us quoted the Duke of Wellington's comment on his own soldiery, 'I don't know what effect these men will have on the enemy, but, by God, they frighten me'. Even when rarely sober, the Skins were frightening. Leslie Woodhead recalled an incident when some of them, well beered-up, erupted into our barrack block to wreak vengeance on a linguist who had done something to annoy them. Having checked each bedroom without finding him, they departed with, 'Dinna worry, Jimmy. We'll find the bastard. An' when we do …'

The food in our Other Ranks mess, if not up to Pucklechurch standards, was good, with the cooks having to cope with our shift work: on the first day 1200–1700; on the second day 0800–1200 and 1700–2200; the third day was free. One week in every month we covered the night shift, 2200–0800. This required eating breakfast in the evening and dinner in the small hours. Although we had to collect our meals from the serving counter, the tables were cleared by locally employed girls, inevitably the target for chatting-up by those already fluent in colloquial German. The civilised atmosphere of the mess was improved by the commanding officer deciding that we need not bring our mugs and irons with us, but should leave them there, to be collected, as in a civilian restaurant, when turning up for meals. Alas, this went too far. Knife by knife, fork by fork and spoon by spoon, they were stolen for the forbidden but widespread practice of eating snacks in the bedrooms. When there were no eating irons left in the canteen, we reverted to bringing them with us, although not held in the left hand behind the back as we had been taught at Wilmslow, with the right hand free for saluting.

There was, in Gatow, very little saluting. At work, we mixed with NCO linguists, although there was rumoured to be a secret room in the Signals Section where a higher form of service life with rings on its sleeve analysed our logs of each day's activity before sending a digest to

Butzweilerhof near Cologne and also via the diplomatic bag to GCHQ near Cheltenham, which then automatically went via the telecommunications link at Chicksands to the NSA computers at Fort Meade in Maryland. In addition, a copy of each day's work was taken to the US SIGINT base at Tempelhof Airport by an armed courier. In case Soviet or East German agents might hijack him and steal the day's take, he was armed with a service revolver and six rounds of ammunition, sealed into a cardboard package. In the event of the seal being broken, the courier would be hauled before a court of enquiry. As somebody remarked, it was taken as read that any enemy agents would be decent chaps, who would politely wait for the courier to break the seal and load his revolver before they tried to grab the classified material he was transporting.

The work for which we had been training since our first day at Crail was carried out on the first floor of the Signals Section, where about fifteen linguists sat at long desks in the set room, wearing headphones and scribbling in pencil on log pads, the transmissions being received on communications receivers like those we had learned to operate at Pucklechurch. 'Operate' is an overstatement: we changed bandwidths and frequencies but, despite the superfluous course in radio technology at Pucklechurch, nobody ever asked us to open up a set or change a burned-out valve. Somewhere, there must have been real technicians who did that sort of thing. With windows sealed up, so that no chance burst of Russian on a speaker could alert anyone outside to what was going on, and several men smoking night and day – which was usual in those times – the set room was unpleasantly stuffy.

The regular NCOs had a bewildering range of ranks, both in the technical grades and as straight corporals, sergeants, etc. One of them sat at the master controls like the teacher in a language lab, instructing each man to monitor a VHF frequency on which there was traffic. One of these controllers, Corporal Benbow, was something of a whizz-kid – very fast getting onto new traffic and allocating it to someone whose incoming traffic was less important. When something really important was happening, he would often grab the frequency and log it himself. A sergeant linguist imparted important instructions to several of the new JTs. One was to yell 'Geronimo!' if we ever heard any form of the verb *perevekhvat*, meaning 'intercept', because it probably indicated a Soviet pilot intercepting a 'ferret' flight in which a British or American aircraft deliberately strayed across the border to test the enemy's reaction time. A more important briefing was on the subject of how to make tea properly, waiting until the kettle had truly boiled.

Inevitably, some intercept frequencies were very busy and kept our brains humming, especially when reception was poor. The problem for others was staying awake between intermittent transmissions and resisting the temptation to retune to American Forces Network (AFN) Berlin because the controller could listen in on any position – although discipline was very relaxed, it was best not to take advantage. The least busy, yet important, frequencies were recorded on giant Ferrograph reel-to-reel recorders in another room, which were voice activated to save tape: they switched themselves on when a transmission began and off at its end, with automatic time-checks recorded at set intervals on the tape. These tapes also had to be logged with times noted, usually by the underemployed night shift.

When we arrived there for our first eight-hour shift, each man was told to take over an active frequency. The previous encumbent removed his cans without a word of greeting and shambled away, yawning with tiredness, for his meal and a doze, ready to return at the end of our shift. On some of the less busy frequencies it was almost necessary to shake one's predecessor awake.

On some days, the whole set room was hectic; on other days and on night shift, one could wander round and make a cup of instant coffee or have a smoke while transcribing tapes recorded on slower frequencies. The calm would be broken by a summons to get back to one's receiver, which had just come alive with traffic. It was not exactly a Battle of Britain 'Scramble, chaps!', with a rush to one's Spit or Hurricane, but it kept us on our toes. Some men with better hearing than me swore they could recognise individual pilots' voices. To me, they still all sounded like Donald Duck, with the difference that I could usually understand what Donaldov in the air was telling Mikhail on the ground in the clipped bursts of traffic.

To escape from the claustrophobia of the stale and stuffy set room, three of us volunteered to man the DF out-station atop a relic of the Airlift: a scaffolding tower that had been built out on the airfield to control the movement of sometimes 200 or more aircraft on the ground at one time. In mockery of the broadcasting tower of Sender Freies Berlin, the main radio station of West Berlin, our scaffolding tower had been christened 'the Funkturm', and served as a direction-finding location because there were no buildings nearby that might create echoes. Nobody had then heard of Health and Safety regulations: the cabin where we worked was reached by a series of open ladders with no safety rails. Once inside, the door was locked and one was alone, with the enemy just 200 yards away. On the other side of the perimeter fence our closest neighbour was a Nazionale Volksarmee tank depot on perpetual standby which guaranteed that, if World War Three suddenly broke out, the operator in the Funkturm would be the first Western casualty in Berlin. Yet the remoteness of the position was balm to the soul of those who could not stand the claustrophobia of the set room.

Out there, we were given the frequencies to monitor by the controller back in Signals Section over a landline, which was known to be tapped by 'the other side'. A simple code was therefore used, so that 'There's a dog in the brown house tonight' might mean 'Monitor, log and get a bearing of Russian traffic on 295 MHz'. Once one had the hang of handling the calibrated steering wheel which turned the dipole aerial on the roof, the job left plenty of time for daydreaming in between assignments, reading a book or worrying what the NVA tankers were up to behind the trees on the border. On dark winter evenings when they kept their engines running to avoid freezing up, with lights flashing and shouting from time to time, it was easy to be paranoid.

Just occasionally an aircraft was visible landing or taking off from the runways below the tower. This was one of two Chipmunk two-seater trainers based at Gatow. The rumour commonly believed on the base, was that the CO used to take one up each week in order to keep entitlement to his flying pay. Much later, we discovered that this was a cover story to account for him flying along the GDR boundary with a British Military Mission (BRIXMISS) officer in the rear seat. Using a long lens camera, on a clear day the passenger could photograph ground activity for quite a distance across the GDR frontier. BRIXMISS was set up to legitimise British officers with a Bulldog Drummond complex, driving beaten-up old cars with souped-up engines, deliberately intruding into forbidden military areas in Eastern Germany. BRIXMISS patrol cars were rammed, forced off the road and occasionally shot at. The counterpart, SOXMISS, gave Soviet officers the similar right to poke around the Western zones – for example, driving frequently past the SIGINT bases in the British sector to photograph them. Both missions were part and parcel of the madness in this corner of the Cold War whenever the temperature increased a degree or more in sympathy with international tensions.

The senior NCO in Signals Section was Warrant Officer Linsell. Rather like Hoey at Crail, he had two sides: unpopular in the set room, he changed into avuncular mode with those who took up his invitation to share his great passion by joining the British Berlin Yacht Club (BBYC). On our first visit to the club under his wing, we strolled along a woodland trail opposite the camp gate, at the end of which lay the Havel Lake with a jetty at which was moored a dinghy to row out to one's chosen boat with the appropriate sails for it. Linsell gave us basic instruction in setting sails, going about, gybing and executing the man-overboard manoeuvre in case someone did fall in. This entitled us to take out two-man sailing dinghies called Pirates with mainsail and jib, and a larger, unclassified boat. There were several other classes which we were not allowed to take out on our own, the largest being Stars, on which we occasionally crewed in a regatta. The entire flotilla, so Linsell informed us, was made up of boats confiscated from 'former Nazis'. When we asked what exactly they were, he answered, 'Germans with nice boats'. Similarly, RN Coders Special based at Cuxhaven enjoyed sailing on the Baltic in boats requisitioned from their Danish owners by the Wehrmacht after its invasion of April 1940 and re-requisitioned by the British at the end of the war.

Linsell having bestowed our membership cards, the next pleasant surprise was to discover the club's all-day bar in which members could buy double rums for 8d, or 3 new pence. Since Ron Sharp and I enjoyed both boating and alcohol, we spent many happy off-duty hours at the BBYC, playing *Swallows and Amazons* games by taking out two Pirates and racing them, to land on deserted islets and on the larger Pfauinsel, or Peacock Island, where the Nazi elite was rumoured to have enjoyed sex orgies – of which we, frustratingly, found no traces. We could also land at Wannsee on the opposite shore of the lake, which had a sandy beach and girls in bikinis. Wannsee was otherwise famous as the setting of the conference on 20 January 1942 in the Villa Am Grossen Wannsee where fourteen of Himmler's top officials under Obergruppenführer Reinhard Heydrich planned the death factories for the Final Solution of the Jewish Problem. Another grim reminder that this was not the earthly paradise it seemed on a sunny day floating to the south-west of the boat club, where a line of buoys denoted the border with the GDR, the most Stalinist country of the Soviet bloc. South of there, the lake narrowed back to river width and flowed on to the town of Potsdam, where I would come to know personally one grim building.

11

EXTRA-CURRICULAR ACTIVITIES

Although our work required intense concentration, the free time afforded by the shift system also gave time for exploring the beautiful woodland along the shores of the Havel, hidden in which were idyllic small, old-fashioned guest houses where elderly Berliners still came for holidays in an atmosphere so different from the city centre, which had been largely flattened by American carpet bombing and was noisy with the machines involved in its reconstruction. If we wanted to go into town, two bus rides from the gate of the camp brought us to what had been Adolf-Hitler-Platz, renamed Reichskanzlerplatz,[1] on which the British Naafi Club was an imposing six-storey modern concrete building with its own cinema showing English-language films. Outside it patrolled a squadron of sex workers, whom we were warned not to touch with the proverbial barge pole unless we wanted to catch an unpleasant and embarrassing disease, although every public gents' toilet had a slot machine dispensing *Männerschutze* – condoms – which were far more difficult for young men to obtain in Britain. Standing outside the Naafi club, one could see all the way down the Kaiserdamm to the Brandenburg Gate, 2 miles distant. With barely a single entire building left standing, in terms of devastation the view more resembled Hiroshima after the bomb than anything we had ever seen in Europe.

After fighting ceased on 8 May 1945 the 2.8 million women, children and very old men who survived from Berlin's pre-war civilian population of 4.3 million called their city '*die Geisterstadt*' – ghost town. People continued to die at the rate of 4,000 per day from starvation and epidemics of cholera and diphtheria. To gain ration cards from the Soviet interim administration, it was necessary for people to work. All women between the ages of 15 and 65 were conscripted as *Trümmerfrauen* – rubble women – who faced the impossible task of sorting through 75 million tons of rubble to save bricks or anything else recyclable and shovel the rest into wheelbarrows for removal by horse and cart, and later trucks. There was no protective clothing; they worked, come wind, come rain, without gloves in whatever blouses, dresses and skirts they had been able to salvage from the debris of their homes.

Much of this debris was used to construct an artificial hill in the British sector, dubbed *der Teufelsberg*, or Devil's Hill, because of the origin of the rubble. Other destroyed German cities had their own devil's hills, but this one was the largest, reaching 400ft high. The site was chosen because American engineers were unable to demolish by explosives Albert Speer's reinforced concrete staff college there, and deemed it simpler to bury the buildings and dispose of the rubble at the same time. When we reached Berlin, the hill, known as 'America's Big Ear', was crowned by aerials of our US opposite numbers, using the height to increase the range of their snooping on Warsaw Pact traffic. To gain a little extra height, the American base included some towers topped by radomes, one of which, with a lower radome on either side, was inevitably known as the 'cock and balls'

In the associated National Security Agency (NSA) base in the US sector, there would eventually be 1,300 highly trained technicians and analysts intercepting GDR, Polish, Czech, Russian and other military traffic and top-level telephone and radio communications inside the GDR. These included telephone conversations between the bigwigs of the Sozialistische Einheitspartei Deutschlands (SED) or Socialist Unity Party, Stalin's puppet party that replaced the former left-wing parties in Eastern Germany, and which ran the country with iron control. Also scooped up were the daily economic and intelligence briefings of the SED Central Committee.[2]

There was plenty of time for us to explore the three Allied sectors of the divided city using the S-Bahn overhead railway, the U-Bahn underground system and buses, in the course of which we found little bars on the station platforms selling shots of *Korn* vodka for a few pfennigs. Distilled from the grain of wheat, rye, barley, buckwheat or oats, a single shot took one's breath away and two spread the illusion of warmth throughout the body on a cold winter's morning. Another cheap and warming drink was *deutscher Wermutwein* (German Vermouth), but the cheapest alcohol was something called *KaKao mit Nuss* (Cocoa and Nut). It sounds, and was, an unattractive mixture, but the extremely low price ensured Ron and I bought regular supplies. Despite a mistranslated poster in the corridor of our barrack block warning that drinking locally distilled spirits could lead to blindness or total death, we suffered no ill effects.

We also discovered the Maison de France cultural centre on the Kurfürstendamm, where French newspapers could be read and books borrowed or bought at the Institut Français counter, with current French films screened in the Cinema Paris. There was also a restaurant, but the best place to eat in the whole of Berlin was the Foyer du Garnison in the French sector. Although in theory the equivalent of the British Naafi, there was no comparison: showing our 1250 ID passes to prove we were NATO servicemen, in the Foyer we could enjoy Parisian cuisine served by real waiters at a heavily subsidised price. For most of us it was the first introduction to snails in garlic butter, French onion soup and other gourmet dishes about which we had previously only read. There was also a duty-free shop in the basement where we bought cheap Phillips electric razors and other modernities that had not reached the general populace in Britain. Since French conscripts were paid much worse than us and the prices were within their reach, we did rather well out of this.

We were also allowed to go into the Russian sector of Berlin, provided we went in uniform, but the Soviet zone, retitled in 1949 die Deutsche Demokratische Republik, was completely out of bounds. Our first visit to East Berlin was on a conducted tour in a coach for British servicemen that picked us up at the Naafi on Reichskanzlerplatz. Crossing the sector boundary at the Brandenburger Tor, we realised rather soberingly that we were physically in enemy territory. The 'Ossie' – East German – female tour guide boasted in detail of the number of rivets in each bridge we crossed and the magnificent industrial achievements of the GDR compared with the Bundesrepublik, which was a blatant lie, the Soviet-occupied zone having been plundered of thousands of complete factories as reparations for the appalling destruction during the war by German forces in Poland, Ukraine and Russia. Frustratingly, she swept us without comment past the remains of the Reichskanzlei, where Hitler's and Eva Braun's bodies had been burned a few hours before the Red Army secured the area. The coach did not stop until reaching Treptow Park, a vast Stalinist memorial to the 361,000 Soviet casualties in the battle for Berlin, where the gargantuan sculptuary was meant to portray those losses as heroic. It was a chilling experience for young men who were aware that most of the casualties were caused by Stalin's obsession to grab territory as far as possible to the westwards before hostilities ended.

The battle for Berlin had also claimed 360,000 German casualties, with half a million German men taken prisoner of war, the survivors of whom returned home after ten years in Gulag camps watching their comrades die of malnutrition and untreated illnesses.

Apart from our coachload of Western service personnel in uniform, all the other visitors in Treptow Park that day wore Soviet uniforms. Some were from the *voyenno-vozdushnye sily*, or Soviet Air Force, including perhaps the very men whose VHF transmissions we snooped on in the set room. On the return journey we had a presumably unintended glimpse of the reality of life in the GDR. The main artery, called Stalinallee, was used for military parades and lined with what appeared for the cameras to be massive new office and apartment blocks. As we saw when the coach turned off the main drag into a side street, they were in fact facades erected for the cameras. Supported by shambolic wooden scaffolding from the back, they were the masonry equivalent of the main streets built for the shootouts in Western films, of which the interiors were shot in studio.

Somehow this, more than anything else, told us why on 17 June 1953 – just three months after Stalin's death – workers in that very street downed tools in protest at their increased working hours for no more pay and their appallingly low standard of living. Strikes being illegal in 'the workers' and peasants' state' of the GDR, they were immediately the target of the dreaded Volkspolizei, or 'People's Police'. But not before the news of their heresy became known. The following morning, nearly 1.5 million striking workers were protesting in the streets of Berlin and 150 other towns and cities of the GDR,[3] waving banners and chanting demands for the government to resign. Believing themselves protected by the nearness of the US, British and French garrisons in the Allied sectors of Berlin and the presence there of Western reporters and camera crews, hundreds of demonstrators actually crossed into the Western sectors to plead for armed support that was not forthcoming, despite the recommendations of a number of Allied officials that arms be supplied to them.

Soviet High Commissioner Vladimir Semyonov and Marshal Andrei Grechko, who commanded the occupation forces, despatched middle-rank GDR government functionaries to several cities in an attempt to calm things down while Walter Ulbricht and the other SED top brass spent 17 and 18 June cowering under Russian protection in the Red Army HQ at Berlin-Karlshorst. Some 20,000 Soviet occupation troops with T-34 tanks and armoured personnel carriers, plus 8,000 men of the GDR's Volkspolizei-Bereitschaften

These spies were all young. The author aged 19
in August 1958 with Soviet personnel at Treptow
Memorial Park, Berlin.

Old spies' get-together. From left to right: Duncan Brewer (Cyprus), the author and Ron
Sharp (Berlin).

R.A.F. STATION WILMSLOW.

A. HETHERINGTON   MANCHESTER.

The ritual end-of-square-bashing photograph. But once Intake 35 got to JSSL Crail, all was top secret with no photos of the camp.

THE · ROYAL · AIR · FORCE · LINGUISTS' · ASSOCIATION

RAFLING
ASSOCIATION

JSSL

Between 1956 and 1959, the
Joint Services School for Linguists
was located at Crail Airfield.
Here linguists were trained for
covert work, their vigilance
contributing to national
security during the
Cold War.

2004

Now out of the closet: the RAFling plaque in Crail actually mentions the 'covert work' linguists did.

There was more to learning Russian than just memorising thousands of words and mastering the complicated grammar. Mayakovsky's play, *Klop* (The Bed Bug) – was performed in Russian by Intake 35 at Crail as a cunning way of avoiding cross-country runs.

The map of occupied
Germany in 1958
shows why Berlin
was so vital for Allied
SIGINT.

Recent history was
not forgotten there.
When aged 9, Dave
Manley's girlfriend
had walked 200 miles
back to the ruined
city in the refugee
stream of raped
women and terrified
children.

To Berliners, the British were largely responsible for reducing their city to rubble.

With all able-bodied men in POW camps or dead, it was the women who had to clear millions of tons of debris.

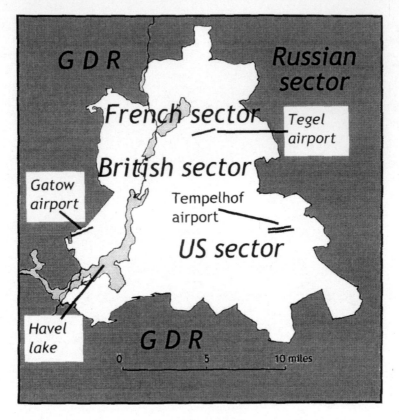

In 1958–59 Berlin was divided into the three Allied sectors and the Russian sector, the whole surrounded by the German Democratic Republic.

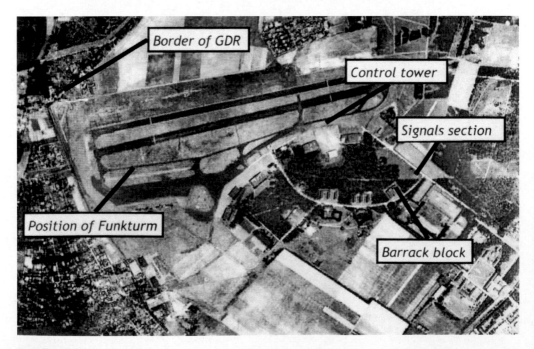

Aerial view of RAF Gatow.

Hermann Goering's comfortable masonry barrack block contrasted with the temporary wooden huts the linguists had known in Britain.

The Signals Section building now. In 1959 the roof was festooned with aerials of different types.

The ultra–Stalinist German Democratic Republic was then controlled by two men named Erich. On the left is SED Party leader Erich Honecker and on the right General Erich Mielke.

Mielke commanded the all-powerful Stasi from his headquarters on the Normannenstrasse.

Seated at this desk with his own telephone exchange, Mielke was known as '*der Meister der Angst*' – the master of fear.

Even on May Day, the workers in this 'spontaneous demonstration' of loyalty do not look happy.

Today a suburban commuter station, Albrechtshof (author revisiting down platform) was a border control point in 1959.

The author was arrested at gunpoint where the two nearer commuters are getting on their morning train to work in Berlin.

Only the barred ground-floor windows betray this building's former function as a high-security Stasi prison, where the author was kept in solitary confinement for six terrifying weeks.

In this bleak interrogation room he was interrogated by the Stasi and KGB about his secret work in Gatow.

Despite the deliberately anonymous street façade, inside the prison life was grim. This is the larger exercise courtyard, overlooked by armed guards.

In the 'extra punishment' cells, naked prisoners were hosed down with cold water in sub-zero weather.

The author in 2008 pointing to the window of his cell.

The interior of the cell where he spent six weeks in solitary confinement.

The real bridge of spies: Glienicke's closely guarded 'Unity Bridge' during the Cold War.

The bridge photographed clandestinely during a spy-swap, with the gent in bowler hat obviously catching the next flight back to London with his 'Joe'.

Glienicke Bridge now is just a suburban bridge between Berlin and Potsdam.

The border control point at Marienborn, now obsolete, is where the author was handed back by the Stasi for debriefing by the RAF.

ROYAL AIR FORCE

R.A.F. FORM 1394.
(Revised November, 1955)

BRIEF STATEMENT OF SERVICE AND CERTIFICATE
ON DISCHARGE

Surname................**FULLER**..   Official No...........**5044557**.........

Christian Names.......**John James**............................   Rank on Discharge ....**J/T**.....

Period of whole-time service. From........**6.5.57**............   To.....~~25.5.59~~....**25.5.59**.....

Trade in civil life.....**Student**....................   4.   R.A.F. trade on entry.....**A & S Asst.**......

Details of any R.A.F. trade training.........................**u/t Linguist**...........................

R.A.F. trade on discharge and brief description of duties (vide Q.R. 616 (6)) and relevant trade structure A.M.O.s)
LINGUIST (A). Translates documents, etc., of a straight-forward nature.
Undertakes routine interpreting duties to assist officers employed on liaison
duties or concerned with the messing and quartering of personnel, requisitioning
etc., when operating in a foreign country.

Assessments of Conduct, Proficiency and Personal Qualities on discharge:— *re. Leave*.

	Exemplary	Very Good	Good	Fairly Good	Poor
(a) **Air Force conduct**	Ex.	–	–	–	–
	Exceptional	Very Good	Good	Fairly Good	Poor

A linguist's certificate of discharge, which tells nothing about his actual work …

DISCHARGE SECTION

UNIT DATE STAMP
24 APR 1959
No. 5 P.D.U.
R.A.F. INNSWORTH
Signature of Airman
R. H. Sharp

Address......*RAF Record Office*.
Barnwood
Gloucester.

Remobilisation Station......................*E*

Signed.........................

Rank.........................*Fed Lt*

Commanding.........................*5 PDU*

WARNING

(To the airman named on this Form)

(i)   You are hereby reminded that the unauthorised communication by you to another person at any time of any
information you may have acquired whilst in Her Majesty's Service which might be useful to an enemy in war
renders you liable to prosecution under the Official Secrets Act.

… and a warning never to talk about it.

paramilitary riot police, were deployed to suppress the demonstrations using water cannons, rifle butts and bullets.

Inside its Karlshorst HQ, Russian intelligence operations now lay with the First Chief Directorate of the Komityet Gosudarstvennoi Bezopasnosti (KGB), or Committee of State Security. Yet, it was the senior KGB officer there who commented, '[The unrest in the GDR] is the reaction of people to the blunders of the country's leadership. Moreover, it was inadmissible to use tanks in such a situation.'[4] In fact, tanks were in the streets to frighten the demonstrators but the gunners usually fired over the heads of the people throwing stones at them. After hearing a broadcast from the US-funded broadcaster RIAS to the effect that there was no longer a viable government in the GDR, Semyonov commented to Ulbricht and the other nervous leaders of the SED that this was virtually true.

Although what passed for 'the forces of order' in the GDR were forbidden to shoot the demonstrators within sight of Western observers, many were gunned down elsewhere when Volkspolizist officers panicked and used their handguns and other firearms. A credible West German report in 1966 alleged there had been 383 people killed during the demonstrations all over the GDR, with a further 106 executed under martial law and 5,100 arrested, of which 1,200 were sentenced to a total of 6,000 years in hard-regime labour camps. Party functionaries, who at first had thought the demonstrators in Berlin were alone in their protests, learned to their horror that a mob in Görlitz, near the Polish border, had sacked the local Party headquarters, the Stasi regional office and the prison. For the believers of the SED, it was tantamount to rioters in Britain sacking churches.[5]

The left-wing poet Bertolt Brecht, who had returned to Berlin after being expelled from the USA for his Communist activities, suggested a solution in verse to the essential problems of the GDR:

> After the rising of 17 June, the Secretary of the Writers Union
> had leaflets distributed in the Stalinallee, stating that the people
> had forfeited the confidence of the government
> and could win it back only by redoubled efforts.
> Would it not be easier, in that case, for the government
> to dissolve the people and elect another?

What happened was not, in effect, so very different. The flight to the West of more than 2 million discontented GDR citizens, many of them qualified professionals, was causing severe economic problems for the SED. Its solution was to make even *thinking* about 'flight from the Republic' a crime punishable with several years' imprisonment. Although the long, so-called 'green' border between the GDR and the Bundesrepublik had already been sealed off, it was still possible in Four-Power Berlin for a GDR citizen to board an S-Bahn overhead railway train in the Russian sector and get off at a station in one of the Western sectors. A single person travelling without baggage might well get away with this, but family groups or individuals unwise enough to take a suitcase with them were liable to be hauled off the train at the sector boundary and face interrogation after instant arrest.[6]

After visiting Treptow Park, we returned to the West and disembarked from the coach outside the Naafi, quiet and chastened by the belated realisation of what life in Communist-controlled Eastern Germany really was like. Literally by crossing a street, one could go from the glitzy materialism of the Kurfürstendamm to grim streets where rubble was still uncleared thirteen years after the war ended – streets inhabited by grey-faced people controlled by ubiquitous Volkspolizisten with attack dogs. In the shops and roadside stalls where they were shopping, there had been little that would have been saleable in the West.

A whole generation later, when the Berlin Wall was breached in November 1989, an adult daughter of the author flew to Berlin to see for herself what was happening. Alighting from a U-Bahn train in East Berlin, she misread the directions for the exit – *Ausgang* in German – and found herself in a stream of Ossies returning from visits to the West, so long denied them. She was shocked at the shouting and screaming of Volkspolizisten harassing them, and by the travellers' lack of reaction, which indicated that this was normal life for them. Allowed to escape from the stream by dint of waving her British passport, she thought it would be a good idea to see what citizens of the GDR ate, and bought a hamburger at a street stall. Totally unlike the tasty German sausages on sale at street corner stalls in the West, she found the GDR bread grey and gritty and the meat inedible, grey and tasteless, and threw it away after a couple of mouthfuls. Yet all around her, the other customers were eating what was obviously for them food of the customary standard. Sometimes a hamburger tells you more about a country than all the statistics.

Proving Orwell's dictum in *Animal Farm* that 'some animals are more equal than others', at the time of my tour in 1958 the paranoid leadership of the SED was constructing for itself a secure estate at Waldsiedlung, north of Berlin. Within a 5km wired and walled perimeter guarded by elite troops of the Feliks Dzherzhinsky Guards Regiment were being built homes with all the luxuries of Western life, from servants to heated swimming pools. If the aim of the coach tours permitted by the SED in 1958 was to vaunt the achievements of its Socialist paradise for the general population, their effect was the opposite.

Not surprisingly, for a few weeks I did not return to the East. It would have been better not to return ever, but that is another story, which continues later. Eventually, with no overt security in those days between the sectors – no checkpoints or showing of passes, but just warning signs in English, French, German and Russian on the sector boundaries – we became quite casual about trips into the East, enticed there by what the GDR called '*der Schwindelkurs*'. At kiosks in the West one could change 1 Deutschmark into 4 Ostmarks, not that there was much in the East to buy. Dave Manley, who spoke reasonable German, used frequently to go into the Russian sector to buy rather scratchy Soviet classical music LPs and also fine quality Supraphon 33rpm recordings at the Czech House of Culture on the Alexanderplatz, which he sold on to other music lovers at a quarter of the Western price for 4s 6d – just over 20 new pence.

The musical tastes of Ron and myself were better served by AFN Berlin, on whose airwaves at 2400hrs every night, when we were not working on night shift, we heard, 'This is Sergeant Joe Grunewald with *Midnight in Berlin* coming to you from the divided city', followed by the immortal Peggy Lee singing Sergeant Joe's signature tune, 'Fever'. Six decades later, hearing the clicking fingers of the intro and her voice singing the opening line, 'Never know how much I love you, never know how much I care', transports me immediately back to that time and the 'very mad affair' of Cap'n Smith and Pocahontas, the Powhattan chief's daughter who died of tuberculosis or pneumonia in Gravesend after being put ashore from a ship taking her, with her English husband and son, back to her native Virginia. We listened, not on the state-of-the-art comms receivers used in the set room but in our bedroom on an antique, bow-fronted, walnut-veneered and probably pre-war Grundig radio the size of an early television set, which had served several generations of linguists after being stolen from a bar in Spandau during one drunken night. In the tradition of those departing when posted home for demobilisation disposing of unwanted effects to their replacements, we had bought it for 10 shillings. It was crackly and drifted off frequency, but had character, so we prized it.

Our more cultured comrades enjoyed numerous visits to the Städtische Oper in West Berlin and several enjoyed a memorable performance of Mussorgsky's *Boris Godunov* at the Komische Oper in the Soviet sector, to which they went wearing civilian clothes in defiance of the Four-Power Agreement, which mandated uniforms for military personnel visiting 'the other side's sector'. There, they found themselves in the auditorium surrounded by Russian uniforms, including air force ones, causing them in the intervals to listen carefully to nearby voices in case they could recognise any.

A previous intake included one semi-pro alto-sax player, who regularly went across 'into the East' in civvies at night to play in a jazz club whose pianist had a day job as our very matey camp barber, Pete Grohmann, who also had talent as a cartoonist. Pete lived in the British sector across the Havel, but had relatives in the East, on whom pressure could be put. As to why he spent his days hanging around in the barber's shop at the end of our billet – his RAF clientele rarely sought haircuts, or bothered to press their increasingly threadbare uniforms – it was generally thought that he was the resident spy because he did frequently pose intrusive questions about what went on in the Signals Section, especially whenever one of us unconsciously used the Russian for yes – *da* – instead of the German, *ja*. His oft-repeated tale of woe, with which we could sympathise, if not identify, was of getting his girlfriend Karin pregnant in their first tumble on the grass, which in their social *milieu* had meant immediate marriage.

PART 4

ONE MAN'S STORY – SOLITARY IN POTSDAM

12

THE SLIPPERY SLOPE

The Coders Special with whom we had trained were stationed on the windy Baltic end of the Kiel Canal, amusing themselves by singing Russian marching songs as they paraded on and off watch past a German Navy mess.[1] Our army coevals were deployed 900ft above sea level at Langleben, site of the Duke of Brunswick's hunting lodge in Lower Saxony, just a few miles from the inner German border, or in draughty huts and camouflaged trailers on the North German Plain, a scant 15 miles from the Litzlinger Heide in the GDR, where the Soviet 3rd Shock Army conducted very realistic exercises that could easily have developed into a zero-warning surprise attack.

Yet we were luxuriating in the comparative lap of luxury that was Berlin, with the Kurfürstendamm as bright and seemingly prosperous as the Champs Élysées – except that where the Arc de Triomphe stood undamaged in Paris was the shattered remnant of the Kaiser Wilhelm Gedächtniskirche. Since the civilian clothes we had brought with us from Britain marked us as occupation forces, those of us who wanted to blend in with the natives bought German cord trousers and windcheaters, which were actually more practical for the Berlin winter.

As young men, relieved to be finished with classrooms, books, vocabulary lists and weekly tests, we quickly adjusted to life on the front line of NATO, ignoring RAF officers and other ranks serving in Gatow, not entirely from youthful arrogance but more because we had become a tightly knit community in the twelve months during which we had studied and played together. The skills at skiving we had acquired along the way contributed to our comfort. By sticking a notice reading 'Night shift sleeping – please do not disturb' on our door on the morning of the weekly room inspection, we never had to tidy and clean the place. As a result, it quickly came to resemble the worst kind of student pad, with empty bottles and food scraps that were only thrown away when they began to putrefy. Our uniforms were unpressed and threadbare, the behinds and the knees worn to a shine, so that we feared being ordered by some officious NCO or RAF police sergeant to buy a new pair, yet the essential job we were doing was like a permanent 'get out of jail' card, so no one ever did have to do that. And the elsewhere universal snarl of, 'Get your haircut, airman!' was never heard in Gatow – at least, not within earshot of any Linguist A.

One of the NCOs in Signals Section had the unforgettable name of Alberto-Maria Zachariah-Ridgely. He was a sensitive and artistic Anglo-Egyptian from Alexandria, whose family had been interned in the Second World War by the British because his mother was an Italian enemy alien and then interned again after the Suez debacle by the Egyptians because his father was English – and finally, expelled from Egypt because his mother was also Jewish. Thrown on the mercy of an unmerciful British Government, they received no compensation. One of Alberto-Maria's passions being photography – he frequently sold pictures to German newspapers – he introduced me to the ground-floor dark room in Signals Section, where he instructed me in the arcane pre-Photoshop science of chemically developing, fixing and printing 35mm monochrome film while listening to his favourite Rossini overtures. *L'Italiana in Algeri* sounds so much more poetic than its English title, *The Italian Girl in Algiers*.

If that was my first step on the slippery path to my undoing, perhaps the second was a tip-off I received from an older linguist about to return to UK for demob. On paydays, we received – in the same Crimean War ritual of laying one's beret on the table and having the money placed in it – our due payment of £4 7s 6d, which seemed like riches indeed, since it was all pocket money. We could choose how much to take in Deutschmarks to spend in town and how much in British armed forces scrip, known as BAFVs, which could only be used on the camp and in the Naafi on Reichskanzlerplatz. We also received cigarette tickets entitling us to purchase 200 British cigarettes per man, per week, at ridiculously low tax-free prices.

Since most of Intake 35 did not smoke, the tip-off was to collect the non-smokers' tickets, buy their entitlement as well as my own in the camp Naafi shop and discreetly take the cartons of 200 cigarettes, wearing German civilian clothes, to a 'forbidden' barrack block, where service personnel were not allowed to go. In there, was the office of the German interpreter who liaised between the camp administration and the locally employed workforce, and who would pay Deutschmarks for as many cigarettes as I could offer, affording me an immediate profit. Another character from *The Third Man*, he was a sweaty, shifty individual who never met my gaze and was constantly opening the door to check if anyone was listening in the corridor, or peering out of his office window to ensure I had not been followed. After my first few deliveries, he offered to pay me not in cash but in East German Agfa photographic films, chemicals and other items, which he bought in the East. He made 100 per cent mark-up, but that left plenty of profit for me when selling them on to other budding photographers, who were still buying them for less than the price of the identical West Agfa products. Proving that my morality was no better than that of dealers on the street corners of an American city, a fateful idea slowly formed in my head: if I cut Sweaty Sam out of the circuit, I could keep his profit as well as my own.

On shift one day in the Funkturm, after getting a previously unheard coded message over the landline, 'Quick! Rabbit on brown shiny bicycle', I tuned to the indicated frequency, logged a long message in German and got a very clear bearing on the source of the transmission. Because my intercept ID indicated that I was a *Russian* linguist, my work was rewarded with the rare accolade of a 'signal from base'. Nobody exactly rushed up to shake my hand and offer congratulations, although one or two did make snide remarks about me now deciding to sign on as a regular – in which event I should have received a huge rise on paydays and also a lump sum representing the difference between my National Service pay and regular rates from my first day of enlistment. I could hardly complain at the jokes as this was the sort of humour I had inflicted on others when the occasion called for it. But it did amuse me that my most valuable day's work in Gatow was not what I had been trained for.

If Pete the Barber was a Commie spy, it was partly due to him that my German had improved enough to log that message. Several times, he invited Ron and me to visit his home at the weekend for a real German meal. Bearing gifts like the Three Kings, we met his mother and the delicious Karin, being married to whom did not seem such bad luck after all. Knowing I had become quite handy with a camera bought from the profits of my trading, Pete asked me to take a picture of Karin bending down to steady Little Peter, a rather wobbly toddler. I crouched down to have the lens at Little Peter's head height, feeling very Cartier-Bresson. The result, however, turned

Pete furious when he saw the print, which showed an unintended up-skirt view of Karin's panties. Among the many darkroom tricks Alberto-Maria had taught me were cropping a print when enlarging a picture and shading a detail that was too dark, to make it lighter, or 'burning in' a part that was too light. Pete calmed down once the flash of his wife's white undies disappeared into the shadow between her legs, but made me promise to destroy the negative under the threat of physical damage to my face if I did not.

In October, our prodigal accountant Dave Bruce managed to talk his way out to join us by dint of persuading his CO in Lincolnshire that there was something wrong about the RAF training a man to speak Russian just so that he could play golf for the Wing. Once he appeared in Gatow our happy band was complete again, with the exception of Duncan Brewer, sweating it out in the sun on Cyprus, but nobody rushed up to crush Dave in a man-hug. It simply was not done.

The educational opportunities of National Service were impressive. Tell that to those who had vegetated for two years in khaki, and the rejoinder would be rude. Yet, thousands of men who left school illiterate had learned to read and write by the time they were demobbed, thanks largely to the army's Education Corps. Others had learned a technical skill like motor maintenance that found them a job in civvy street. Not only had we been taught Russian language and literature far beyond what was necessary to do the job, but those of us wishing to sit the German O level exam were offered free travel back to the British zone and accommodation at RAF Butzweilerhof to enable us to do the dictation and oral exams, with the German–English and English–German translation components tackled later, after our return to Berlin. The journey on the BMT was memorable for a poison dwarf, armed with a bolt-action rifle that looked to us like the Lee–Enfields with which we had drilled in basic training, explaining to us, 'If the Russkies come aboard, I can drop 'em, easy. Ten aimed shots in thirty seconds, no kidding! Change the mag and ten more. Just like that. Two mags in just over a minute!' The consequences would have been appalling, but fortunately he did not have to demonstrate his skill, so the trip to Butz was really a three-day holiday.

As the delightful Berliner autumn turned into Central European winter, the landscape changed rapidly and cycling out to the Funkturm on icy *Kieselsteine* was actually dangerous. From somewhere a beaten-up Volkswagen was procured to drive us to and from our duties at the out-station. Only the regular NCOs had RAF driving licences, but they were easy-going fellows and allowed us to take the wheel now and again and practise spectacular skids on the icy, deserted hardstanding between the control tower and the Funkturm. The first snows of winter transformed the woodland around the Havel, where I enjoyed many solitary walks in a fairyland of skeleton trees, between which the mainly pristine snow showed occasional tracks of wild animals: rabbits, birds and a fox or two. Beyond a rime of ice on the shore, the blue water lay still under a clear blue sky.

Christmas came and my parents' generosity in inviting two German POWs – actually former Waffen-SS men – for lunch on what my mother called 'the Saviour's birthday' in 1946 was surprisingly reciprocated. A notice was pinned up in the barrack block informing us that many Berliner families were willing to host a British serviceman for lunch on Christmas Day. I accepted, and bearing tins of Maxwell House coffee and some cigarettes met the Sanitz family, living in a fourth-floor apartment in the traditionally Communist Stadtviertel of Wedding, in the French sector. Herr Sanitz was a loco driver working for the East German Reichsbahn. His 16-year-old son spoke quite good English and it was pretty obvious that my invitation was intended to give the lad some conversation practice. His older sister had acquired a 4-year-old daughter-without-Daddy, who was captivating, and while the Christmas lunch of meat balls and boiled potatoes was nowhere near as good as the fare that day in our canteen at Gatow the welcome of these real working-class Berliners was warm.

Ron, however, duly arrived at the house of his unknown hosts, to find a rather frigid middle-class reception. An alcohol-free lunch was followed by what the Victorians called parlour entertainments: one person played a piece on the piano, somebody sang a couple of *Lieder* and a poem was recited. When it came to Ron's turn, having mastered neither the keyboard nor having a singing voice, he recited a salty limerick that was greeted with silence. He told himself the reaction was because the family did not understand English; it later transpired that they did. His first act on leaving as soon as he decently could was to down a shot of Korn on an S-Bahn platform.

Although some men told tales of open hostility from young Germans in the British zone, that was rare in West Berlin, where most people were glad the Allies had saved them from Stalin with the Airlift in 1948. I never had any trouble with the natives, perhaps because I dressed in the same clothes as they did and not the Harris tweed jackets and grey flannels that others had brought from Britain, which were the sartorial equivalent of waving a Union Jack. But, just in case, Herr Sanitz insisted on walking me back to the nearest S-Bahn station, to catch my train back to Spandau. Strolling along together,

I asked him, 'What will you do if Nikita Khrushchev squeezes the Western Allies out of Berlin as Stalin tried to do with his Berlin blockade in 1948?' The verb was well chosen: Khrushchev likened Berlin to the testicles of the Western Powers, and used to say, 'When they annoy me, I just squeeze Berlin'.

'What could I do?' Herr Sanitz asked.

'Move to West Germany,' I replied.

'Douglas,' he said. 'Berlin is my home. How could I leave it?'

At least that explained why everyone had not fled the GDR. Not having much sense myself of what 'home' meant to most people, I never listened to the BBC programme *Two-Way Family Favourites*, re-broadcast on the British Forces Broadcasting System every Sunday at lunchtime. Famous as the programme that had brought together the delightful presenter in London, Jean Metcalfe, and her future husband, the avuncular Squadron Leader Cliff Michelmore, presenting at the Hamburg end of the link-up, it was tuned into by millions every week, but I could not stand the syrupy sentiments sent through the ether: 'Chin up, lad – We miss you', answered by, 'Not long to go now, Mum and Dad'. Even the signature tune, 'With a Song in my Heart', was enough to make me retune the ancient radio in our room. Was I jealous of the men in Intake 35 who wrote to their parents each week without fail? No, I just did not understand normal family affection and thought it odd that Herr Sanitz would rather keep his family in their drab and gloomy rented fourth-floor walk-up under a Soviet-style government than take the quite generous start-up subsidy from the Bundesrepublik Government to every Ossie who requested political asylum – as they did in their thousands each week. It was to stop this haemorrhage of skills and labour that the infamous Wall would be built over one weekend in August 1961, putting a brutally sudden stop to the refugee flow and turning the Marxist-Leninist paradise into a prison state for nearly three decades.

Our two keen churchgoers in Gatow were welcomed by the congregations of English-language churches and chapels in the British sector, although John Fuller found the Anglicans more centred on Britain than heaven, with regular singing of the National Anthem. Defecting from the established Church pro tem, he accompanied John Anderson to the more amenable Methodists at Wesley House in Spandau. German students of both sexes also frequented Wesley House to meet British and American members of the occupation forces and improve their knowledge of English.

When 22-year-old Ingrid Beletzki was persuaded by another girl to come along to a social evening there, she was definitely not hunting for an

English-speaking boyfriend. Although her family had invited lonely Allied servicemen for a meal the previous Christmas, she strongly believed that a decent German girl should not actually go out with occupation soldiers – for good reason. We had arrived from Britain believing – most of us – that whatever the Germans had suffered in and after the Second World War, 'they had it coming to them' for starting that war and, with the selfishness of youth, were not particularly interested in their stories.

Ingrid's father avoided later harsh treatment as a Jew by volunteering for the Wehrmacht in 1939 and thereafter being protected as a serving soldier, although seeing his young children from that moment only on rare and brief periods of home leave. Contact was lost entirely after he was posted missing, believed dead, on the Eastern Front in 1941, shortly after the birth of the younger daughter. Ingrid's mother took the three children of the marriage to live in her mother's home, where all three generations were bombed out in a night-time RAF raid. Despite the shortage of accommodation due to the bombing, Ingrid's mother found an empty apartment, where they were again bombed out.

At this point she contacted the foster parents of her husband who owned a small farm near Landsberg an der Warthe in Ostbrandenburg on the east bank of the Oder (now Gorzów Wielkopolski in Poland). It seemed a logical move for a family twice bombed out, since this rural area was unlikely to be targeted. With the rapid advance of the Soviet forces in 1944, Germans in the area began fleeing westward to seek sanctuary, believing that a stand by German forces on the western bank of the wide Oder River would halt the Soviet advance. But the local mayor was a Nazi who said this was unjustified panic and anyone 'running away' was a traitor. That the panic was entirely justified became clear when the retreating Germans demolished the bridge across the Oder River at Frankfurt an der Oder, leaving no escape route from Landsberg back to Berlin. The small farm was now a refuge for about fifty people, sleeping on floors and scavenging for anything to eat during the day. Landsberg was heavily damaged by the advance of the Soviet troops, intent on raping every female of whatever age and looting anything that took their fancy. The bodies of women killed by their rapists, or incidentally, were left lying in the streets. Near the farm was a former camp for French POWs, which had been taken over as an insane asylum whose inmates sheltered some of the surviving families, including Ingrid's, because the Russians left them alone there.

By February 1945 many children and adults were ill from malnutrition, including Ingrid's 4-year-old sister. After the German surrender in May 1945 and the Allied Conference in Potsdam from 17 July–2 August, it was clear that Ostbrandenburg would be on the wrong side of the new Polish border imposed by Stalin, which followed the roughly north–south line of the Oder and Neisse rivers. With a temporary bridge erected by the Soviets across the Oder, the three generations of Ingrid's family set off to walk in a stream of 1.5 million other refugees over 200 miles back to Berlin through a landscape littered with the debris of war – disabled artillery and tanks, shattered and burned-out houses and the unburied corpses of farm animals and German soldiers. With between 12 and 20 million more Germans expelled officially or unofficially from Poland, Czechoslovakia, East Prussia and elsewhere in Central Europe, nobody cared about their plight.

Pushing a small handcart with their pitiful belongings, the elderly grand-mother, mother, 9-year-old Ingrid, her 7-year-old brother and much weakened little sister slept in the fields, finding food on some days, on others just water and sometimes not even that. Incredibly, they made it back to the chaos of largely destroyed Berlin, where the epidemic of diphtheria – then an often fatal disease – hospitalised all three children. By that Christmas, the younger sister was dead and their mother was in hospital with diphtheria, so Ingrid and her brother lived with their grandmother. Emerging from hospital in poor health, their mother worked as a *Trümmerfrau*, clearing rubble in all weathers with her bare hands to earn starvation rations for herself and the two surviving children in what was now the French sector of Berlin. Many German POWs in the Siberian camps were kept as slave labour until 1954, but in 1951 Ingrid's mother received a Red Cross card informing her that her husband had been repatriated with other former soldiers so ill they were not expected to live. He was a broken man, with a severe heart problem and psychological problems which caused behaviour that disturbed the two surviving children, to whom he was a complete stranger.

With that background, it is easy to understand that Ingrid wanted nothing to do with a soldier, especially a foreign one. Yet, when her friend introduced her to Dave Manley at Wesley House, saying that he was looking for someone to give him German lessons, she could not refuse in front of him because, as a well brought-up German girl, she considered that would be impolite! That moment of politeness changed the course of her life. Dave fancied her straight away and courted her with such persistence that their relationship survived his three years at Oxford University after demob.

13

A SENSE OF BELONGING

In Gatow, we knew that Christmas had been banned in the atheistic USSR, although GDR citizens who had the courage to attend church did bravely assemble to celebrate 25 December under the suspicious gaze of the several hundred thousand unpaid informers working for the Stasi, known as *inoffizielle Mitarbeiter* (IMs) – unofficial collaborators – and the cameras of Stasi officers, some carried openly and others secreted behind the windows of hundreds of surveillance vans. New Year's Eve, called Sylvesterabend in German, was however the accepted occasion on both sides of the border for drink and jollity. We were warned by the NCOs that just about every transmission logged on 1 January would be drunken mumbles ending in '*S novym godom*' – 'Happy New Year' in Russian – because over there vodka ruled OK. Apparently a previous intake had picked up a message the year before in slurred English from some well-lubricated Soviet military person, 'And to all our listeners in Gatow, Happy New Year!' A more alarming sense of Slav humour was when an anonymous *starshi serzhant* (sergeant major) of a Soviet tank regiment read out over the network some co-ordinates for 'fire at will', and these, when plotted by a British Army analyst, turned out to designate the Signals Section in RAF Gatow.

But alcohol was not only king on their side of the border. On New Year's Eve the RAF Police in Signals Section were pretty sloshed too. One of them was an odd fellow named Roger,[1] who never had promotion beyond corporal because he could not pass his driving test. For whatever reason, he took his eyes off the road each time he changed gear in order to check what his hand was doing on the gear lever – with results that varied according to the speed of reaction of his instructor. Well primed with the spirit of New Year and convinced by alcohol that he had at last cracked his driving problem, sometime after midnight Roger grabbed the keys of the police Land Rover and disappeared into the night. We heard the motor start and then silence. A good fifteen minutes later he reappeared, somewhat dishevelled, bruised and with cuts on his face, having driven off the road and wedged the Land Rover firmly between two saplings, losing his cap in the process. His mates thought this a big laugh until one of them noticed that in the crash or while crawling out through the rear doors of the Land Rover because the front ones were jammed shut by the trees, he had lost his service revolver, which had been torn off the securing lanyard when snagged on something. To lose a loaded firearm was a court martial offence that would probably see him doing a couple of years in a military prison. At this point, several equally sloshed linguists hurriedly ran upstairs so that we could testify to having 'seen nothing' – and were horrified when the police followed us into the forbidden territory of the set room to sober up with large mugs of tea before setting out to play Hunt the Revolver in an attempt to save Roger's bacon.

Life in Gatow – indeed in Berlin as a whole – was inevitably claustrophobic. Although irregularly shaped, the three Western sectors measured roughly 15 miles west to east and 15 miles north to south, totalling roughly 220 square miles. From the base, one could travel a few miles to the north and eastwards, but to the west and south our mental maps were blank and more terrifying than the terrae incognitae of medieval cartography, marked only with '*hic sunt leoni*' – 'here be lions'. Indeed, with the exception of the BRIXMISS teams, entering the GDR was *strengstens verboten* – forbidden territory indeed – a geographical, cultural and political black hole in the centre of Europe.

Appreciating that a Berlin posting could produce a kind of stir-craziness, the powers-that-be had wisely built two spells of leave into our posting in the divided city. In that time the United Kingdom was insular, both geographically and culturally. With no low-cost airlines or package tours, foreign holidays were enjoyed only by the very rich: summer at Auntie's villa on the Côte d'Azur or at Biarritz; winter skiing with the high life in the then empty Alps; a leisurely, week-long transatlantic crossing by steamship. It is true that Sergeant Mick had told us of a previous linguist named Michael Korda, who chartered an executive aircraft to take a group of his pals to the south of France for a weekend jaunt, but that was the stuff of legend. In any case, his father was the famous Hungarian film producer Alexander, the boss of

London Films, whose output was seized by its creditor, Prudential Assurance. Korda père coolly then bought the films back for 1 shilling in the pound of their notional value. The rich get richer …

Yet we sons of families, none of whom could have been called rich – and sons also of wartime rationing just recently ended and the grim post-war austerity of the Attlee years – were living in the centre of Europe, with so many travel possibilities that would have seemed – no, would have *been* – impossible for us a couple of years earlier. So, plans for leave expeditions were as varied as were we. German-speakers headed into the ancient cultural centres of Western Germany or visited Hitler's hideout, the Berghof at Berchtesgaden in the Obersalzberg. Those with a love of mountains toured the Western zones of Austria. The Latinists and Greek scholars visited Italy, staying in cheap hotels and flea-infested youth hostels as the price of soaking up on a budget the atmosphere of a Rome still devoid of tourists. Our Marco Polo, John Fuller, armed with a rail pass and determined not to waste a day of it, even made a solo run as far as what had been Magna Graecia – southern Italy and Sicily – to marvel at the wonders of the Greek ruins at Taormina and Agrigento – and be scared of the Mafia when followed by mysterious strangers in the narrow streets of Sicilian towns.

My interest in the French language had led me to make several low-budget forays to Paris before National Service. Knowing the city well and loving it, I defied two sets of parental disapproval to invite my fiancée – we had become engaged on my last leave before departing from the UK – to meet me there. From Berlin, the best route was to take the American Military Train to Frankfurt and then travel by civilian trains into France. The AMT started from Lichterfelde-West, where the US Army had built an entire terminal exclusively for its own use. Even the station was an experience, guarded by gun-toting MPs in their 'snowdrop' helmets, who checked my 1250 ID and travel pass, waving me inside with 'Enjoy your trip, Doug'. Passing through the portal was like stepping through a cinema screen: from Sergeant Joe Grunewald's grim divided city in the centre of Europe to the celluloid state by the Pacific. Everyone seemed to be sun-tanned and chewing gum. Compared to ours, their badge-infested uniforms looked as though they were tailored in Hollywood. Loudspeakers blared out the voice of British broadcasting star Vera Lynn singing her greatest hits: 'We'll Meet Again' – that prayer of so many separated couples during the Second World War – and '*Auf Wiedersehen*, Sweetheart', which had been the first recording by a foreign artist to reach No. 1 in the US Billboard Charts in 1952. To my own surprise,

I found the nostalgia induced by her voice and the syrupy lyrics disturbing. Surely I had not come to feel that Berlin was in any sense 'home'?

Emerging from America-on-wheels at Frankfurt, I was already at the halfway point in my journey, with 350 miles to go. Once across the frontier, I enjoyed the sound of French spoken all around me, and stopped off at several towns, revelling in the space and freedom that was mine to enjoy after the cramped sameness of Berlin. Here were no uniforms, no discipline, no Russian voices intruding into my dreams. It was such a change from the communal life of the past eighteen months that, with Vera Lynn's voice in my head, I felt almost lonely.

But Paris was – as always for me – a warm and familiar place, despite grey skies and drizzle most of the time. In 1958 Britain we would probably have had a problem booking into a small backstreet hotel as an obviously unmarried couple of 20-year-olds, but this was Paris, celebrated in literature and on the silver screen as '*la capitale mondiale de l'amour*', and Parisians had an unshakable belief in their own myth. Taking our passports, the manager behind the cramped reception counter asked from where we had come, in that time of so few foreign tourists. I told him I was doing military service in Berlin, while my girlfriend had come from Britain. Young love! Immediately, he had to fetch his missus from the basement, where she was doing the laundry. She and the maid all but swooned at the romance of a conscript crossing Europe to spend a few days with his girlfriend.

I wanted my fiancée to share my enjoyment of the Louvre Museum, Montmartre, Pigalle, the Luxembourg Gardens, the Buttes-Chaumonts, the Champs Élysées and other *grands boulevards* created by Baron Haussmann, the ruthless planner who destroyed medieval Paris to create an elegant capital worthy of Napoleon III's nineteenth-century Second Empire.

If the hotel staff thought it odd that we rose early for each day's sightseeing instead of passing the precious daylight hours in unbridled passion in our room, they obviously wrote it off as that eternal mystery for the Gallic mind, '*le phlegme habituel des Anglo-saxons*', but it was a hard job to persuade them we did not require coffee and croissants brought up to the room for a leisurely *petit déjeuner au lit*.

The time passed all too quickly until we were saying goodbye at the Gare du Nord in a scene from *Brief Encounter* (which was actually filmed at much less romantic Carnforth Station). With the smells of coal smoke, lubricating grease, oil and steam in my nostrils, I felt like Trevor Howard, minus the trilby hat, standing there on the platform and waving goodbye to my Celia

Howard as the locomotive chuffed its way out of the station, bearing her to the cross-Channel ferry at Calais.

Lingering my way through Metz and Strasbourg to Frankfurt and the AMT, I was alone again, except for Vera Lynn in my head. It would be eons longer than I then knew before Trevor met Celia again, so 'Auf Wiedersehen, Sweetheart' was quite appropriate but, as the steam trains chuffed and rumbled their way bearing me eastward towards the divided city, I was still grappling with the malaise that had troubled me on the journey from Berlin. John Fuller, more given than me to spiritual reflection, came close to what I was feeling when he wrote, half a century later:

> To work, sleep and play in the company of the same group of people for twenty-four hours a day over a period of eighteen months is a community-forming experience which can either ensure one never wants to meet those people again or implants a deep shared friendship like no other. Fortunately those of us on the Russian Course had sufficient similarity in background, attitude and intelligence to forge an enduring circle of friendship. That twelve or more of us continue to meet together each year some fifty years[2] later is testimony to that. The intensity of shared experience is like no other, and one begins to appreciate the nature of the camaraderie described by those who served together in the war, though thankfully for us it was without the day-on-day fear or anxiety. Once beyond the stresses of basic training, our National Service experience was, one has to say, really quite enjoyable, and made so principally by the quality of the community in which we lived.[3]

I had never experienced the feeling of belonging to a group, but had always been an outsider, looking in — as, I suspect, many writers are from their earliest years. At school, I knew no feeling of kinship with my classmates. Being unable to comprehend team games, I felt a deep sense of alienation when they revelled in the *crack!* of leather on willow or argued about scores and scorers of winning goals in football matches played before they were born. Writing is a solitary occupation. Observation, rather than involvement, maketh the kind of man or woman who practises it. So I had not run around on muddy rugby pitches with Intake 35's Fraternity of the Oval Ball. I did not understand that other game, let alone play it with the bridge addicts. I enjoyed alcohol too much to spend evenings with the teetotallers. I did not go to worship with our believers or sing in choirs like some or tread the boards in Dmitri's plays as so many did to escape sports afternoons. I was, in short, *not* what Dr Johnson called 'clubbable'.

Yet, I was aware of missing their company, these men in many ways so unlike me who had shared a rare and demanding experience, putting aside our reluctance to wear a uniform and accepting a modicum of discipline while we pitted our wits against the silliness of Bull and the perversities and intricacies alike of Russian. Did we compete in the weekly tests? Once the spectre of RTU was behind us after the First Major Test, nobody showed much interest in the results pinned up on a noticeboard, for we were competing, not with each other but with the Russian language in a shared but unvoiced determination to crack the verbal code of the Slav mind.

So, the other men of Intake 35 were, in John Fuller's words, a community or group to which I did not fully belong but with which I was very much at ease.

Back in the set room, Paris seemed a dream. In Gatow's disorientating shift system, time seemed to have stood still, except that a man called Dave King had replaced me in the Funkturm trio while I was away, and had the gall to log the start of his shift as 'Entrance of the Demon King'. It was hardly worth descending all those ladders, whose icy iron rungs froze the hands on the way down and again when climbing back up, just to relieve one's bladder, so at the Funkturm we peed over the edge of the platform, observed perhaps by the NVA tankers, but no one else, although since then half the airfield has been sold off as a housing estate. During my absence, Ron had, from boredom, logged his calls of nature with entries like 'The evening light beautified the golden cascade', threatening in some oblique way my status as The Poet in the Tower.

In a reaction to the euphoria of freedom, travel, Paris and normal civilian life for a couple of weeks, I fell into a slough of despond, shambling zombie-like to the Signals Section for my shifts and wandering about Spandau and Central Berlin in my free time, nipping into bars for shots of *deutscher Wermutwein* 'to keep the cold out'. The art films that had been such a source of delight in Crail were replaced by awful commercial films on the Kudamm, useful for German vocabulary but totally uninspiring. A warm and friendly lady called Jane who arranged entertainments in the camp Naafi endlessly played her selection of Frank Sinatra records and brought in a local man with 16mm projector showing English-language rented films every so often. Inevitably, these included *High Society*, the last film made by the Ice Princess Grace Kelly before she became an ill-fated real-life princess by marrying

Prince Rainier of Monaco. Male leads were Louis Armstrong, Bing Crosby and, of course, Frank Sinatra. Jane also arranged Bingo evenings – then called Housey-Housey – which failed to attract any linguists and were for the 300-plus other servicemen on the base, of whom we were largely unaware.

My visits to the Sanitz family continued, although Ron did not return to his frigid Christmas hosts. I learned a great deal from these trips to Wedding because the Sanitzes sensed that I was not a hostile soldier, but a neutral civilian in uniform, and came to trust me enough to unearth their photo albums of relatives going back several generations, including the album normally kept hidden, in which were photographs of several male relatives wearing Waffen-SS insignia during the war. They had all died on the Ostfront, after living out God-knows-what horrors there, but to my hosts they were still joke-telling Onkel Fritz and generous Opa Herrmann. There was a brief silence when I said, '*Ich hätte ihrer Feind gewesen*' – born a little earlier, I should have 'been their enemy' – and a dead one, by the look of them.

To change the subject, I asked about the fall of Berlin, remembering too late that almost every woman in Berlin had been raped by Russian soldiery – some in front of their children, some repeatedly and many dying in the process. Frau Sanitz retired to the kitchen, busying herself with the washing up, while her husband deflected the conversation by telling me about a neighbour's 15-year-old boy who had been conscripted into Himmler's ultimate insanity, the Volkssturm, in the last terrible days of the Reich, together with men old enough to be his grandfather. There was a gallows humour joke at the time that these pensioners were Hitler's most precious soldiers because they had 'silver in their hair, gold in their teeth and lead in their legs'. But swearing in boys in uniforms far too big for them and 'arming' them with a single one-shot Panzerfaust between twenty, what was the point of that? '*Ich schwöre Dir, Adolf Hitler…*', they chanted, dedicating themselves to die for the sick and trembling madman in the Führerbunker. Chased shit-scared into the building by two Tommy-gun-toting Red Army soldiers, not very much older than them, the neighbour's boy and a pal also wearing a Volkssturm greatcoat were pursued up to the roof, six floors up, and not shot, but thrown off it, their bodies left in the street below for days because no one dared move them.

Invitations shared with Ron to visit Pete the Spy's family were always fun, although it was difficult to reconcile Pete's laddish working persona with him in correct weekend paterfamilias guise. On one visit I made there alone because Ron was on shift, the family thought I could not follow their chatter in Berliner dialect. Although slightly beered-up, I listened intrigued as they all agreed that Hitler had been a great leader, 'Because then we had no unemployment. Remember? Everyone had a job. Everyone had money. *Na, ja,*' they nodded.

I felt like saying, 'Everyone had a job because the factories were turning out armaments night and day in preparation for the war the little corporal was planning, and which killed Pete's dad, together with between 70 and 80 million other people', but what would have been the point? Realising that I was certainly following the gist, if not all the twists and turns, Pete shut them up and walked me back to the S-Bahn station for a train to Wannsee. This was part of the city's integrated transport system, so one could buy an *Umsteiger* ticket that covered the train and both the ferry crossing to Alt-Kladow and the bus ride back to Gatow on the other side of the lake. On that calm day with clear blue, cloudless high-pressure sky, it felt unreal to be drifting across the Havel on the twenty-minute crossing and wondering whether I would ever see the romantic city of Potsdam with its several grand palaces, which lay frustratingly just around a bend in the river. Little did I know what lay ahead.

Although during most of the winter the weather was too changeable to go sailing, Ron and I still hung out at the BBYC, mainly for the double rums at 8*d* a time. Perhaps it was the rum talking when we decided one afternoon to grab the sails for *Harwich* from the boathouse and take her out. *Harwich* was a larger, heavier and more stable boat than the Pirates we usually sailed, but our doubts commenced when, no sooner had we left the mooring and hoisted the mainsail than a violent squall hurtled us away from the shore at quite a lick. Out on the lake, the waves were far bigger than we had appreciated. Sobering up, already soaked to the skin, we dropped the mainsail, nearly capsizing in the process, and managed to come about because it was too windy to risk gybing, even on just the jib. Tacking our way against the wind, we reached the lee of the trees around the club and moored to the buoy under the amused gaze of the barman and a drinking pal.

14

APRIL FOOL!

As the days lightened in March, King departed on leave and I was relieved to be freed from the claustrophobia of the set room with its alarums and incursions. Yet, stuck out there in the Funkturm on the edge of the airfield for eight or more hours on two days out of three, the feeling of unreality grew. What was the point of logging so conscientiously all the clipped and distorted routine transmissions about the height of the cloud base and some tyro's circuits and bumps? Why was I sweating to DF every possible transmission before it ended, instead of just writing in the log that reception was too bad? Was the updated Order of Battle which our work there on the front line of NATO allegedly made possible really the shield that protected the world from nuclear holocaust? Alone on shift in my isolated tower, I mulled over Eliot's poem *Burnt Norton*, debating with myself whether perhaps time present and time past were both present in time future, and the future itself somehow within time past. Written down now, it does sound mad, but he wrote it, not I. Probably I was a little mad – although, how do you define 'a little mad'? In today's street parlance, I was having a prolonged 'bad trip' without abusing any substance except alcohol, but the divided city of Berlin *was* a mad universe with its own crazy logic, separated from the real or sane world by 100 miles of empty void, which one could only cross with the right papers. Otherwise, there was no way out.

For those of us in the middle of it, the Cold War was an insane stand-off. Of course, it was better than the alternative, the military expression for all-out nuclear conflict between the USSR and NATO. That I was not the only one sliding into deeper and deeper depression was evident one night when another Intake 35 linguist, who had already a history of severe depression at university, did go clinically mad and had to be taken away in the small hours by men in white coats. Yet, most of the others seemed to be calmly looking forward to demob, some ticking off the days on demob charts and all apparently as well balanced as ever, so far as I could tell.

I had experienced a similar state of mind before. At Crail, oppressed by the claustrophobia of hours in the classroom and nights in hut Benbow 3 with twenty or so other men making it impossible to enjoy for long the solitude I needed as much as others needed company. Unable to sleep, I had gone for long midnight walks to the Balcomie shore, beating my fists against the roadside telegraph poles to feel the reality of pain after staring at the waves, in whose cold embrace lay the 'undiscovered country, from whose bourn no traveller returns'.

It was not something I could talk about, even to Ron. Least of all to him, for he seemed so damnably sane – as he still did in Gatow. However, towards the end of March he had to go into the British Military Hospital in Spandau for a stay-in operation. With hindsight, I suppose it was partly the absence of my stable roommate which meant I had no anchor keeping me – or at least my behaviour – within what a psychiatrist later called 'the bounds of normality'. While Ron was being tucked up again and again in bed by the rather too attentive male nurses in the BMH, I thought that one more sortie into the East might drum up some cash to take back to Britain. What was the motive? Cash, boredom or bravado? I cannot say, and it is no excuse that the young often have the illusion of being invulnerable. It was a crazy idea, for I had noticed before Christmas a tightening up of controls at the boundaries of the Western sectors, where the infamous Wall would be built in August 1961.

That the idea was crazy became brutally clear just before midnight on 30 March when I watched from the shadows as several S-Bahn trains departed from the suburban station of Albrechtshof back into the British sector, some searched by frontier guards and some not. The gloom of the whole station was broken only by four 60 watt bulbs – two on each platform – because the GDR had a permanent shortage of electricity and bulbs. Eventually, I took a gamble, stepped into the light and boarded a train just after the previous one had been searched and left. It started to move, and then stopped with a loud squeal of brakes after a garbled announcement over the loudspeakers on the platform. The doors opened and an East German border guard with rifle slung worked his way along the carriages, checking the few passengers, one after another. I tried to estimate my chances of getting off while out of his direct line of sight and pretending I was waiting for the next train.

But I had left it too late. He stood in front of me, demanding, '*Papiere!*'

A thousand thoughts raced through my brain, not one of them useful. On the platform, someone was calling for him to hurry up. Hoping he would give up after seeing me reach into an inside pocket and pretend to pull out some ID, I realised the game was up when he said, '*Schneller*' – 'Hurry up'. I handed him my RAF 1250. He looked at it, compared the photo with my face, then barked, '*Heraussteigen!*'

I followed him off the train. He walked ahead of me, confident as only the servant of an all-powerful state that I must follow as a dog follows its master. The train doors closed and it gathered speed. Was his rifle loaded? If not, how long would it take for him to chamber a round and shoot me if I made a run for it? The crazy thought of jumping onto the buffers between two carriages was discarded as too dangerous. Pretty sure no one could see what I was doing midway between the two street lights on the up platform, I slipped my hand inside the duffle bag I always carried on these expeditions and pulled out the bag of East Agfa films and other goods I was carrying, dropping it plus some GDR currency from my trouser pockets over the low concrete wall at the edge of the platform. Since the motivation was to prevent myself being accused of smuggling or illegal possession of Ostmarks, I must already have resigned myself to being arrested and searched, but the action was instinctive, rather than reasoned. Up the stairs and over the metal footbridge to the other platform I followed the frontier guard docilely. What else could I have done?

In the ticket hall – a bare, freezing room with no seats or heating, lit by a single bulb – two other border guards inspected my 1250 without much curiosity, one of them talking to an officer on the telephone. He shoved my ID card into a pocket, picked up his rifle, loaded a round into the chamber and ordered me to walk ahead of him. '*Wohin gehen wir?*' I asked – 'Where are we going?' That did surprise him; in the GDR people did not ask questions when being arrested. Ignoring the question, he prodded me out of the door, ordering me three times to turn left until we were walking along parallel with the tracks. Being lower than the embankment on which the station was built, the road was even worse lit than the platforms. As we passed my stash, I was hoping that anyone except a guard would find it in the morning and stuff it – films, cash and all – into one of the shabby briefcases in which working men seemed to carry their sandwiches. That is probably what happened, since the subject never came up in interrogation.

A couple of hundred paces along this road, we stopped at a guardhouse in which a dozen or so East German guards and two Red Army soldiers were smoking and chatting. The conversation stopped, everyone staring at me when I was pushed inside. One of the Russians took my 1250 and said to his comrade, '*Smotri!*' – 'Look what we've got here!'.

At a desk in the corner a lieutenant of the Grenzschutzpolizei was talking on the phone. Replacing the handset, he came over to me. I had read somewhere that the last refuge of men from bourgeois families in the GDR was serving in the border guards, which apparently had no class hang-ups. The lieutenant was young, smart and polite. He offered me a cigarette and lit it for me. I apologised for the disturbance, '*Entschuldigen Sie bitte, dass Ich Sie gestört habe*'. It was a lunatic thing to say, apologising for being arrested, but I was desperate to make some connection with this stranger who held my fate in his hands.

'*Es gibt nichts zu entschuldigen,*' he smiled, clicking his heels and giving a slight bow. My head was spinning. I had never seen heel-clicking before. This had to be a scene from an operetta or the BBC radio show *It's That Man Again*, when two terribly polite gents could not decide who should walk through a doorway first, 'After you, Claude.' 'No, after you Cecil.'

'*Morgen fruh,*' the lieutenant said, '*die roten Mützen kommen für Sie.*'

The red caps would come for me in the morning? I clung for a moment to this reassurance, although somehow knowing that it was the equivalent of the copper's 'Just come down to the station with us, sir, and we'll have this sorted out in fifteen minutes'.

One of the guards led me outside while the one with the loaded rifle kept me covered. The insane idea came to me that I could push the nearest man against his comrade, to put him off his aim while I ran off into the darkness. But how many other guards were there between me and the border, which was the only area in the whole GDR that was brilliantly floodlit? The unarmed guard opened the metal door of what looked like a windowless garage. Inside was a wooden bench with a blanket. Nothing else. As the door clanged shut behind me, I knew I was not going home in the morning.

The single bulb was switched off from outside. It was cold in my temporary prison, even with the grubby blanket wrapped around me. I drew up a mental balance sheet. On the credit side, I had not been questioned, so when I was, I could tell any story without contradicting myself. The best one was surely to say I had fallen asleep on a train, got out at the first station in the GDR and slipped across the footbridge when no one was looking. If asked what were my duties at RAF Gatow, I could say … what? A bedding store, that was it! I would be a clerk in a bedding store – a harmless, bored National Service conscript of no danger or interest to anyone. Much later in Vietnam, US servicemen were advised to become 'grey men' if taken prisoner by the Viet Cong or North Vietnamese Army, pretending to have low intelligence, low rank, no classified information, no political beliefs – and not try to be heroes or defy their captors. These were tricks that no shot-down pilot could play, but they worked for thousands of others whose military duties were unknown to their captors.

My duffle bag had been taken away, but I still had my wristwatch. It was just after 3 a.m. when the light was switched on, the door opened and a guard called me outside. Bundled into the back seat of a dark-coloured car between two guards with rifles between their knees and another guard in the front passenger seat, holding my duffle bag, I did not bother to ask where we were going. There was no other traffic on the dark streets. Nobody spoke. Occasionally a street lamp broke the darkness of the night. Outside the town, after some time I noticed moonlight reflecting off the surface of small lakes, which meant we were travelling south, with Gatow and the Funkturm over there on my left, not very far away.

After about thirty minutes, we drove into a large town which, I guessed, had to be Potsdam – not that I was fated to see very much of it for fifty years. Even there, the streets were poorly lit and surfaced in *Kieselsteine.* Nothing I could see seemed to have changed since the 1930s. There was no sign of life in the streets, no all-night cafes or bars, just an all-pervading gloom with an occasional poster at an ill-lit intersection vaunting the prowess of the SED or the success of the current 5-Year Plan. The driver pulled up outside a carriage gate in what seemed to be a residential street, and hooted. A light came on. The double doors opened and we drove inside. After the doors had closed again, I was told to get out and found myself in a courtyard surrounded by high walls. The frontier guard in the front seat handed my duffle bag to a man in a different uniform, who motioned me inside the building and showed me into what seemed to be a sparsely furnished courtroom with a large portrait of Lenin on the wall.

For quite a long time, he and I stared at each other. I blinked first. He was the personification of everything I had been trained to fight. Odd sounds – shouts or cries – broke the silence from time to time. A couple of times, the man who had taken the duffle bag poked his head round the door, but said nothing. Checking that the prisoner had not hanged himself, I wondered?

My pulse elevated, I was aware that I should have been planning my next move, but my conscious mind was a blank.

After an hour or so, a nondescript man of average height, wearing a raincoat over a cheap suit and carrying a briefcase, entered and told me in English to follow him to a smaller room with a bare wooden table and two wooden chairs. 'Sit,' he said. I sat in front of the table, he sat behind it. He examined my 1250, comparing the photograph with my face, and emptied my duffle bag onto the table. Picking up my camera, he said, 'So, Mr Boyd, you are a NATO soldier, based in Berlin. What are you doing in the German Democratic Republic with a camera?'

Did I look like a spy? Hoping to build the 'grey man' story of being a stupid conscript who had made a stupid mistake, I trotted out a story about having had a few drinks, falling asleep in the train, waking up in Albrechtshof and innocently strolling across the footbridge to catch the next train back into Berlin.

He made a few notes. When he had finished, I tried a question, 'What is this building?'

'You are guilty of the crime of *illegaler Eintritt* – illegal entry into the German Democratic Republic.'

'Is that a crime?'

'If I came to Britain without a visa, that would be a crime. So yes, Mr Boyd, you have committed a crime. Also, in your bag, you brought a camera with you. So a charge of espionage may also be made in your case.'

That the crime of illegal entry existed in a country from which 2 million-plus citizens had fled and been proclaimed guilty of '*Flucht aus der Republik*' seemed ironic. Failed escapes were punished with up to seven years in hard-regime prisons for men and women, their children being taken away and placed in State-run orphanages, many never to be reunited with their parents.

'What is the penalty for illegal entry?' I asked.

'Under paragraph 8 of the GDR law dated 11 November 1957, it is up to three years in a labour camp.'

That jolted me fully awake. 'Are you a lawyer?' I asked.

'Why do you ask?'

'Don't I need a lawyer, to advise me?'

Then I had no idea that, in the courtroom where I had been kept waiting and all the other thousands of courtrooms of the GDR, the 'defending counsel' was a State servant who was not allowed to meet his 'client' or see the printed accusation or any other relevant paperwork before the trial – at

```
                                                  DSTO
                                                  0003
                                                          94266    ✳
Eingang  Fernschreiben / Fernspruch / Funkspruch  Streng geheim!
              FS-Nr. 192        vom 31. 3.     1959  Dringlichkeit:          ᴄ
Absender:  BVfS.- Potsdam, Abteilung VII/3                 - 1 APR. 59      ᴸ
An         MfS.- Berlin, HA.- VII-                         1200         ℬ,
                                                           Abt.3
                             Berlin       den     1. 4. 195 9


Betr.:    Englischer Besatzungsangehöriger

Am 29. 3. 1959 wurde bei der S - Bahn - Kontrolle am Kontrollpassier-
punkt Albrechtshof gestellt :
B o y d , Douglas  geb.am 24. 8. 1938 in Eling/London
                   B. ist Angehöriger der Royal Air Force und steht
                   im Rang eines Junior/Technician (Corporalgefreiter)
                   und ist auf dem Flugplatz Gatow stationiert.
```

Excerpt from the *streng geheim* telex from Stasi Potsdam to Stasi Central announcing the author's arrest.

which neither he nor the defendant was allowed to speak. His role was simply to approve the procedure and endorse the sentence.

'I shall advise you,' he said.

'But you say you are not a lawyer.'

'I am an officer of the Volkspolizei …' – few people in the West then knew of the Stasi, in which he was an officer, but for me it was worrying enough that he was a Volkspolizei officer – '… and here, I ask the questions, Mr Boyd, not you. Tell me what are your duties at RAF Gatow?'

I protested that I was not allowed to talk about military matters. After a little sparring, I added that I was the clerk in charge of a bedding store, where my duties included updating the inventory of blankets and sheets and pillow cases that had been issued to the personnel, polishing floors and occasionally making tea and coffee for the officers.

Lieutenant Becker – I learned his name only fifty years later – made no comments. It was nearly dawn when he pressed a bell-push on the table. A warder entered and said, '*Komm*'. He led me along a corridor into the main block of the prison. On either side of the corridor were cell doors. Above my head there was no ceiling for four floors, just wire netting at each level to prevent people jumping to their deaths, and pipework of all dimensions. It was like the engine room of a large ship, but when I said this to the warder he gave me an odd look that said plainly I must be an idiot. That was encouraging: if I could keep up that act, maybe I would get out alive. We stopped at the far end of the building after several twists and turns, outside the door of cell No. 20. He unlocked the door and motioned me inside.

Cell No. 20 in the Stasi's Lindenstrasse interrogation prison in Potsdam measured just three paces by two, the floor space encumbered by a bed of the type one might find in a doctor's consulting room under a small barred window, high up in the end wall, plus a small table and a chair. There was no running water, just a smelly lidded can to serve as my toilet. The grey dawn light came through the dirty window. Over the door was a low-wattage light that was left on, day and night.

No ex-prisoner ever forgets the first time the cell door slams shut and is bolted from the outside. The absence of a handle on the inside symbolises the loss of freedom. To that, the Judas hole, through which the guard can see but the prisoner cannot, adds loss of dignity and privacy. Identity shrinks to a cell number. I used the can and lay down on the bed, my pulse still racing. Next to cell No. 20 was a plate lift. I heard it creak several times as the prisoners' breakfasts were brought up from the basement kitchens.

After half an hour the cell door was thrown open by a different warder, who came straight from a Second World War POW escape film: riding breeches tucked into polished knee-high riding boots, a cap so 'slashed' that it added several inches to his height and, by his side, a black Alsatian dog. Only the swastika insignia was missing. He stepped aside, leaving the dog to watch me, and took a tray from someone standing outside my field of vision, which he placed on the table before backing out of the cell without a word and relocking the door. I decided to call him, in the privacy of my mind, 'the SS man'.

On the tray was the breakfast with which I became all too familiar: a chipped enamel mug; a small enamel jug of what looked like coffee but was made from roasted acorns; two slices of black bread and a dollop of brown jam on an enamel plate, with a spoon to spread it. I poured the ersatz coffee and swallowed some of the tasteless dark liquid. Realising that I was hungry, I spread some of the jam on the bread and bit off a mouthful. The bread was coarse and gritty, the jam impossible to analyse, but probably made from a mixture of vegetables and fruit, which was always in short supply in the GDR.

After my traumatic night and calmed by the food and drink, I dozed fully clothed on the bed until I was awoken by the SS man and his dog bringing my midday meal and removing the breakfast things. Lunch consisted of a plate of noodles on which reposed two grey and tasteless meat balls. Such was my ravenous hunger that I ate it all up.

If I had been depressed before, that was nothing compared with the sense of desolation that now weighed me down. I was a prisoner in the most repressive Stalinist state of Europe, charged with a crime that apparently could get me a three-year prison sentence. To make everything worse, I was a prisoner in a country with which Her Majesty's Government had no diplomatic relations, which was the political equivalent of the earth opening beneath my feet and swallowing me up. Outside Lieutenant Becker's file, I did not exist. There would be no mail to me, or from me, and no parcels to raise my morale. No British or other consul could visit me, or protect me. I was as alone as a prisoner in the Siberian Gulag, upon realising which I felt an almost tangible fear, blocking all intelligent thought.

It was 1 April 1959 and I was the biggest April Fool in Europe.

15

THE PROMISE OF A GIRLFRIEND

After a complete immersion stay with a French family on a school exchange visit at Easter when I was 14, I was bilingual and became fascinated by the ideas and writings of French philosopher Jean-Paul Sartre, who was very fashionable at the time. A key concept in Sartre's philosophy of existentialism was what he called '*le délaissement total*', or total abandonment: we are, each of us, alone. Waking on my second morning in the prison, I realised that I was *living* total abandonment. The guards probably did not know my identity, so hardly anyone knew where I was, or even if I was still alive.

Back in Gatow, were they checking to see if a boat was missing at the yacht club or dragging the Havel, in case I had drowned myself, accidentally or on purpose? With Ron in the hospital, it was quite possible that no one had yet noticed I was missing. As I later learned, he was visited by a couple of RAF officers, who obtained the surgeon's consent to Ron being driven by ambulance back to Gatow a couple of days early. There, he was required to be present in our room while the officers went through all my belongings in the search for a clue as to what had happened to me. He had, of course, no idea where I was or exactly what I had done.

One of the questions addressed to him was, 'Have you ever known J/T Boyd incapable through drink?' Ron put on his most innocent expression and assured them earnestly that he had not. As loyalty, a barefaced lie counts high, although he later justified this one to himself and me on the grounds that we almost always went drinking together, glass for glass, so that he had therefore not consciously 'known' I was incapable, since he was in the same condition.

The net spread wider. A letter from Duncan in Cyprus having been found in my locker, he was grilled there by two RAF Police officers, but could tell them nothing about my disappearance.

In the Stasi prison, the second day was a copy of the previous one. Two different guards brought my breakfast and midday meal, the latter a watery stew with two bits of potato and some strands of meat floating in it. I tried talking to them. The first one took no notice, but just left, re-bolting the door; the second put a finger to his lips and glanced behind him at the open doorway, which I took to mean that he was not allowed to talk to me because silence was a part of the prison regime. The last meal of the day, served at 5 p.m., was even less memorable than the previous two but by then, with senses on high alert, I had worked out that the kitchens were below my cell and staffed by women, whose voices reached me faintly up the shaft of the plate lift from time to time. Later, I discovered that unlike the detainees of both sexes being held in solitary confinement above ground level, the women of the Arbeitskommando down there were not political prisoners but criminals serving their term – although what they were guilty of, I was not to know.

The smallest change in routine was an event. On Day Three, towards midday, a warder opened the door and motioned me outside. 'Kopf auf dem Kinn,' he barked – literally, 'Head on your chin'. It was an order to lower my head to my chest so I could see only the floor immediately in front of my feet. Walking behind me along the corridors between the cells whistling, he made me stop and pushed me into an alcove, facing the wall, when we heard a different warder whistling, so that I could not see another prisoner being marched along in the other direction. This was normal practice in KGB prisons, copied by the Stasi, to depress prisoners' morale by allowing no detainee to catch sight of a fellow sufferer or possibly recognise a familiar face – or, indeed, any face without a warder's cap above it – except for that of an interrogator.

Lieutenant Becker was sitting behind the table in the interrogation room. He motioned me to sit down on the bentwood chair in front of the table. Later, I learned that it was specially made: beneath the woven split cane seat was a lint pad, designed to absorb my personal body odour when sweating and nervous, and which would be placed in a hermetically sealed glass jar using sterile forceps, immediately after the interrogation.[1] The Stasi had a bizarre collection of several hundred thousand of these pads, each labelled with the prisoner's name and number, the idea being that any pad could be taken out of the jar and used to give tracker dogs the scent, should this particular person ever be on the run. That only a tiny percentage of the pads were ever used gives some idea of the all-pervading paranoia of the GDR.

'How are you feeling?' Becker asked.

'Scruffy,' I replied.

'That's a word I don't know.'

'I need a shave.'

He nodded. 'I'll tell the guards. Now you must do something for me in return.' He took me again through my account of how I had come to be at Albrechtshof in the middle of the night. What was the name of the bar where I had been drinking? Who were my companions there? I said I would rather not name them in case they got into trouble. He shrugged and changed direction.

'You didn't tell me where you work in Gatow.'

'I'm not allowed to talk about it.'

'Mr Boyd, you must learn to be …' He could not find the word in English, '… *vernünftig*.'

We eventually worked out that the word meant 'sensible'. If I wanted to be well treated, I had to co-operate. I took a deep breath. If Pete the Barber was not a spy, there were bound to be other informers working for the Stasi among the local employees on the base. Sweaty Sam, for example. So it was best to keep close to the truth: I told him that I worked in the Signals Section building, as a clerk, and repeated the list of my boring chores in the bedding store.

'Why is it called Signals Section?' he asked. 'What does that mean?'

'I've no idea,' I replied. 'I just work in the bedding store on the ground floor. I'm not allowed upstairs.'

'What are the names of the officers there?'

I gave him the name of the CO of RAF Gatow, since that had to be public knowledge, but said that I did not know any other officers by name, playing on the fact that I was only a National Service conscript, ticking the days off my demob calendar to 5 May 1959, the date of my longed-for *Entlassung* – a German word we had all learned, meaning demob. I added, 'I expect that's the same in your army. Conscripts just want to go back to civilian life at the end of their service.'

'Wrong,' he said. 'In the Socialist countries, we are proud to serve the State because the State serves the people. It is different in the West, where the workers and soldiers are exploited by the rich.'

I nodded agreement, and told him how I had had to leave school early and go to work in a bank because my parents had no money to support me. Although true, this was not the entire truth: my principal reason to leave school was a deep disillusionment with the A level syllabus and the way modern languages were then taught at Oxford. However, it seemed to be what he wanted to hear.

'Here in the German Democratic Republic,' he said, 'all young people can go to university. It is not necessary to be rich.'

'I'm impressed.'

He seemed pleased with me, adding, 'You must be bored in your cell.'

'It's better,' I grinned, 'doing nothing there, than polishing floors all day.'

He smiled. 'Would you like some reading material?'

'Yes.'

'Have you seen the *GDR Review*? It's a magazine, very popular in the West. Hundreds of copies are sent every month to Britain. It tells the truth about our country and the impressive achievements of socialism in the GDR. I think you will enjoy it.'

He pressed the bell-push, the door opened and a warder marched me back to my cell, pushing me into alcoves, face to the wall, when we heard another approaching guard whistling. In the cell, my midday meal was cold. Unappetising when warm, the soggy noodles and grey meat balls were almost inedible, but there was so little fat in them that I was able to force myself to eat most of what was on the plate.

In solitary confinement, every small event is a respite from boredom. That afternoon, things looked up, twice. A warder brought a mug of tepid water, a small piece of gritty soap, a safety razor and a towel about the size of a face flannel. Better than nothing, I thought, until finding that the blade of the razor was blunt from much previous use and painful to use as it scraped rather than cut through my beard stubble, nicking the skin in several places. Unknown to me, it was infected from some other prisoner's barber's rash, which would torment me for a long time to come. I tried to see whether the blade could be removed, but it was somehow locked into the safety razor, to stop a prisoner slitting his wrists with it.

The second 'event' was to have a copy of the previous day's SED daily paper *Neues Deutschland* brought to the cell. Any reading material was welcome, but this was, if anything, even worse than *Pravda* and *Izvestiya*: verbatim reports of politicians' speeches and sycophantic accounts of their heroic performance in bettering the lot of the workers, leavened – if that is the word – with articles on incredible feats of GDR athletes and sports players. As the world learned after the collapse of the GDR, their performances were enhanced by dangerously high doses of anabolic steroids and hormones that changed the sex of many or rendered them permanently sterile. That afternoon, two editions of the *GDR Review* were delivered by one of the silent guards. One, two months old, was in English. The other, in German, was for the current month. I devoured them both from cover to cover. There were articles on GDR folk dancing ensembles touring other socialist countries, welcomed by trades union officials and committees of 'heroic workers' in Azerbaijan, Poland and the Baltic States. Transparently impossible statistics were claimed for the GDR steel and lignite industries. The story of a GDR coal miner – *Bergarbeiter* was a new word for my German vocabulary – who regularly exceeded his daily quota of coal by 120 per cent reminded me of reading about Stakhanovite heroes of the USSR in the library at Crail.

Subconsciously, I started to hum the tune of 'Stenka Razin', until realising with alarm that I must put out of my mind anything to do with Russia or the Russian language in case a hidden microphone betrayed my knowledge. Somehow – perhaps by some kind of auto-hypnosis – I suppressed everything learned at Crail, at Pucklechurch and in Berlin so efficiently that I could hardly construct a sentence in Russian after my release. It took a long while to recover the deliberately lost language that had filled my head for most of the last two years. I had been reciting to myself that morning FitzGerald's translation of *The Rubaiyat of Omar Khayyam* as a mental exercise, and now restarted it:

> Awake, for morning in the bowl of night
> Has flung the stone that puts the stars to flight:
> And Lo! the hunter of the East has caught
> The sultan's turret in a noose of light.

Then I was stuck. 'And thou beside me in the wilderness …' – how did that verse go? My mind was blank. Then, like an exhausted creature from the depths, another verse resurfaced:

> Myself when young did eagerly frequent
> Doctor and saint, and heard great argument
> About it and about; but evermore
> Came out by the same door as in I went.

Two more lines surfaced:

> I often wonder what the merchant gets
> One half so precious as the goods he sells.

And that was it. Of the hundred or so verses, I could recall no more. I tried some of my favourite French poetry – Rimbaud, Baudelaire, Verlaine and others. A few lines came to mind, but not a single complete poem. I have no explanation to offer, but that was how it was. As I fell asleep that night, the last thing I saw was the English edition of the *GDR Review* lying on the table. The fact that there was an English edition of anything in the prison library was immensely heartening because it had to mean that other English-speakers were, or had recently been, there. So I was not alone!

Waking on Day Four to the familiar faces of the SS man and his dog, I decided that it was necessary to take control of myself, to combat the waves of pure terror that constantly welled up inside me. I could not get out of the cell, but I could decide what to do in it. Having slept fully dressed because there was only one blanket, I stripped to vest and pants, recalling all the physical exercises the PTI had made me do in the hangar at Pucklechurch, and mentally gave thanks to him as I worked through a double regime of bending and twisting, including knee-bends and press-ups and running knees-up on the spot. Grateful to that anonymous PTI, whom I had detested at the time, for showing me all the exercises, I ended up sweating, my vest and pants damp with perspiration, so when the mug of water was brought for me to wash my face I used the water afterwards to rinse my underwear, wringing it out as hard as possible and draping it over the radiator – which was not hot, but warmer than the air in the cell. The remaining problem was how to clean my teeth, the best solution being to rub them with the damp towel. After two hours of activities I had *chosen* to do, the pendulum of my morale had swung back to positive – and rose slightly on seeing through the grimy window a con trail high in the sky. With every word the pilot said probably being logged in the set room, it felt good that *I* knew something *they* did not.

The pendulum of morale swung up again that afternoon when I was taken out of the cell and down some steps into a small, cobbled courtyard with walls 5m high. The metal door clanged shut behind me. It was the first time I had been in the open air since my arrest. With high buildings on all sides, I was like the man in Oscar Wilde's poem, *The Ballad of Reading Gaol*, who 'looked with wistful eye upon that little tent of blue that prisoners call the sky'. At least I was not on a treadmill for hours every day, as Wilde had been. I took deep breaths, thirstily drinking in the sight of the blue sky and some sparrows flying about, trying not to see the warder with his sub-machine gun staring down at me from the observation box perched atop the courtyard wall. That the birds were not prisoners proved that even the GDR Government did not control everything, as did an anarchic clump of grass growing in a crack between the cobbles. To complete a tour of the yard took twenty-eight normal paces. I started by walking briskly round it, then walked slowly, then walked briskly again, changing direction each time.

Back in the cell – I refused to call it mentally *my* cell – I rubbed myself down with my cord trousers and put on my vest and pants, which were almost dry. The latrine bucket had been emptied while I was in the yard. Otherwise, the rest of the day was anticlimactic, my morale dropping hour by hour.

Waking on Day Five when the breakfast arrived, I ate the black bread and brown jam, drank the ersatz coffee – and wondered how to fill another twenty-four hours. Day Six dawned grey and raining, so no exercise in the courtyard. Days Seven and Eight and Nine were the same. Morale plunged, and plunged further on the next several days. There were moments when I would, from utter loneliness, have told Lieutenant Becker anything he wanted to know for the sheer relief of exchanging words with a fellow human being. Fortunately, he lacked the interrogator's flair for gauging the state of a prisoner's morale, so none of his visits coincided with my moments of despair. I had, of course, no idea that the immense bureaucracy of the GDR's Ministerium für Staatssicherheit was gearing itself up on my case.

By the next time Becker came to the Lindenstrasse, I had got a grip on myself again – not least because on one occasion I was let out for exercise in the large courtyard overlooked by cell windows on four levels, where it was even possible to run a complete circuit. Although the windows were all blocked up, some by glass bricks and some by frosted glass, I thought it worthwhile to play the trick used by POWs in Second World War films, and whistle a tune that any other Western prisoner might recognise, while close to the windows. Beginning with 'God Save the Queen' and going on to 'La Marseillaise' and 'The Star-Spangled Banner', I heard no answering whistle, but on my second attempt there was a just recognisable reply to the National Anthem: someone up there was British!

That lift to my morale kept me going several days, but after more than a week of not seeing Becker or exchanging a word with anyone – it was my third week in solitary – I decided to go on hunger strike, as a way of attracting attention. At first, to prevent my resolve weakening and taking a few mouthfuls, I tipped the food into the latrine bucket, but that meant the warders were not aware I had not eaten. To get my message across, it was necessary to leave the food on the plate untouched, which required stronger resolution. Several days of this – time had begun to blur, with days and nights confused

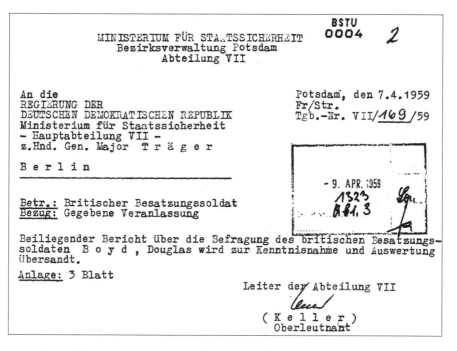

MINISTERIUM FÜR STAATSSICHERHEIT
Bezirksverwaltung Potsdam
Abteilung VII

BSTU
0004 2

An die
REGIERUNG DER
DEUTSCHEN DEMOKRATISCHEN REPUBLIK
Ministerium für Staatssicherheit
- Hauptabteilung VII -
z.Hnd. Gen. Major T r ä g e r

B e r l i n

Potsdam, den 7.4.1959
Fr/Str.
Tgb.-Nr. VII/169/59

- 9. APR. 1959
1323
R.#.1. 3

Betr.: Britischer Besatzungssoldat
Bezug: Gegebene Veranlassung

Beiliegender Bericht über die Befragung des britischen Besatzungs-
soldaten B o y d , Douglas wird zur Kenntnisnahme und Auswertung
übersandt.

Anlage: 3 Blatt

Leiter der Abteilung VII

(K e l l e r)
Oberleutnant

Letter of 7 April from Becker's superior, Oberleutnant Keller, who was head of Abteilung VIII of the Bezirksverwaltung Potsdam, to Major General Träger – his boss at Hauptabteilung VII in Berlin – forwarding 'for information and evaluation' the 'report on the questioning of the British occupation soldier Boyd, Douglas'.

– brought me to a state where I no longer felt hungry, or even interested by the food on the table, but stayed lying on the bed and staring at the ceiling for most of the day.

This brought a visit from a rather grandfatherly man in civilian clothes, who introduced himself as the prison governor, come to plead with me to eat because it was important for my health. Spooning some of the midday noodles into his mouth, he pronounced them good, telling me the food was the same that he and the warders ate, indeed the same as he ate at home with his family. I let myself be persuaded, eventually agreeing to eat if 'der Offizier' – meaning Becker – would come and talk to me. The governor promised to arrange that, so I ate as much of the noodles as I could manage to force into my shrunken stomach – and ate some of whatever was brought for the evening meal also before falling asleep.

It was still not seven o'clock when I was taken to the interrogation room next morning. In his cheap suit, with raincoat slung over the table, Becker

> **BSTU**
> **0006**
>
> Fragen nach Einzelheiten aus seiner Arbeit und der Einheit be-
> antwortete er, trotz vorheriger gegenteiliger Versicherung, nur
> zögernd, ausweichend und wenn schon, dann sehr allgemein. So er-
> klärte er, seine Arbeit bestände in der Anforderung von Verpfle-
> gung und Ausrüstungsgegenständen sowie in der Erledigung von Auf-
> räumungsarbeiten (Teekochen, Fußböden bohnern usw.). Eine hinrei-
> chende Erklärung dafür konnte er nicht geben. Er erwähnte nur,
> dass dies in der brit. Armee "so üblich sei", da für sehr viele
> Soldaten keine geeignete Verwendungsmöglichkeit vorliege.
> Ähnlich verhielt es sich mit Fragen nach Bewaffnung, Belegungs-
> stärke, Kommandopersonal usw. Hierbei nannte B. lediglich den
> Namen des Kommandeurs der Einheit

Extract from report dated 6 April. Abbreviated translation:
Despite reassurances, [Boyd] answers questions about his work and the unit with reluctance, evasively and very generally. He explained that his work consists in requisitioning catering supplies and [other] items of equipment, making tea and polishing floors, etc. He explained that this is normal in the British Army, since there are no specific duties for many soldiers. Similarly, he gives no information about weaponry, staff numbers, officers, etc. – except for the name of the commanding officer of the unit.

looked the same at any hour, when he came at midnight or even earlier in the morning – but never in the middle of the night, as was done to break hard-regime prisoners' sleep patterns. He made no reference to my hunger strike, asking instead what I had thought of the latest *GDR Review*. Trying to be a good pupil, I said it was very interesting and that I had learned a lot about life in the GDR.

'You know,' he said thoughtfully, 'you could acquire citizenship and stay here, helping to build socialism.'

I feigned interest, asking, 'How could I do that?'

'I could arrange for you to be given a job on a collective farm in Saxon Switzerland – as a tractor driver. There are many Westerners living there.'

As I knew from reading about it in the *GDR Review*, the beautiful hilly area of Saxon Switzerland lay in the far south-eastern corner of the GDR, near the Czech and Polish frontiers, from where it would be difficult, if not impossible, to make a successful run to a Western frontier.

'I can't drive a tractor,' was my feeble excuse.

'They would teach you,' Becker said. 'And you'd have a pretty blonde girlfriend waiting for you there.'

Having heard the rumour of a State-run brothel somewhere in East Berlin, where Western military defectors were given beer to drink and girls for sex as an inducement to talk about their work, I asked how I could be sure the pretty blonde was waiting for me in Saxon Switzerland.

Becker smiled again. 'She will be an obedient Party member.'

A warder opened the door and said there was a phone call for Becker. He left the room and did not return for several minutes. It was almost impossible to resist the urge to walk quietly over to the window, just to look out onto the street for a moment, but I assumed I was being spied on through a hole in a wall or by a hidden camera, and that his absence was some sort of test, so made myself stay docilely seated by the table. When he returned, I said I had thought about his offer, but had a girlfriend waiting for me back home. He asked whether I would like a shower and some books to read. I said yes to both questions, and was surprised when he pushed across the table a packet with several cigarettes in, saying, 'Matches are forbidden. You'll have to ask the guards for a light.'

Failing to realise that feeding my need for nicotine was actually a punishment which would reawaken the craving, I thanked him. He hit the bell-push, a warder came. I had politely requested several times to be handed over to the BRIXMISS team in Potsdam, but for once I actually argued with Becker that I should not be detained in a prison. It was the only time he ever laughed out loud, as did the warder waiting to take me back to the cell, who agreed with him that, '*Hier ist kein Zuchthaus.*'

I retorted, 'If it is not a prison, what is it, a hotel?'

Both laughed anew when Becker said that it was a kind of hotel. Officially it was an *Untersuchungsgefängnis*, or interrogation prison. It was fortunate that I had at the time no idea what went on in the main wings of the Stasi's Lindenstrasse Prison – ironically dubbed '*das Lindenhotel*' by its long-suffering inmates – and the far more vicious prisons for convicted prisoners, to which they were sent all over the GDR after being inevitably found guilty at their trials.

As I walked back along the corridors with the guard, a strange, middle-aged man was standing at the corner just before the first cells. About 5ft 6ins tall, corpulent and wearing a crumpled suit, he had a bald pate and hair fluffing out at the sides and back of his head, reminding me of the Russian film director, Sergei Eisenstein. It was the only time I was allowed to see anyone in the corridors, apart from the guard escorting me. Who that man was, why I was allowed to see him and why he watched me walk past without speaking is a mystery to this day.

That afternoon I was taken out of the cell and shown into the shower room. A posh title for just another cell with a shower fitting in the ceiling and a not very efficient drain hole cut into the concrete floor. The air was damp and chill. Black mould was growing on one wall. The warder watched me undress, handed me a minuscule piece of soap and a small hand towel that was already damp from previous use, then turned on the overhead shower. The water was cold. Thirty seconds later, he turned it off just as it was getting warm. I dressed and was marched back to the cell, feeling damp but clean-ish for the first time since my arrest.

On the table lay three books, all in German. One was Jack London's *White Fang*, another was a tale of the Old West by the popular German author of Westerns, Karl May, featuring his characters the Apache Chief Winnetou and his white blood brother, Old Shatterhand. The third was an even more bizarre choice: an economics tome about the Tennessee Valley Authority set up by US President Franklin Roosevelt in 1933, about which I had never heard. With the absence of a dictionary requiring that I puzzle out the meanings of unknown words and increase my German vocabulary the hard way, the books were mind-food for some time to come. By that afternoon, I realised that, whatever else was happening in the prison, I was on a very 'soft' regime. Did that mean I was shortly to be released?

Becker had set up a library service for me. As soon as I finished one book, I told a warder, who removed it and another appeared in the cell during my next exercise period. One was a book of Party-approved poetry. None of the poems would have been particularly memorable under normal circumstances. Yet memorising them also gave the brain something to do and some lines here and there still stick in the memory nearly sixty years later.

That night I wondered what would have been my fate, had I fallen for the 'blonde girlfriend' offer. In 1963 US authorities released information about eighty-one American servicemen who had defected to the GDR. By the end of the Cold War, that figure was believed to total 150 men, of whom thirty-five were American, including one black serviceman who committed suicide although married to a local woman. As Markus Wolf, head of the Hauptverwaltung Aufklärung – the Stasi's external espionage arm – once remarked, people are intrigued by betrayal, but everyone hates the traitor, including his case officers. Immediately after arriving in the GDR, the defectors were interrogated in Potsdam as I had been and some of them were filmed for propaganda purposes before being driven to a 'traitors' hostel' in Wallstrasse, Bautzen.

One of the few who had any Western secrets to give away was Intelligence Corps Corporal Brian Patchett, employed as a Russian linguist in the Royal Signals Detachment at RAF Gatow, whose defection was announced by the GDR news agency on 6 July 1963. Patchett was a very disturbed young man with no friends, who regularly wet his bed and who had been sacked for unreliability by his only employer in civilian life. His defection was possibly triggered by being dumped in June by Rosemarie Zeiss, the 21-year-old Berliner girlfriend whom he had met when she was working in the Gatow Naafi. None of his former comrades seemed very surprised when Patchett's absence was announced as he had often expressed Communist ideas in arguments with them. He was one of the defectors happy to be filmed condemning British and American SIGINT operations in Germany, with which he was familiar. It is thought that he returned to Britain at some point, although his current whereabouts are unknown.

Most Western defectors were of low rank and often with a service record of 'woman trouble', alcoholism and brawling. After interrogation in Potsdam, they were transported to Bautzen, where Western radio and television programmes could not be received, and from where escape was almost impossible. This would have been my destination, had I accepted Becker's offer. Living in a 'traitors' hostel', life there was grim, with hours of political indoctrination on three days a week and boring work in local factories on the alternate days. On the single free day each week, recreation was a choice between ping-pong and ping-pong. Although there was an International Cultural Centre in Bautzen, this held little appeal for most of the defectors, who were more interested in booze and brawling.

With minimal wages equivalent to about £10 per month to spend in two grimy bars in the town, fights frequently broke out there between defectors and locals and between defectors who had come to hate each other. Several committed suicide. Some obtained work in a locomotive factory or in a shoe factory near Bautzen, meriting reasonable quality accommodation by GDR standards, while others stayed in the shared rooms in Wallstrasse, being used as low-grade farm workers, occasionally sighted and photographed by BRIXMISS officers driving past. The best 'success story' was of one genuinely politically motivated American who was given work as a journalist because he could write the Party line. A few returned to the West, facing imprisonment. Most simply disappeared after the fall of the Wall, so their fates are largely unknown but are unlikely to have been very happy.

16

VISITORS FROM MOSCOW

In the third week of April – I had long since lost count of the exact day – a warder opened the door in mid-morning and motioned me to come out. I had just shaved as well as possible with the blunt razor blade and mug of tepid water after doing half an hour of exercises. So far, it had been a good morning with minimal boredom and my spirits were as high as they ever got in the prison. Only a couple of days previously, Becker had been to ask me some questions that did not seem to lead anywhere and given me a whole packet of cigarettes, so I did wonder what he wanted after such a short interval, and guessed he had come to give me news of my release.

On the usual march along the corridors I was thrust into an alcove once and, a minute later, passed a warder with another prisoner facing the wall in an alcove. The warder, trying to block my view of the other prisoner with his body, glared at me when I tried to look but out of the corner of my eye, head down, I saw the bottom of a skirt and bare legs. This was the first time I knew there were women in the prison apart from the ones working in the kitchen. I was still mulling this over when my warder opened the door of the interrogation room. Instead of Becker, sitting at the table were two men in civilian suits. To my 20-year-old eyes, they looked middle-aged. A woman in the same age bracket was standing facing me. I was still in positive mood and thought briefly that they had come to tell me I was being released.

Instead, after the door closed behind me, the woman said, '*My predstaviteli praviteltsva sovietskovo soyuza*'. That was Russian for 'We are representatives of the government of the Soviet Union'.

I have never been more terrified, before or since. It was difficult to keep the fear from showing on my face, so I put on a silly grin, to pretend I had not understood. While I flattered myself that I had bluffed Becker that I was a lowly clerk doing a boring administrative job, these KGB officers knew exactly what went on in the Signals Section of RAF Gatow. The two men fired questions at me in rapid succession, using the woman as translator. They asked about my family, took me through my education to the point where I left school to work in the bank, and affected to sympathise with my story of how my father's illness and the family's impoverishment – which was real enough – prevented me from going to university. As Becker had done, they assured me that in the Soviet Union everybody could go to university. I said that must be wonderful, but harped on my previous role as a bank clerk when they asked why someone of my intelligence had been given such a lowly job as clerk in a bedding store.

Knowing that conscripts in the USSR were used as drudges and mercilessly bullied by older servicemen, including NCOs, resulting in several hundred known suicides each year, I said, 'I suppose the RAF thought I could keep a reliable record of stores after adding up figures all day in civilian life'. They did not comment, so I added, 'Perhaps other bedding clerks sell stuff, but they thought I'd be honest, having worked in a bank'.

It was so plain the men did not believe a word I said in this pantomime that I could feel sweat on my palms, several times wiping them surreptitiously on my thighs while pretending to change position. From time to time, the woman pretended to forget to translate a simple question. '*Zanimayetyes sportom?*' – 'Do you play sport?'; '*U vas skolko lyet?*' – 'How old are you?'; and so on. Each time, pulse racing at the narrow escape, instead of answering I smiled as though it were all a joke while I waited for her to put the question into English, while three pairs of ears monitored my voice and three pairs of eyes watched for me to show the slightest sign of understanding Russian.

The interview went on for a good couple of hours – which were really a very bad couple of hours – until they came up with a plan that accorded with my pretended activities in Gatow. After a warning that the GDR could keep me in prison for months or even years without trial, they offered to 'spring' me out of the prison in a few days' time and drive me back to the border with the British sector of Berlin, from where I could find my own way back to Gatow, and account for my absence by a story of being shacked up with a girlfriend, with whom I had at last fallen out. Yes, I would be punished, maybe even court-martialled, but that was better than staying in the Lindenstrasse Prison for an unknown length of time, wasn't it?

I agreed, but asked, 'Why would you do this for me?'

'Because,' the older man answered, 'in the Great Patriotic War,[1] your country and ours were allies. So we are your friends and the Germans are your enemies and ours. That's why.'

I pretended to see the 'logic' of that. At the end of this real-life nightmare, I agreed to go along with their plan to 'spring' me from the prison. There was just one condition, they said: I must on no account tell 'the interrogating officer' that they had been in the Stasi prison and talked with me, in case he spoiled 'our' plan.

Back in the cell, I was drenched in nervous perspiration and shivering with fear. I just hoped it had not been obvious to the Russians. Did it even matter, since they would have known perfectly well the principal activity of the RAF in Gatow? The very last thing I wanted was to fall into the hands of the KGB, which would lead to many years locked away in some remote work camp in the Gulag. So, I kicked up such a fuss with the guards after being returned to my cell that Becker came next morning to see what was wrong. His normally expressionless face showed emotion for the first time when I told him of the Russians' visit.

'They had no right to be here!' he exploded. 'This is not their territory.' His reaction seemed to confirm my guess that, even in the neo-Stalinist GDR, the half a million Russian troops stationed there were regarded as occupation forces, not brothers-in-arms. Or so I thought at the time, but there is another possible explanation for his reaction.

'In any case,' I said, 'my demob date is 5 May – two weeks or so away. After that, I shall no longer be a NATO soldier in Berlin, but a civilian.' As a ploy, it was both desperate and pathetic, but I was panicking to get out of the prison before the Russians could play some trump and claim me. As confirmed by my Stasi file, recovered many years later, Becker's masters in Department 3 of the Stasi's 7th Directorate recommended shortly after the KGB trio's visit that I should be returned to the West through Dr Ludwig, president of the German Red Cross, and Mr Gruenter, president of the American Red Cross in Europe, who could pass me on to the appropriate authorities. The Red Cross was a back-channel used by British and GDR governments from time to time, since they had no reciprocal diplomatic relations.

During the later years of the GDR, there was a colossal traffic in human lives called *Häftlingsfreikauf*, or purchase of prisoners. For humanitarian reasons, the West German Government purchased the liberty of 33,755 prisoners held in GDR prisons and 250,000 of their relatives and other people, at a total price of 3.5 *billion* Deutschmarks. Neither side talked about it because that would have made the GDR Government look ridiculous for ruling the country so badly that it needed this 'invisible export' and because the West German Government would have been accused of subsidising the economically unviable GDR.

These clandestine deals were handled by a very discreet lawyer named Vogel, who had offices in both East and West Berlin. Like most lawyers, he took a fee from each deal, which made him the richest man in the GDR. So it was no surprise to find in my Stasi file a 'proposal' dated 28 April 1959, which mentioned that I had repeatedly asked to be handed back to the British Military Mission in Potsdam. It also stated that no useful purpose was being served by my continued detention, and that I should be handed back through the Red Cross. The proposal was signed by ... Vogel. After that, the only other sheet in my BStU folder records the despatch to the Stasi archives in June 1962 of the file on '*Grenzverletzter Boyd*' – 'border-violator Boyd'.

Da ein weiteres Festhalten des B. keinen operativen Nutzen bringt wird vorgeschlagen, ihn auf diplomatischem Wege durch den Präsidenten des Deutschen Roten Kreuzes, Dr. L u d w i g , Verdienter Arzt des Volkes, Dresden, an den Präsidenten des Amerikanischen Roten Kreuzes in Europa, Mister G r u e n t e r, den entsprechenden Behörden zu übergeben.

Einverstanden: ....   (V o g e l)
                                     Ofw.

However, since nobody told me at the time what was going on, I became increasingly uneasy and unable to sleep. By now I had lost any clear sense of the date or how long I had been in prison, as was intended. Dozing on my bed early one morning, just after breakfast, I became aware of a brass band playing not far away. The sound grew in intensity then died away and was replaced by another and another until it seemed everyone in Potsdam must be marching around the town, playing oompah music. Through the fixed window of the cell, outside sound was none too clear and it was impossible to tell direction, but it eventually dawned on me that it must be May Day – the international feast of labour. The sound of the bands continued all morning, leaving me with the determination to badger Becker on our next meeting with the countdown to my demobilisation from National Service in four days' time, at which point he would no longer be holding prisoner a member of NATO armed forces, but a civilian. It was not much of a legal point, but better than nothing – or so I thought.

He came to the Lindenhotel next morning and I greeted him with the news that, in another three days, I should be a civilian and therefore of no danger to the GDR under any circumstances. He made a note in the file on the table between us, as though this was news to him.

After a pause, I said, 'I heard the parades yesterday.'

'There were no parades, Mr Boyd.'

'But it was May Day, wasn't it?'

He gave a small nod, which was as near as he ever came to answering a question of mine.

I added, 'And I distinctly heard the bands marching around, out there in the town.'

'Mr Boyd, parades are militaristic. So we do not have them in the GDR because this is a peace-loving country. What you heard were spontaneous demonstrations of the workers.'

Years later, when I saw a photograph of the parades in Potsdam on that 1 May, it seemed sad that 'spontaneous demonstrations' could be so grim. Not a smile in sight, just Party functionaries in grey suits with grey faces marching along holding up massive photo portraits of Party leaders. And wasn't it amazing how fast the workers had enlarged these to poster size for their *spontaneous* demonstration?

Calculated from the known first day of May, I counted down mentally: three days to go, two days to go, one day to go. Demob! I really believed that morning that I would be released. Different scenarios played themselves out in my head: a smiling Becker shaking my hand at the border between Potsdam and the British sector; British MPs in a jeep coming to collect me from the prison, and so on. By dusk that evening I was in profound gloom, which grew worse on each successive day. Knowing nothing of Vogel's proposal, unaware that the wheels of the Stasi were grinding slowly and extremely small, I fell into a real slough of despond. Some meals I ate, some I ignored. Some days I slept, some nights I could not sleep. Allowed into the courtyard for exercise, I sat in a corner, moping. In the cell, I did none of the exercises that had so boosted my morale earlier. I was perfectly aware that this complex of behaviour was despicable and that awareness pushed my morale down even further.

At 6 a.m. on 12 May 1959, when my breakfast was brought by the SS man, I was already sitting up on the chair because sleep eluded me that night. The black Alsatian dog padded up and sniffed my crotch as though checking where to bite when given the command, and I did not bother to move away. In fairness to the dog, I probably smelled pretty high from neglecting my toilet.

'*Mach's schnell!*' It was the first time the warder had spoken to me. Instead of leaving, he stood waiting while I ate the bread and jam, and drank some acorn coffee, the dog watching. Then, '*Komm mit!*'

Expecting to be taken to the interrogation room, I was led instead along the corridor past it and into the small courtyard just inside the main gate of the prison. There stood Becker with two Stasi heavies in the front seats of an ancient Mercedes. On the passenger's lap was my duffle bag. Was I being transferred to a different prison? It seemed possible. Ushering me into the rear seat without saying where we were going, Becker handed me a packet of sandwiches as we erupted through the gate with a screech of tyres on the cobbles of the Lindenstrasse. I ate the sandwiches, in which slices of garlic sausage tasted delicious after all the bland prison food, as we sped out of Potsdam and along an autobahn crossing open countryside, but even this did not completely dispel the gloom.

'*Hat's geschmeckt?*' Becker asked, when I had finished eating. I replied that the aftertaste of garlic was delicious, which led to a surreal discussion in which he explained that the German word *Nachgeschmack* means a *bad* aftertaste. It is strange, the details that stay in the memory.

Sitting in the back seat on the other side of Becker was a rough-looking British soldier, also in civvies, who was eating similar sandwiches, although missing several teeth. I realised that it must have been he who whistled back 'God Save the Queen' that day when I was in the big exercise yard. His army career, as he told it to me during the journey, was a series of promotions up to sergeant and demotions back to private for getting drunk and smashing up bars in Berlin. He ended, 'So, when I've 'ad enough of the bleedin' army, I go across to the uvver side for a few weeks' rest.'

It seemed incredible to me that such a man had worked out a way of commuting between the two blocs of the Cold War for his own convenience. Of course, he could be a Kiplingesque spy, in which case his cover was brilliant. When Becker leaned forward to talk to the front seat passenger, I asked my strange companion behind his back where we were being taken.

'They're 'anding us back at the border,' he grinned. 'You'll see.'

He seemed to know what he was talking about, but I did not dare to believe it. Becker sat back, looking uneasy. 'There's a problem, Mr Boyd. I've forgotten to collect your identity card from another office. All your other possessions are in your bag there, but not the ID card. Will that get you into trouble?'

Why would he say that, if I was not going to be handed back? After all the stress, I wanted to giggle at the lunatic idea of my interrogator worrying about a detail like that. In case he was going to drive back to Potsdam, to get it, I tried to stay cool, assuring him that men lost their 1250s all the time and were just issued with another.

'Are you sure?' he asked. 'In the Nazionale Volksarmee, it is a serious offence to lose an identification card.'

The soldier gave me a wink. 'Lost me bleedin' pay book twice when I was on the piss,' he told Becker. 'They just give you anuvver one after a bollocking from the sergeant major.'

After about three hours – but everything that morning is slightly blurred – the ancient Merc pulled up at what did look like a border checkpoint, although somewhere in the back of my mind I wondered whether it was all an elaborate scenario – for what purpose, I could not guess.

'Told ya,' the soldier pointed at two red-capped British MPs standing by a building 200 yards away. 'Those bastards are waitin' for me. I even know the buggers' names. That one …', he pointed.

One of the heavies grabbed his arm and propelled him into the border guards' office, which looked like the prefabricated cabins seen on building sites. I followed, and sat down at a desk with Becker, while the heavies stationed themselves on either side of the single door. According to the wall clock, the time was 11.30. Becker asked whether the soldier or I had any complaints. It was so like an orderly officer asking the same question in the mess that I was only just able to suppress that insane urge to giggle.

I replied, 'No complaints, thank you.'

The soldier asked, 'Got a fag, then, mate?'

Becker handed each of us a last East German cigarette and lit them both. Reaching beneath the table, he took out my duffle bag and handed it to me. For God-knows-what reason – sheer nerves, probably – I said that I might come back to the GDR for a holiday. Looking surprised, Becker said, 'That would not be a good idea, Mr Boyd.'

We puffed on our cigarettes, nobody speaking, until the door opened at 11.40 and a tall and distinguished woman in the blue uniform of the

International Red Cross entered, introduced herself and shook hands with the three of us at the table. 'Twenty minutes to go,' she said brightly to me. 'I like to be early.'

Becker tried to engage her in a conversation designed to elicit some approving comment on the GDR or its government. Each time, this astute and charming lady, whose name I never memorised, found a diplomatic way of answering a slightly different question, never using the expression 'German Democratic Republic'. Without giving him a single quotable quote, she chattered on while the clock slowly ticked away the seconds to the agreed handover time. All Becker's leading questions were parried with her innocent queries. One sticks in my mind, 'Do you drink tea in Eastern Germany? Really? How very interesting. I thought you drank coffee.' It was hard to contain the hysterical laughter that bubbled up inside me when I realised from her oh-so-English small talk that she had to be genuine. And if she was, then so was everything else. I was finding it hard to breathe when she stood up, saying, 'Gosh, look at the time. It's noon. We must be off.' She made it sound as though apologising to the vicar that we had to leave the village fête a little early.

I shook hands with Becker, who had been pretty decent really, and said unnecessarily, 'Perhaps we'll meet again.'

He shook his head. 'Good luck, Mr Boyd!'

The two heavies stood aside as the three British citizens left the office, walking down several steps and continuing in silence across the no-man's-land between GDR territory and the British-occupied zone of Germany. On the British side of the crossing point designated Checkpoint Able, the Red Cross lady was there one moment and gone the next, before I could thank her; or perhaps I was too slow to realise exactly what was going on.[2]

The two MPs greeted my companion in misfortune, 'You again, you bastard?'

He grinned at me, 'Told ya they'd be pleased to see me.'

My reception committee consisted of two men in civilian clothes. The taller one said, 'Welcome back, Boyd. I'm Flight Lieutenant Burton, commanding the RAF Police in Gatow.' The other man – grey complexion, grey coat and grey suit – did not introduce himself, so I mentally named him Mr Grey.

I looked back across the border. There was no traffic passing, just Becker getting into the ancient Mercedes with the two heavies. He stood for a moment with the rear door open, looking across no-man's-land in my direction. There was something in his body language like a dog watching its master leave without it, and I felt sorry for him, stuck in the greyness of the GDR.

Dealing, as Becker presumably did, with numerous Westerners who had fallen into the clutches of the Stasi, did he lie awake at night after they went home, wondering what marvels they were seeing, what food they were eating, what clothes they could buy in the shops, what freedoms they took for granted – in short, what life was like in a democracy?

Burton took the wheel of a civilian car parked behind the British border control buildings, Mr Grey sitting beside him, with me on the rear seat. 'It must feel odd, to be free again,' Burton said as we drove off, an RAF Police Land Rover trailing us for the first few miles. Receiving no reply, he asked, 'You all right, Boyd?'

I mumbled something about being out of practice at talking, which was true. But in addition, my head was spinning. After six weeks of living at prison pace, I had not yet fully taken in the helter-skelter events of that morning. Yet, suddenly I remembered that the film in my camera had included some shots of the airfield at Gatow. It would not have taken long for anyone to work out that they had been taken from the platform of the Funkturm, which would have given the lie to my statement to Becker that I was not permitted to go out onto the airfield. More to the point, if Burton had the film developed and printed, and found those pictures, he could charge me with … I didn't know what. Surreptitiously, I loosened the cord at the neck of the duffle bag. The film had been taken out of the camera and developed in some Stasi laboratory, to check I had not photographed anything in the GDR. It was coiled up with an elastic band round it. Avoiding any sudden movement that might attract attention in the rear-view mirror, I reeled through the thirty-six exposures to find the shots of the airfield and snapped the film fore and aft of them. Replacing the two longer pieces of film in the duffle bag, I dropped it on the floor. The problem was, how to get rid of the seven incriminating frames.

'Do you mind if I open the window a little?' I asked. 'I'm feeling a bit travel sick.'

'Go ahead,' said Burton.

Winding down the window a few inches and palming the strip of film, I slipped it out through the gap at the top of the glass, checking that the Land Rover behind us did not stop. What else had I forgotten? I could not think.

We stopped for lunch at a wayside beer garden-cum-restaurant, where the first taste of beer was almost inebriating. Asked what I wanted to eat, I was so unaccustomed to making any decisions that I could not think of an answer, but nodded when Burton suggested Bratwürst with potato salad. The fresh air, sunlight, simple tasty food and a glass of beer were like a dream. But my senses were still on high alert, which is why I could hear everything Mr Grey and Burton were saying to each other in low voices at the other end of the table.

'The last time I was on a border like this,' Mr Grey said, 'was Czechoslovakia in '48.'

'The Communist coup d'état?' Burton queried. 'What was your role?'

'Waiting for one of our chaps, who did *not* make a home run.'

'What happened to him?'

'We never caught hide nor hair of him again.'

A few minutes later, after a couple of glances in my direction to check whether I was listening to them – I probably appeared still in a daze – Mr Grey mentioned Prime Minister Harold Macmillan being warned by the security services that Nikita Khrushchev, who frequently referred to West Berlin as 'an intolerable espionage swamp', might 'play one of his tricks' by having me marched into the General Assembly of the United Nations towards the end of April to confess my role in Berlin. That explained the visit of the three KGB officers, which could have led to my fifteen minutes of fame or infamy!

The urge to laugh hysterically which had possessed me earlier was gone. I wanted to cry with sheer relief.

17

A MEETING WITH THE BOSS

Our destination that afternoon was the British occupation forces' HQ at Rheindahlen – a four-hour drive from Helmstedt – where I was dropped off at a billet occupied by several RAF Police NCOs, one of whom was to be my escort/guard for the next few days. He was pleasant enough, and took me to the mess for the evening meal. Perhaps he had done this sort of work before, because he asked no questions. One of the other men in the billet seemed curious to know why I was under guard, yet being treated with kid gloves, so I told him I had been ill.

That night, I slept and woke up several times, unsure whether the events at the border were a dream. In the morning, the billet, the other men getting washed, shaved and putting on uniform, seemed at first an illusion. Reality set in when my escort walked me after breakfast to an office where Burton began debriefing me. There was no sign of the civilian who had been at Helmstedt with him. I had decided in the car the previous day to tell the same story that I had told in Potsdam: that I must have fallen asleep on the train and failed to get off at Spandau. Burton uttered no comments, just made notes, but gave away, perhaps deliberately, that he spoke Russian. When he described Becker as being '*nemnozhko krasny*', meaning 'a little bit Red', I could not understand what he meant. Although aware that I should have understood the words, my mind was blank in that direction, and never fully recovered all the linguistic knowledge I had deliberately dumped in the cell.

That afternoon, Burton put the critical question to me, 'Have you at any time divulged details of your work in Gatow while you were in the GDR?'

'I don't think so,' I replied.

'What does that mean?'

'Well, the first few days are very clear, and the last ones too, but in the middle everything is rather hazy. So I cannot be 100 per cent whether I was drugged and questioned without my knowing.'

Agreeing that it was quite possible, he continued the very low-key debriefing. On the following day my escort drove me to a British Military Hospital somewhere on the base – which was as large as many towns – where I was given an electroencephalogram test and was afterwards interviewed by a wing commander, who was a psychiatrist tasked with assessing my mental state. His rank was equivalent to a lieutenant colonel in the army, but the atmosphere was so relaxed that I wondered whether I had been given some sedative. After looking at the printout of the encephalogram test, the wing commander asked whether I had had one before, and did not seem surprised when I told him that I had undergone a similar test at Great Ormond Street Hospital in childhood because I suffered from petit mal, a mild form of epilepsy. He nodded, as though that made sense to him, and asked whether I still suffered from blackouts.

Since this seemed like a sort of alibi for my story of not getting off the train at Spandau, I said I wasn't sure, but if I did, they were of very short duration. At the end of the two-hour interview, I asked what conclusion he had reached. He looked at the test printout and at me. 'I'm going to say that you are within the bounds of normality, but it's possible you had a blackout on the train.'

During the debriefing I had gone over everything with Burton, including my thought that I had been sent back because of the Russians' visit to the Lindenhotel. Much later, it occurred to me that the Hauptverwaltung Aufklärung of the Stasi, which was its external espionage arm, must have had several spies in place at Gatow. So, an alternative explanation was that it did not want a security clamp-down there to jeopardise their sources if I disappeared into the maw of the KGB with scandalous results. One can never be sure, in what CIA counter-espionage boss James Jesus Angleton called 'the wilderness of mirrors'.

I had been handed over at Helmstedt on Tuesday, 12 May. Three days later, on the Friday morning, I was driven to Burton's office, where he told me that the top brass had arranged for me to be flown back to Britain that day, so I could spend the Whitsun weekend with my family. Quite apart from the total absence of Russian from my brain, I was still having trouble with reality. If he had said they were going to shoot me, I don't think I would have protested.

He reminded me that everything I had learned or experienced in the past two years was still subject to the Official Secrets Act. This was somewhat super-fluous, since former Coders Special William Miller and Paul Thomson had published in the May 1958 edition of the Oxford University student magazine *Isis*, which was devoted to nuclear disarmament, a two-page account of naval intercept activities, for which they were prosecuted under Section 2 of the Official Secrets Act 1911. Tried by no less eminent a lawyer than Lord Chief Justice Goddard, they were sent to prison by him for three months. Since it was obvious that the Soviets had their own SIGINT operators – one of whom I later met in London – unlike the two coders, I had no qualms of conscience about our snooping in Berlin. So, there was no intention on my part to talk out of turn. I asked what to say if journalists asked me questions.

'They won't,' Burton reassured me. 'A D Notice has been issued to all the broadcasters and newspaper editors asking them not to mention your little escapade or your return to Britain.'

At the time of my unsought adventure, most people believed that there was no political censorship in Britain, but the system introduced in 1912 (and still in force today) enabled Admiral George Thompson, then secretary of the D Notice Committee, to drop a note to the press and broadcasting organisations 'requesting' no mention be made of my youthful misadventure. Thus, few people had any idea that I had been through the Stasi mill and was fortunate enough to come out in one piece. Nor did I volunteer the information, even to my own family, because during the debriefing I had been told not to talk about it to anyone until I had grandchildren. Now I do have that blessing. In any case, the collapse of the USSR makes it all irrelevant today – or does it?

Burton also hazarded that my relatively gentle treatment in the GDR might indicate that I would be regarded by 'the other side' as a sleeper, liable to be contacted at some future time and asked to perform a favour in return. 'In that event, ring this number and ask for Mr Shepherd,' he said, handing me a slip of paper with a number on the Shepherds Bush exchange in London.

Driven to an RAF airfield, I was escorted by a uniformed RAF Police sergeant onto the tarmac, where a twelve-seater twin-engine passenger plane was standing with propellers idling, ready for take-off. A seat had been kept for me. The aircraft was full of officers in uniform with plenty of rings on their sleeves, who looked at me as though I had the plague. I was the only passenger in civvies – rather scruffy ones at that, after living in them for six weeks. We taxied out to the runway and took off. Like most people in those days, I had never flown. It seemed hysterically funny that my only flight during the two years with the *air* force was a reward for being in an enemy prison, but this was neither the time nor the place to laugh. Looking out of the windows, it was worrying to see how much the wings flexed when we dropped in what was then called 'an air pocket'. More worrying was a squadron leader who made his way back from the front of the cabin, bent down and growled at me, 'I know who you are, J/T Boyd. I don't know what you're doing on this aircraft, but they kicked my best chum off to give you his seat. So, when we land at Brize Norton, I'm going to see that you are arrested and put behind bars, where you deserve to be.'

After our landing at Brize Norton air base, he hurried over to the terminal buildings to do his worst, from which I was rescued by an RAF Police NCO with a waiting car, in which he drove me off the base to Oxford railway station. Equipped with a rail warrant, I caught the first train to London and travelled on to Canterbury, finishing my journey home from the prison in Potsdam sitting on the No. 4 Canterbury–Whitstable bus on which I had travelled to school each day. My parents told me that two men from the security services, dressed in civilian clothes, had visited the house late one evening for the purpose of checking whether I had deserted and come home. My mother started to ask me questions about my misadventure until stopped by my father saying, 'He's not allowed to talk about it'.

On the following Tuesday, I used the other rail warrant I had been given at Brize Norton to travel to Gloucester for my formal demobilisation. Identifying myself at the RAF office on the station, I was not directed onto a service bus, filling up with other men being demobilised, but driven by a police corporal in a Land Rover to RAF Innsworth, north of the city. While other men being demobbed stood in queues for two days to hand back their uniforms and kit – I had no idea where mine was – I was whisked to the front of each queue by a flight sergeant nearing retirement age, and signed off the strength of the RAF, item by item, in less than two hours. The last call was at the pay office, where I was amazed to be given my back pay for the time I had been in prison at Potsdam. Although it did not amount to much, I felt quite rich.

The flight sergeant drove me back to Gloucester railway station, where he seemed to find his last task difficult, given that I was a mere junior technician. Finally he managed to say, 'Air Chief Marshal Sir Hubert Patch, the Air Member for Personnel [AMP], would *like* to have a chat with you, if you are free next Monday at midday.'

Sir Hubert's wish to meet me was correctly phrased, since I was officially no longer a serving member of the RAF under his command, but the subtlety escaped me because I was still in a daze. I said that was okay. The flight sergeant handed me two warrants: one for the journey back to Canterbury and a return warrant for the trip to London on the following Monday.

In those days, the RAF was governed by the Air Council, of which Sir Hubert Patch was the member responsible for personnel matters – a job he had started only a few weeks previously after a very varied service career. I duly arrived early for my appointment at Adastral House in Theobalds Road, Holborn, trying to look reasonably smart, wearing a blue pinstripe suit I had bought when working in the bank, which fitted me badly because I had lost a lot of weight in prison. Stepping out of the lift on the top floor, I was greeted by a short and very dapper man in a three-piece suit, who gushed, 'I'm the PA to the AMP'. I had no idea what he was talking about. After waiting ten minutes or so in his office, I was shown into the great man's sanctum. Although he was in uniform, the office and its furnishing resembled a London gentlemen's club: carpets on the floor, some paintings on the walls, a drinks cupboard and deep, brown leather armchairs in the conversation area.

A large and imposing man, Sir Hubert did not shake hands, but told me to sit in one of the armchairs, seated himself opposite and said, 'Right, Boyd, you've got ten minutes to tell me about it'. His face has faded from my memory, but his piercing gaze has not. He was not the sort of man I would have chosen to lie to, but I could not change the story I had told Burton in Rheindahlen. After not interrupting me for several minutes, he fired several questions at me about the KGB officers' visit to the prison, before telling me that opinions in the top hierarchy of the RAF were divided between the majority who considered I should be put away in Colchester Military Prison for a couple of years for contravening the Official Secrets Act by being in a Warsaw Pact country while doing top-secret work and … the others. Fortunately, he was one of the latter and the decision of what to do with me was his alone.

'I believe you did not give anything away,' Sir Hubert said. 'You were damned stupid to get yourself in that mess, but you came out of it well. What are you doing now, looking for a job?'

'Yes, sir.'

'You're an unusual young man. I'll give you a reference.'

And that was my last contact with the RAF as a National Serviceman. On the train back to Canterbury, I thought it was kind of Sir Hubert to make the offer of a reference – which certainly contributed to getting my first job in the film business. Then I thought, it was probably a way of keeping tabs on me for a while. Who knows?

18

GOING BACK

In 2006, seventeen years after the collapse of the misnamed German Democratic Republic, Florian Henckel von Donnersmarck's award-winning film *Das Leben der Anderen – Other People's Lives –* was acclaimed as a shatteringly accurate portrayal of the four decades of grey and depressing life imposed on the citizens of the GDR by the SED hierarchy.

The film's central character is Georg Dreyman, a highly privileged playwright. After the fall of the Berlin Wall, he goes to the organisation responsible for the Stasi archives, known as die Bundesbeauftragte der Unterlagen des Staatssicherheitsministeriums der ehemaligen Deutschen Demokratischen Republik – the Federal Commissioner for the Archives of the Ministry of State Security of the Former German Democratic Republic – understandably abbreviated to BStU. The fall of the Wall spurred hundreds of Stasi officers, terrified that they would be murdered by their erstwhile victims, to shred thousands of files containing details of their own activities, those of their unpaid informers in the GDR and secret agents of both sexes in the West. Officers even took incriminating files home and then to their allotments in the suburbs, where they burned them on bonfires to the amusement of other allotment holders, who knew exactly what they were up to. Although thousands more of the surveillance files covering most of the population of the GDR were destroyed by delirious crowds invading the Stasi's offices and prisons after the fall of the Wall, Dreyman is hoping to find his file intact, and discover in it clues to why his Stasi-blackmailed lover killed herself.

In the BStU reading room, a clerk wheels in a trolley piled high with 2in-thick document folders.

'Which one is mine?' Dreyman asks.

The clerk replies, 'They all are.'

And so are all the folders piled high on two more trolleys. That brief scene, lasting only a few seconds, is a measure of the relentless spying on *everyone* in Erich Mielke's police state, for Dreyman had belonged to the elite stratum of society, being a personal friend of Margot Honecker, whose husband Erich ruled the GDR. Even that had not saved Dreyman from the Stasi's scrutiny.

Watching Donnersmarck's gripping film gave me the idea of requesting my own Stasi file from the BStU. It was not simple. First, I had to prove my identity with a photo of my passport and give dates and place of arrest and date of release from Stasi custody. Also required was the name of the prison where I had been held. There had been three interrogation prisons in Potsdam, a city of about 100,000 population in 1959. All had been used by the NKVD/KGB and then handed over to the Stasi in 1952. A Google Earth map helped eliminate two of them, since the brief glimpses of its surroundings indicated that the one where I had been held was in a street in the centre of town and the others were further out. Having proved who I was, I was warned that there was a two-year waiting list, with priority given to people involved in law cases to do with inheritance or for something they had done during the existence of the GDR. It was also necessary to collect the file in person from the BStU's office in Berlin-Mitte, since its policy was not to send any document by mail, but only hand it to the person concerned.

In 2008, when it was decided to hold the fiftieth annual reunion dinner of Intake 35 in Berlin, I re-contacted the BStU and pressed some buttons to jump the queue. Knowing the respect with which many older Germans still treat old comrades' associations, I informed the BStU that I was coming to Berlin at the end of September for a reunion with my former service comrades, but that my age and poor health made it unlikely I could ever make the journey to Berlin again.

The ploy succeeded, perhaps conjuring up visions in the BStU offices on Karl-Liebknecht Strasse of us elderly former linguists sitting at a long table in a beer cellar, singing the old marching songs and beating time with our *Biersteine* on the table. The reunion was to be, like all the others, a rather more sober affair. Although it is true we had learned Russian marching songs at JSSL, we had done precious little actual marching and never while singing. The trick worked: the two-year waiting list dissolved in seconds and

I received the reply that I could come whenever it suited me during my stay in Berlin for the old comrades' reunion. I duly arrived at the BStU offices in the Karl-Liebknecht Strasse and was greeted by a charming 40-something female official named Hilde Altmann,[1] who stayed with me while I read through the file.[2] The reason for this was that many people are anguished when they read in their file that they were betrayed to the Stasi by a spouse, a child or a parent acting as an *inoffizielle Mitarbeiter*. At another table in the reading room was an elderly man in tears, reading his file. He kept mumbling, '*Wir waren nur arme Menschen*' – 'We were just poor people'. Yet poverty was no protection from the Stasi.

I had only myself to blame for falling into the Stasi's clutches, so there was nothing traumatic in my file. After reading it, I asked Hilde whether she had lived '*im Westen oder im Osten*' during the long years when Germany was divided, before 9 November 1989.

'*Im Osten*,' she replied. Her husband had lost his job after being blacklisted by the Stasi for reasons never divulged to him.

After Honecker was deposed shortly before the fall of the Wall, his replacement Egon Krenz promised an easing of travel restrictions for GDR citizens. The border with Czechoslovakia was reopened and an amnesty announced for all who had left. Confusing announcements were made – that all travel restrictions would be either eased or abolished by Christmas. On 9 November, SED spokesman Günther Schabowski was asked at a press conference being televised live when the travel restrictions would be finally withdrawn. He answered, 'Immediately'.[3] This was not the Politburo's decision. The official explanation of Schabowski's lapse is that he had not been adequately briefed on the details of the new policy; it is equally possible that, as a lifetime Communist and dedicated SED functionary, his brain could not absorb the details of the new heresy, so that he panicked in front of the cameras and said the first word that came into his head.

Within minutes, GDR citizens were streaming towards the Wall, expecting the barriers to be open. The border guards had heard over the radio or seen on television Schabowski's press conference. Lacking any contrary instructions, they allowed the first trickle to pass though. With West Berlin television cameras covering the incredible scene and their images being seen in East Berlin, tens of thousands more rushed to the Wall and walked freely into the West.

On that night, Hilde had not seen the televised press conference and knew nothing of Schabowski's faux pas, but received a telephone call from her mother-in-law, whose apartment overlooked a checkpoint, saying, 'Hilde, you must come here right away'.

Incredulous, the two women watched out of the window as the crowds streamed through into West Berlin. Expecting some violent reaction from the border guards or Volkspolizei riot police, they were too frightened to go down and join them. When I asked her what she had felt then, Hilde's face lit up with remembered joy. 'It was,' she said, 'the most wonderful night of my life.'

Afterwards, I took a taxi with my wife to visit the former headquarters of the Ministerium für Staatssicherheit on the Normannenstrasse. This boring office building, resembling the head office of a large company, is now a museum which tourists can visit for a profoundly depressing tour of exhibits, including the interrogation chairs and their scent pads stored in sealed glass jars, concealed cameras in briefcases, handbags, magazines and even buttons, sound recording devices for bugging conversations at a distance, telephone taps, machines to steam open letters and re-seal them without leaving any trace – in short, all the apparatus of a one-party police state, whose government was determined to control millions of people by perpetual terror. Missing, of course, are the lists of the hundreds of thousands of *inoffizielle Mitarbeiter*, who spied on their spouses, parents, children, pupils, students, neighbours and colleagues.

Upstairs on the first floor is a *Tigerkäfig* – a cell with no walls, just bars where prisoners could be chained for as long as their captors wished, out of reach of the toilet. A few steps away from there is a map showing all the Stasi regional offices in the GDR, like a measles rash everywhere. Another map shows all the hundreds of prisons – resembling perhaps more closely the buboes on the skin of a plague victim – where hundreds of thousands of innocent people suffered for years to atone for the crimes they had not committed.

A few paces from there, but in another world, is a massive office with private telephone switchboard beside the imposing desk, carpets on the parquet floor, a large conference table and comfortable conversation area. This office for a mid-twentieth-century tycoon was the centre of Mielke's spider's web, from which the terror he created radiated out in all directions. Visitors wanting to know whether he was punished after the end of the GDR are amazed to learn that he was not. He was, however, prosecuted for two murders he had committed in 1931 and sentenced to six years in jail under conditions far less uncomfortable than in his own prisons, and released in 1995 to live out his last five years on a state pension in a retirement home situated between his former office and the Hohenschönhausen interrogation prison in which he had personally abused so many victims.

On the following day I visited the prison in Potsdam where I had spent those six terrifying weeks in 1959. It is now a memorial to the 4,000 people sentenced there to forcible sterilisation in the Nazi era and the thousands imprisoned there by the Gestapo prior to 1945, by the KGB from 1945 to 1952 and by the Stasi from 1952 to 1989. Fortunately, during my incarceration I was unaware of the appalling suffering of many inmates because I was held in a separate wing as a pawn to be traded in due course for some political advantage. Had I then known how brutally the Stasi treated citizens of the GDR undergoing interrogation elsewhere in the prison, I should have been too terrified to argue about anything.

My visit coincided with a national holiday called *der Tag der deutschen Einheit*, although it is not the precise anniversary of the political reunification of the two Germanys in 1990. On that day in 2008, the courtroom where I had sat staring at Lenin was in use as a lecture hall, where a paid guide was talking an audience of some fifty men, women and children through a history of its use by the Stasi, before taking them on a tour of the prison. Since her commentary was hardly news to me, I slipped out halfway and turned left to walk ahead of the crowd along the well-remembered corridor past the interrogation room where I had tried to form a relationship with Becker, past the corner where I had seen the unexplained Eisenstein lookalike, past the rows and rows of cells to the far end of the building. Cell No. 20 had been converted into a broom cupboard, for which it had about the right dimensions. According to the man in the ticket office, it was one of the few cells still kept locked, but only to stop visitors nicking the cleaning materials. On this visit I could also walk up the metal stairs to the three upper floors and take in the photo cell, where new arrivals were photographed for their prison IDs, the punishment cells and cells with two bunks where up to eight people had been locked up. How did they sleep? That was part of the humiliation and a way of weakening them to give in and admit the 'crimes' of which they were accused. In British terms, they were all on remand, awaiting trial, but in the Stasi's eyes they were already guilty.

Information boards for the visitors spelled out how, under the KGB during 1945–52, conditions were the same as in Soviet prisons:

In each 7-square-meter cell usually four or five prisoners were crammed, sometimes more. The cellars and the chapel were also used as cells. To prevent prisoners seeing out, windows were fitted with wooden shutters. In the corridors, carpeting deadened the sound of the guards' footsteps.

The only toilet facility was a pail in each cell. The light was kept on, day and night. In the winter the cells were hardly heated. During the long months of interrogation hearings, both men and women had to wear the clothing in which they had been arrested. No personal hygiene or clothes washing was allowed. In the cells were fleas, lice and bedbugs.

Food consisted of dry bread in the morning with a thin watery soup at midday and in the evening. The resulting malnutrition caused most prisoners swiftly to succumb to illness, for which no medical treatment or care was available.

Interrogations were conducted by Soviet officers in the courtroom block, usually at night. Sleeping in the day was forbidden. Any resistance was punished. During interrogation, prisoners had to confess the crimes of which they were accused. No legal advice was permitted. Normal methods of the interrogating officers included threats, beatings and torture. Many prisoners suffered painful 'special treatment'. Some died from this treatment; others committed suicide.

Another board recounted the Stasi's use of the prison:

Between 1952 and 1989, a total of 5,705 men and 952 women[4] were incarcerated in the Lindenstrasse prison. Two thirds of them were less than thirty years old. Most prisoners were from the working class. Only 1 per cent of prisoners were accused of crimes such as robbery and murder. [Most such cases were investigated by the Criminal Police, so] these were cases where the Stasi suspected treasonable motives behind the criminal acts.

About 10 per cent of prisoners were accused of industrial sabotage, anti-social behaviour and desertion. The other 90 per cent were political prisoners: 2,000 were accused of trying to flee the GDR; more than 1,600 of espionage; 900 of 'agitation'.

This information is extracted from prisoners' details in the Stasi local office, now held in the archives of the BStU Potsdam. Details for the year 1989 are incomplete.

Statistics compiled by the Stasi and now held in the BStU archives indicate that my stay *im Lindenhotel* was during a quiet period, when *only* seventy-two men and thirteen women were held there for weeks and months without any kind of trial, compared with the peak after the uprising on 17 June 1953, when 519 men and fifty-three women were crammed into the limited number of cells.

I ended my worrying unaccompanied tour of the prison on all four floors by walking across the large exercise yard where I had whistled 'God Save the Queen'. It is now the setting for a commemorative sculpture entitled '*Opfer*', or 'Victim', which has been erected beside the three brick-built 'extra punishment' cells where naked prisoners were hosed down with cold water in sub-zero winter weather and left with no clothes, blankets or other protection. How long could someone, already malnourished, survive that ill-treatment?

Outside the courtroom/lecture hall, I met an elegant and attractive woman who introduced herself as Gabriele Schnell. She had heard that a foreign former prisoner was visiting and wanted to meet me in her role as an unpaid volunteer who collects and preserves the accounts of former prisoners and has published several volumes of them, to remind people of all the suffering. I promised to send her an account of my six weeks in solitary, and gave her one of my books. In return for this, she presented me with her book, *'Das Lindenhotel': Berichte aus dem Potsdamer Geheimdienstgefängnis – Reports from the Secret Service Prison in Potsdam*. This chilling collection of *Häftlingsberichte* – personal accounts by detainees – makes my time in the prison seem like a mild inconvenience.

19

OTHER PRISONERS' LIVES

My weeks in the Lindenstrasse prison were endured in varying stages of terror, occasionally going well into the red, as on the day when the Russians came. But I was fortunate in being a foreigner who managed to convince the Stasi that I was an idiot, and was therefore saved from the customary treatment for arrested citizens of the GDR or foreigners caught in espionage operations. The following cases give some idea of what they experienced while in the Stasi's clutches, although innocent of any act that would be a crime in a democracy.

Arrested with eight other Potsdam pupils by Soviet NKVD officers on 2 May 1946, 16-year-old high school pupil Peter Runge was interrogated in the Lindenstrasse Prison every night for three months, accused of the crime of wearing a white carnation on May Day. Kept in solitary, he had no way of knowing that he was not alone. On 8 August the verdict of five Russian officers at his military trial was that he was a former member of the Hitler Youth organisation – belonging to which had been obligatory under the Nazi regime for boys of his age – and had worn the white carnation as a protest against the forcible integration of the German Communist and Socialist parties to form the SED.

On 20 September his name was placed on a list of criminals to be transported to the former Nazi concentration camp at Sachsenhausen, where he was confined in a barrack hut containing some 200 other men, many of them ill. Not until 17 January 1950, after three and a half years of detention, was he released after receiving extra rations for a few days to make him

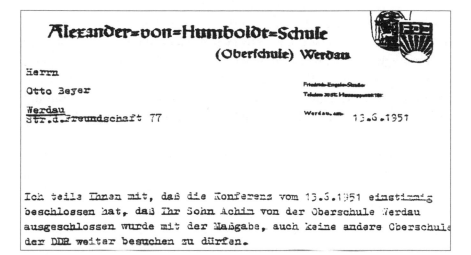

Letter expelling Achim Beyer from every school in the GDR.

look less undernourished, and handed 15 Marks for his railway fare from Sachsenhausen to Potsdam.[1]

Achim Beyer was a secondary school pupil in Werdau, a small town in Saxony. On 13 June 1951 the Alexander von Humboldt Schule wrote to his father informing him that Achim had been expelled 'and would not be admitted to any other school in the GDR'. What the boy had done to 'merit' expulsion is unknown, but in no civilised country would he have been barred from *any* further education. A copy of the expulsion letter is to be seen in the former Stasi HQ building on Normannenstrasse in Berlin.

This was a punishment often used against children and adolescents from religious families, which ensured that they could find no remunerative adult employment in a country where being unemployed was a crime.

Fritz Sperling was the 40-year-old deputy president of the old Kommunistiche Partei Deutschlands (KPD), or German Communist Party, before the Second World War. One of the party faithful who had suffered much during the Hitler regime, he was elected to the executive committee of the SED when it was set up by the Soviet occupation forces in April 1946. After five years' faithful service, he was leaving a hospital in the Soviet sector of Berlin on 26 February 1951, after treatment for a heart condition, when a friend tricked him into getting into a car that drove off and delivered him to Hohenschönhausen Interrogation Prison – the largest in Berlin. As a Moscow-trained Communist who had been imprisoned by the

Nazis pre-war, he had at first no idea that he would be held there for many months. On arrival, he was forced to strip and locked into a cell containing only a rough wooden plank on which to sleep and a latrine bucket. In the daytime he was allowed to sit on the plank bed, but not lie down or lean against the wall. At night, he had to lie with face and arms visible through the spyhole, which meant being unable to cover his chest despite the severe heart trouble.

Given Sperling's standing in the SED, Stasi boss Erich Mielke came in person to order him to confess and 'sacrifice himself for the good of the Party'. Sperling's protests that he had never betrayed the KPD or the SED were unavailing. From February 1951 until December 1952 he was interrogated almost daily by NKVD officers, who deliberately punched him on the ribs over his heart while his hands were cuffed behind his back, so he could not protect himself. Transferred to a freezing cell in one of two punishment prisons at Bautzen, he was again not permitted to lie down in the day, although suffering from severe sleep deprivation.

The Soviet, and later Stasi, warders in Bautzen frequently beat prisoners for no apparent reason. As a form of humiliation, prisoners were not allowed toilet paper or sanitary towels. Extra punishment saw a prisoner placed in *Arrest* – which meant confined in a cage of iron bars with no privacy at all, known as *der Tigerkäfig* (tiger cage). To increase the prisoner's suffering, he or she might also be fettered hand and foot to the bars of the cage for up to three weeks in such a way as to be unable to reach the toilet, and thus be forced to foul him- or herself, afterwards being insulted by the guards as 'a filthy animal'.

Sperling's poor health deteriorated rapidly in prison, leading to a further heart attack in September 1952, after which he was denied medical help for five weeks. Sentenced to seven years' imprisonment as a war criminal, fascist and 'agent for crimes against peace', Sperling was pardoned but not rehabilitated after Khrushchev's denunciation of Stalin's crimes in February 1956. He died two years later at the age of 46 from the aggravation of his heart condition during detention.[2]

Nothing much changed when the three Potsdam interrogation prisons were handed over to the Stasi in 1952. At the age of 16 in 1946, Karl Fricke had seen his father – a teacher and therefore obliged to be a member of the Nazi Party – arrested by NKVD officers. Fricke Senior was condemned to twelve years of forced labour, dying in 1952 in prison from untreated dysentery. Karl grew up to be a journalist living in West Berlin, who made a speciality of articles and radio broadcasts critical of the SED. Aged 25, he considered himself of far too little importance to be at risk of kidnap in April 1955, when he received a telephone call from an occasional source. Since this man had been imprisoned in the Soviet Union for five years pre-war and handed back as a known Communist to the Nazis – as were many others under the German–Soviet Non-Aggression Treaty of 1938 – and then been immediately sent to a Nazi concentration camp, Fricke had no reason to suspect that he was a Stasi agent. Visiting his apartment to borrow a book otherwise unobtainable in the West, Fricke was drugged and recovered consciousness seven hours later in a brightly lit room, surrounded by four or five Stasi officers, who proceeded to insult and swear at him. After twice being beaten up, he was thrown into a basement cell without fresh air or daylight, and left to recover.

Although he had no idea where he was imprisoned, Fricke was to spend 455 days and nights in Hohenschönhausen under threat of a twelve-year sentence if he did not confess. Interrogations in the unnatural and painful position of sitting on his hands every afternoon and from 10 p.m. to 6 a.m., with sleep in the daytime forbidden, left him weak and confused. Suddenly, the interrogations stopped for three months, in what the Stasi called 'leaving the prisoner to stew' as a way of wearing down his or her resistance. Allowed only one piece of toilet paper per day, a lack of elementary hygiene added a severe skin infection to Fricke's suffering. As extra punishment, he was twice locked for several hours into a mini cell no more than 50cm², where he could not sit or change position to relieve the discomfort. In July 1956 Fricke was sentenced in a closed trial by the Supreme Court of the GDR to fifteen years' hard labour, afterwards reduced to four years. He was released when he was bought free by the West German Government in a deal brokered by Vogel during 1959.[3]

At 5 a.m. on Friday, 28 May 1954, 34-year-old Georg Rabach was hauled out of bed and arrested by Stasi officers for the crime of being a Jehovah's Witness. Taken to the Lindenstrasse, he was interrogated until his trial on 21 July, at which he was sentenced to nine years' prison for 'agitation'. Later, he learned that this sentence was mild: a fellow Jehovah's Witness in Leipzig was given a show trial in Berlin and sentenced to fifteen years' imprisonment, of which six entire years were spent locked in the same cell.[4]

Walter Janke was the 32-year-old head of the East Berlin publisher Aufbau. He was arrested in December 1956. Three years after Khrushchev had denounced Stalin's crimes at the XXth Party Congress, Janke was made to strip naked before a huge portrait of the dead Soviet dictator. After his clothes were removed, officers examined inside his mouth, his throat, armpits and his anus. Janke could have done without the distinction of a personal visit from Mielke, who said he was guilty of counter-revolutionary activities, spraying him with spit as he screamed that the Stasi had broken stronger men. The interrogation continued until seven o'clock next morning, when Janke was confronted with an indictment seven pages long. Refusing to sign it, he was held under interrogation in Hohenschönhausen until July 1957.[5]

Dieter Junker was an 18-year-old apprentice arrested while cycling to work at 5.30 a.m. on 14 June 1957 by three men in leather coats travelling in an old BMW. Taken to the Lindenstrasse and ordered to wait in the courtroom – as I was twenty-one months later – he was given to understand that he would be sent home that evening, but was instead locked up at 10 p.m. in a cell so small that the only floor space not taken up by the wooden bunk permitted him to take just two steps. After two days, interrogations began, sometimes twice a day. Given prison clothing with shoes two sizes too large, he tended to stumble when escorted along the corridors, for which the penalty was to be kicked behind the knees each time by the warder, causing him to fall full length. Interrogation switched to nightly sessions, sometimes lasting until morning, after which he was forbidden to sleep during the day. According to a Stasi document dated 14 June, he was being interrogated because his father was accused of espionage, about which he actually knew nothing. After three and a half months' detention under interrogation, on 23 September 1957 Dieter was released.[6]

When she was 38 years old, Waltraud Krüger applied for a legal permit to leave the GDR, which was then itself a crime. On the catch-22 logic that a Communist state was as near heaven as one could get and therefore anyone wanting to leave it was clinically insane, she was forcibly confined in the sick bay of a Stasi interrogation prison, where she was held down by several nurses while a psychiatrist gave her an injection – of what she did not know. Undressed by a nurse, she did not recover consciousness until next morning when the psychiatrist began a course of injections of the anti-epileptic drug Luminal, which had been used to kill people in the Nazi euthanasia programme. A declaration that she wished to remain in the GDR was placed in front of her. When she refused to sign, the Stasi doctor and nurses tied her down on the bed and put in a drip.

Soon, she was no longer aware if it was day or night, and things got worse with another drip in her leg veins that was excruciatingly painful. When the needles were pulled out, she screamed, hardly able to recognise her swollen discoloured legs. With all the drugs, she could often not understand the interrogators' questions, yet refused to sign anything. Forcibly fed after losing much weight, she was informed that her daughter Anita had also been arrested, having 'confessed' that she had written several letters to the West – which, with the Stasi's rigorous postal censorship, would have been impossible. Waltraud was also told her husband had been arrested.

The interrogator warned her that in Western Germany sick people like her received neither medical care nor money.

'In which case,' she retorted, with a last spark of defiance, 'why don't all the people in the West come and live in the GDR?'[7]

What had happened to Waltraud's daughter, Anita, was almost unbelievable. From the several hundred thousand IMs – the Stasi's unpaid informers – a young man had been tasked by his controller to seduce and marry her in an effort to convince Anita to stay in the GDR.

Now a shadow of the woman who had been arrested, Waltraud eventually agreed to end her hunger strike if given assurances that nothing would happen to her husband and daughter. Although she now ate, the Luminal injections continued. On 14 July, after five weeks of this treatment, Waltraud was given back her clothes and fumbled her way in great pain to the main doors, where she was placed on a stretcher and lifted into an ambulance for an unknown destination. Seated beside her was her equally mistreated husband, but they were forbidden to speak to or touch each other. In January 1981 the family was given permission to leave the GDR legally with Anita, after their liberty had been purchased by the Bundesrepublik.[8]

Heide-Marie H. was a 32-year-old photographer, arrested on 3 December 1978 when a frontier guard ordered a West German friend of hers to open the boot of his car at the Drewitz border crossing to the south of Potsdam. Ordered to climb out, Heide-Marie was told to strip and given a body search before being put into a car with blacked-out windows and driven away. With no idea where she was, she was placed in a cell in the Lindenstrasse Prison in the middle of the night, her clothes and wristwatch having been confiscated. Potsdam being her home town, she recognised the street outside through the window at her first interrogation.

On 8 January she was ordered to write down the names of those involved in her escape attempt and other friends, which she refused to do, although one of her friends was an unpaid informer, code-named Rita, who did provide several names. Because her present residence was in Leipzig, Heide-

Marie was placed in an 80cm^2 cell in a prison van after four days, without being told where it was going, and then locked up with another woman in a Stasi prison in Leipzig.

The interrogations were irregular, leading to her appearance in court on 2 March 1979. That morning, she 'made up' her eyes with charcoal from some used matches as eyeshadow, to give herself just a little confidence. The hearing was in camera. She was awarded twenty-two months' hard labour and transported in a prison van to a yard in Zwickau Prison, where she and many other women were bathed in the glare of floodlights and ordered to undress, to be sprayed for lice before being driven to another prison at Hoheneck. There, the women were given different prison clothes, including a triangular headscarf to be worn at all times. The labour of the prisoners was effected within the prison walls, where several state factories had set up production lines. Here Heide-Marie was horrified to find that most of her fellow prisoners had been incarcerated for ten years, during which they were used as virtually cost-free labour, doing everything from tailoring clothing to assembling electrical motors. She was released from prison exactly one year from the date of her arrest, after a humiliating strip search, in which her body cavities were explored by a guard to make sure she had not secreted anything in them.[9]

In its role as '*Schild und Schwert der Partei*' – 'Sword and shield of the Party' – the Stasi had the distinction of actually creating a whole new class of criminals. All youths and young adults were considered guilty in principle of *staatsfeindliche Aktivitäten* – treasonable activity – for merely dreaming of sharing in the fun of their coevals in Western Germany by being able to freely buy chewing gum, Levi jeans and tee-shirts, or to hear and dance to Western music. To cure them of this last 'crime', at a national conference on dance music in 1959 at Lauchammer, the SED announced the invention of its very own *Lipsi-Schritt* – a far more decorous ballroom dance in 6/4 time, which was expected to wean the youth of the GDR away from 'the undesirable capitalist influence' of the current Western dance known as 'the twist'. Like most of the other heavy-handed SED imitations of Western fashions, it was a laughable failure, which did not stop Becker from dangling before me the prospect of dancing the night away to *Lipsi-Schritt* tunes on a collective farm in Saxony with the promised pretty blonde girlfriend.

Young people were arrested, interrogated at length and given prison terms for 'crimes' such as flying paper aeroplanes in a crowded street with sarcastic messages written on them, for writing to a human rights organisation in the

West, for building an improvised radio transmitter that broadcast Western pop music in a radius of a few hundred metres on a summer beach, for going to a jazz club, for wearing punk clothing or having body piercings or long hair. The list was endless, and one cannot even say the penalties were overly severe because in a democracy these acts were not crimes at all.

In June 1961, before the Wall was built, 20-year-old Johannes Weber met a girlfriend who lived in West Berlin and regularly went there to visit her. His last visit was on Saturday, 12 August. The following day he learned that visits to West Berlin were now impossible for GDR citizens because the Wall was being built and access was already barred by barbed-wire fences, guarded by soldiers ordered to shoot anyone attempting an illicit border crossing. Johannes was innocent enough to criticise the Wall that prevented him seeing his girlfriend again on a birthday card sent to his father that was intercepted by the Stasi. Arrested on 23 August, his clothes and possessions taken away after the humiliating body search, he was interrogated for eight hours without a break or a drink, accused that he had '*in hetzerische Form ... die Regierung der Deutschen Demokratischen Republik zur Absicherung der Grenze nach West-Berlin stellen genommen und diese Massnahmen verleundet*'. In plain English, he was accused of criminally slandering the government of the GDR by criticising the construction of the Wall.

By now terrified, Johannes pleaded that he had only wanted to be able to meet his new girlfriend again, and had no political motives in what he had written on the birthday card. On 25 August he was condemned to eighteen months' detention in a high-security political prison at Bautzen, known to its prisoners as 'the yellow misery'. After his eventual release, he found that friends and colleagues all treated him as a criminal because they were unable to believe that his only 'crime' was an imprudent sentence written on a birthday card. It took forty years before he was declared innocent by a rehabilitation court after German reunification, but by then his life had been ruined.[10]

After the rapid erection of the Berlin Wall on 13–14 August 1961, 27-year-old Sigrid Paul was no longer able to visit her baby son in a West Berlin clinic where, for the last five months, he had been receiving medical treatment not available in 'democratic' East Berlin. After nine weeks of rejected requests to visit him again, she was allowed to go and hold him in her arms for a brief time, but then had to decide whether to stay with him in the West or return home to her husband. Believing that the boy would soon be better and able to come home, she returned to East Berlin but was not allowed to visit her child again. After eighteen months of anguishing about the baby's progress, both parents were invited by some students to join their escape via a tunnel being dug by them underneath the Wall.

On 28 February 1963 she was on the way to work when two men forced her into a black car with such violence that a bus driver stopped his vehicle for her to jump on, until he realised the 'kidnappers' were Stasi operatives. Delivered to the interrogation facility at Berlin-Lichtenberg with her watch, handbag, belt and shoelaces removed, Sigrid was questioned all day and all night about the students by a team of men in relays, who did not believe that she knew hardly anything about the arrangements. After twenty-two hours without rest, she was placed in an unlit cell inside a closed prison van.

After a long drive, she was let out in another prison, where she was made to strip naked and bend over in a crouch so that a grinning guard could check nothing was hidden in any bodily orifice. Given coarse men's prison underclothes, she was taken to an unheated cell and told her name was now 93/2 – 93 for the cell and 2 for the number of her plank bed in it. Spied on regularly through the Judas hole, she had no idea where she was. With little or no sleep, after two weeks she was so exhausted and desperate for news of her family that she signed everything put in front of her. That conditions could be even worse, she understood in May 1964 when ordered to clean away blood and excrement in a cell of which the walls were lined with thick rubber, where they locked up prisoners who had gone out of their minds.

Tried in July 1963 with no prior knowledge of the charge, she was sentenced to four years in prison for 'conspiracy to flee the Republic'. The worst thing was the unending yearning to see her son. How did he look? How big was he? Could he talk yet? What did his voice sound like? Had his teeth grown? What did he know about his parents? Did he even understand what a father and mother were?[11]

Interned from March to August 1963 and from October 1963 to October 1964, Sigrid was put in a prison van very early one morning. The guard would not say where she was going, but at Berlin-Rummelsburg she was kept waiting in a filthy cell without bunk or stool for about twelve hours. Given back her things which had been taken away at the time of arrest, she found herself outside on the street, apparently free. By an administrative oversight in the BStU after the demise of the GDR, Sigrid eventually learned the name of her main interrogator and tracked him down, but he refused to talk to her.[12]

Christian Kohler grew up in a Catholic family living in Lausitz near the Polish border. Because of the family's religion, he was not allowed to sit the

Abitur school-leaving examination. Instead, he became a nursing auxiliary and began work in 1974 at the age of 20 in a nursing home, where he was hard-working and popular to the point of being promoted to deputy head of the institution one year later. Because the work was arranged in shifts, he often had two or three days off together and would take advantage of this to hitchhike around the country. In punishment for this, his all-important identity card was replaced by a temporary one, which was an immediate signal to any official that he was 'politically unreliable' and therefore to be treated harshly. When he had to apply for permission to travel to Communist Poland on a walking tour in 1976, a police check revealed a compass and maps in his pack, resulting in his arrest.

Advised during interrogation that someone like him had no future in the GDR, Christian applied formally to the Interior Ministry to be allowed to emigrate to Western Germany on the grounds that he did not feel a full citizen of the GDR. The request was refused. He protested. Having been told that his case would be dealt with in a few weeks, he was instead informed that he was being investigated by the Criminal Police for refusing, as a conscientious objector, to perform military service. His case notes made a mention of his 'faded trousers' and 'hair down to his collar', proving that he was a 'State-hostile person'. In August 1979, Christian was forcibly conscripted into the Nazionale Volksarmee, where he refused to handle weapons. The army proving more humane than the Stasi, he was ruled to be unsuitable for military service and released.

While working for the German Red Cross in Potsdam, he joined the Babelsberg Peace Council, taking part in a silent protest against rearmament with fifteen other members. Regarding their arrest by the Stasi as unconstitutional, he went on hunger strike in the interrogation prison until his health was in danger. Protests at his detention by church members and politicians in West Germany were ignored after he was sentenced to eight months' imprisonment in closed court on 22 March 1984. Ironically, his liberty having been purchased by the Bundesregierung Government, Christian was expelled to West Berlin on 18 May 1984, but wanted only to continue his struggle for human rights in the GDR. He was unable to return there, and on 4 April 1985 he committed suicide at the age of 30.[13]

In 1983 Markus Riemann was the 22-year-old son of a pastor. Under the discrimination against religious households he was not allowed to attend university, and had to scrape a living as a gardener in Havelstadt, a suburb of Potsdam where he shared a rundown flat with his girlfriend. He and a group of environmentally conscious friends were worried at the nationwide pollution caused by the GDR's mining and burning of lignite. Since it was normal for every church to have a fir tree on display at Christmas, one of them suggested making people aware of the damage to the GDR's forests from acid rain by displaying in church some conifers poisoned by industrial pollution. Five of the friends spent the night in the house of a local pastor while collecting the dead trees, not knowing that the pastor's telephone line was permanently tapped by the Stasi. When they stepped off the train in Potsdam, each holding a brown tree 1.5m high, they were arrested and interrogated all night long on the grounds that exposing environmental damage was 'hostile to government policy'.

The whole impressive might of the MfS swung into action, with a team of officers searching their homes and seizing such 'evidence' as Markus' record collection, an empty loose-leaf binder, an address list, photographs, letters and even empty envelopes, and his copy of the New Testament. Several pastors went to the Town Hall to protest against the arrest of the five youngsters and told the official in charge of 'Church affairs' that at the Midnight Mass their congregations would be told not just the familiar Christmas story, but also about the arrests. The 'Potsdam Five' were then released, with the dead trees confiscated as 'evidence'. The story did not end there, however, because fines were imposed on Markus and two other boys totalling 2,000 Marks for 'failing to respect public order in that on 17 December … they conspired to display five environmentally damaged trees in Potsdam churches'.[14]

From the beginning of the 1980s the technical college for training nurses and social workers in Potsdam was kept under particularly close scrutiny by the Stasi, although the students were just ordinary kids seeking low-level professional qualifications. In September 1985, 20-year-old Carola Dessow began her studies there, perhaps because her estranged mother was a nurse in Leipzig. Carola already had some black marks in her Stasi file, which recorded that she had frequented folk clubs where songs touched on freedom and peace. Unknown to the students, the college deputy principal and Carola's class teacher were both IMs, who reported to their case officers that she sometimes voiced opinions which did not conform with official policy; also, she failed to read the SED newspaper Neues Deutschland every day; she refused to learn to shoot an air gun in sport lessons and was also overheard alleging that the GDR was not a democracy.

A full-scale Stasi operation was mounted to trap this dissident student nurse, on the grounds that she might 'infect' the student mass. Another girl student was enlisted to report the names of her friends. One morning, while all the students were in the classrooms, a fake fire brigade inspection of the accommodation block was conducted, the 'firemen' being Department XX Stasi officers in borrowed uniforms. A janitor, who was also an IM, opened the door of Carola's room with a pass key. Photographs were made of handwritten and typewritten papers found among her possessions, including a draft 'letter to the government of the GDR'.

At that time when mechanical typewriters were used, the Stasi had an entire department that held specimens of text produced by every typewriter in the GDR, each of which had minor irregularities, such as a particular letter microscopically higher or lower than the others. Thus, any typewritten document could swiftly be traced to its author, making him or her immediately liable to a prison sentence of not less than two years under sections 219 and 220 of 'the GDR Law Book'. Carola could have been arrested there and then, but the Stasi's perpetual paranoia dictated a necessity to catch all her 'fellow conspirators'. An additional IM was therefore ordered to join her circle of friends. The Stasi captain in Department XX who was in charge of the operation noted in his 'Appreciation of the Working Plan' in August 1986 that the *several* IMs watching Carola had been unsuccessful in 'penetrating her circle'. Checks were run on all Carola's friends in Leipzig, Potsdam and elsewhere, in case any of them had requested an exit visa.

In January, another clandestine search was made of Carola's room. The incriminating papers were still in her locker with new ones on the subject of Chernobyl. The deputy principal of the school was 'informed of this by a student' and a four-page plan of operation drawn up. At 7.30 a.m. on 22 January a student IM telephoned the Stasi district office to confirm that Carola was in class. The janitor and an MfS senior lieutenant entered her room and checked that the incriminating papers were still there.

Twenty minutes later the deputy principal ordered Carola to her room, where the papers were 'discovered' and notification was immediately sent to the Ministry for Health Education, the SED district office in Potsdam and the college administration. Carola was taken in for questioning and, on the following day, a report on her case marked 'Urgent' was sent by teleprinter to the head office of Department XX. But this was accompanied by the appalling news that the student body and most of the teachers argued that Carola should neither be suspended from the college, nor arrested, but allowed 'voluntarily' to leave.

Hers was the comparative good fortune to be found out near the end of the Stasi's reign of terror, and thus avoid serving several years in prison, which would earlier have been the case. On 19 March 1987 she packed her remaining belongings and left the college, officially denied *any* further education.[15]

Hundreds of thousands of citizens suffered like the people detailed above, but few spoke after release about their suffering for one good reason: not to make things worse for those left behind. Everyday life in the GDR grew increasingly controlled, the armies of IMs grew more intrusive and the penalties for 'crimes' that would not have been criminal in a democracy grew more vicious – and often, quite simply mad. Even after *Die Wende* in 1989, most East Germans were so glad to have the long nightmare ended at last that few outsiders learned what it had really been like.

Being locked up in solitary confinement is always depressing. Being a prisoner in the Lindenstrasse *Untersuchungsgefängnis* was also terrifying. I had unwittingly put my head in a noose and, had I appreciated then just a fraction of the power wielded by my jailers, I might have given up all hope. Sometimes ignorance is, if not bliss, at least a considerable mercy.

20

EX BELLO FRIGIDO IN PACEM

The first member of Intake 35 to use Russian in civilian life was Harvey May. Demobbed in April 1959 with impeccable timing, he started work the following month at British European Airways' (BEA) Cromwell Road terminal. Three days later, BEA began London–Moscow services on 14 May using Vickers Viscount 806 aircraft, flying via Copenhagen. At the end of the summer, Harvey saw an internal advertisement for Russian-speakers because, although English was used internationally for communications between air traffic control organisations and aircraft in their airspace, the USSR insisted on using Russian. This meant that each BEA flight to Moscow had to carry an interpreter. Harvey became one of three on-board radio operators, translating communications both ways between the British flight crews and Russian air traffic control.

At the beginning of April 1960 this service was taken over by Comet 4Bs. Most of BEA's captains at the time were ex-RAF types. Approaching Moscow-Vnukovo Airport one night, Harvey received a weather report of light snow showers and translated this. The captain, sporting a splendid Second World War handlebar moustache, turned to Harvey and said, 'I say, old boy, ask the chaps down there what is the braking coefficient. There's a good chap.' Harvey asked the question several times in his best Russian, but received no reply from the ground, possibly because this was classified information – or perhaps no Soviet pilot bothered with such details, which would explain the number of crashed aircraft visible just off the runways of Soviet airports in those times. Happily, the Comet did not become one of them.

Also in 1960, Ingrid married Dave Manley and had to face considerable hostility in her adopted country from everyone she met, except for Dave's immediate circle of friends. To just about anyone else in Britain, fifteen years after the end of the war the word 'German' still equalled 'Nazi'. Austerity Britain was not much fun at the time anyway: rationing had not ended until 1954; the ranges of clothing in the shops were limited and the British sizing system in imperial measurements was incomprehensible to a continental person accustomed to the logical metric system. Apart from in the delicatessens of a few large cities, most of the food she was accustomed to eating back home was unobtainable and she found the rows of identical houses festooned with television aerials very depressing.

Despite her traumatic childhood and the several interruptions in her education, Ingrid had fair schoolgirl English, but found shopping extremely difficult in those days when there was only a handful of supermarkets in Britain. Elsewhere, it was necessary not only to visit several different specialised stores to fulfil a shopping list, but also to ask the shop assistants for the articles she wanted *and* express the quantity needed in the confusing avoirdupois system of pounds and ounces because very little food was then available pre-packed.

As a schoolboy, I had earned pocket money by delivering customers' grocery orders on an errand boy's bike and served in a grocer's shop, cutting butter from a huge slab to the desired weight and patting it into a tidy brick shape on greaseproof paper for the customer, also weighing sugar from a sack into blue paper bags. Even keeping track of the housekeeping money in British currency, with farthings, ha'pennies, 12 pennies to a shilling and 20 shillings to a pound after the simplicity of 100 pfennigs to the mark, was not easy, but Ingrid stuck it out, believing that Dave's languages and her background meant they would settle in Germany or another European country with their children. But things did not work out like that. Dave travelled and worked in several countries throughout their married life, leaving her and eventually a son and daughter stranded in Britain.

Of all the linguists in Intake 35, John Anderson undoubtedly made the most diverse use of his time at JSSL Crail, teaching Russian in British schools from 1966–72 and setting up Russian language O level teaching at five comprehensive schools in Bradford, with the keener pupils able to study for A levels at Bradford University. In 1985 he spent a month in Leningrad/ St Petersburg on an exchange visit with the Herzen Institute. In 1990 he led the first home-to-home exchange with the city of Tver. In 1997 he taught

English to Russian student teachers in Minsk, numbering among his students a former KGB agent in Angola. In Addis Ababa during 2002, Russian was his only common language with the chief librarian of Ethiopia's Civil Service College. Yet his most bizarre use of the time at JSSL was teaching English to a female Ukrainian tram driver stranded in Botswana after her African husband deserted her. He also takes Russian groups on tours of York Minster.

John Toothill also travelled to Russia while a student at university, after checking with the RAF for permission and being warned never to be alone and not to take a camera with him.

Brian Howe took his wife to Russia in 1985, visiting Moscow, Leningrad and Sochi.

Apart from those intrepid travellers, most of my other comrades-in-tongues said that, at the very least, having Russian on their CVs certainly made them stand out from the other candidates when applying for jobs.

Returning from Cyprus a year after the rest of us had been demobbed, Duncan Brewer was contacted by the RAF with the offer of re-enlisting as a flight sergeant posted to Canberra jets flying 'ferret' missions across the Iron Curtain. He politely declined, later working for a while as a translator for a construction company building plastics factories in Krasnoyarsk and Mogilev and also being employed as consultant on the production of the 1981 Warren Beatty film *Reds*, set in post-Revolution Russia.

During my stay in Berlin, I had intended to apply after demobilisation for a post at GCHQ near Cheltenham, working on the analysis of SIGINT from the out-stations like Gatow. However, by the time I was demobbed, the recently introduced procedure of positive vetting sensibly barred from working at GCHQ anyone who had been in a Warsaw Pact prison, like me, and possibly been brainwashed there. Instead, I first became a very incompetent statistician for the Rank Organisation World Film Distribution Division, my most impressive performance being to lose £5,000 in the Philippines. But I had fallen on my feet, as the saying then went, for this was at exactly the time the company was attempting to open up the Soviet market. As the only Russian-speaker in a wide radius, I was soon in demand to translate incoming correspondence and contracts and check the translated subtitles the State film company, Sovexportfilm, was going to use in the Russian versions of films like *The Importance of Being Earnest* – translated as *Kak vazhno byt' seryoznym*, meaning literally 'How important it is to become serious' – poor Oscar!

Since Moscow would not pay hard currency, but only barter one Soviet film for one British film, I also attended screenings of those offered in exchange as an interpreter for the top brass. This was less demanding than it might seem, since after the first couple of reels¹ the executive vetting the film, who was suffering from overexposure to colleagues in Hollywood, would say something like, 'Okay, Doug, *stumm*. I don't need to know any more. If it's a movie, it moves.' In this way, I came to the attention of the top managers, resulting in promotion to the post of polyglot international sales rep. It was fun flying around Western Europe with my own expense account to negotiate contracts for licences in films, also dealing in London with people from Film Polski, Čescoslovensky Filmexport, Hungarofilm and even Sovexportfilm. Television was just beginning to erode cinema audiences, so the British production companies formed a watchdog organisation wittily christened FIDO. The Film Industry Defence Organisation was dedicated to *never* selling British films to television. But money was money – whether marks, francs, lire or whatever – so I became the deniable junior executive selling television rights in Europe while the management swore this would never happen in Britain.

Life was very enjoyable for a young man in his early twenties but palled when one year turned out to be pretty much like the last. In January 1965, while Sir Winston Churchill lay dying just a few miles away, I was interviewed in a darkened room on the sixth floor of Television Centre in Shepherds Bush for the job of heading the BBC Eurovision office in London. My background in negotiating contracts with European television stations and my knowledge of several languages made me a likely candidate for the job but, in the Corporation's civil service way of doing these things, my interview was by a board of three individuals, whom I could not see clearly in the gloom. Drawn from the Appointments Department, the chairman of the board sat at the large and imposing desk, while in easy chairs upholstered in Thai silk sat another man from Establishment and a gaunt middle-aged woman. A large television set in the corner of the room was relaying the latest minute-by-minute news of Sir Winston's decline. The woman in the gloom apologised, saying that she had to know the second something happened on that front.

It did seem an odd sort of job interview, but I murmured, 'Of course'.

The man at the desk asked a few straightforward questions about my CV and motives for wanting to join the Beeb, as did the other man, but it swiftly became obvious that the mysterious woman was senior to them. Her questions were far more probing. Unused to the BBC way of doing things, I might well have been disconcerted, had I not just enjoyed a fairly alcoholic expense account lunch with a friend, the afterglow of which enabled me to relax and go with the flow. After forty-five minutes, including long pauses while the trio listened to the television commentary, leaving me alone with my thoughts, I was dismissed and told that I should be informed by mail of the outcome. According to former linguist Geoffrey Elliott, there was a 'bluff brigadier who lurked in Broadcasting House in the Cold War years secretly vetting job applicants for the BBC'.[2]

Possibly because the Brig delayed the decision on my job application for obvious reasons, in the Corporation's typically Olympian fashion it took until 1 April before I reported for my first day of work. Informed by her secretary that the formidable woman, whose face I had been unable to see clearly at the interview, was to be my boss, I learned that she was in Italy, spending the week at the Florence fashion shows to buy her new summer wardrobe. Since nobody else had any idea that I had been appointed, let alone what I was supposed to be doing, I was introduced to my staff of five women who plainly were unimpressed and rather hostile, and told to go away and come back a week later, when the boss lady was back. For the second time in my life, I felt like a real April Fool.

Once I had my feet under the desk, my previous experience in dealing with European television organisations and my knowledge of languages led to professional contacts with satellite state officials who continued my education in the history of their countries' relationship with the 'bear next door'. During the Cold War, they were routinely debriefed by their KGB-controlled secret police on their return home and some were full-time intelligence officers working under commercial cover. This could have been awkward. It never was, so there was no need to call the mysterious telephone number and 'ask for Mr Shepherd'. Many a pleasurable evening was spent with these colleagues from behind the Iron Curtain, drinking their wine, vodka and *slivovitz* and eating their national delicacies in smoky restaurants filled with the smells and the sounds of their homelands – folk music and voices arguing – while their émigré compatriots planned revanchist counter-revolution over *shashlik* and *slivovitz* at the other tables. Some became good friends – perhaps because my unsought learning curve in Potsdam gave me some understanding of, and sympathy for, their situation, spied on by the KGB clones imposed on their countries by Moscow. Thus, one way and another, my training at JSSL Crail enabled me to experience the Cold War from both sides.

At the end of my debriefing in Rheindahlen, I had been warned never to travel behind the Iron Curtain, at risk of being rearrested by the KGB or one of its clones. Yet, during my years as a television producer/director[3] with the BBC in Manchester I did take a camera crew for a week's filming in Bulgaria, then still behind the Iron Curtain, and came safely home despite betraying my knowledge of Russian to the Bulgarian Television 'liaison producer' – i.e. spy attached to watch our every move – and persuading a pretty, bikini-clad blonde Russian girl to appear in one brief scene on the beach at Slunchev Bryag to accompany the words 'sail on, silver girl' in the Simon and Garfunkel hit 'Bridge over Troubled Water'. She was understandably shy, but the real problem was having to negotiate permission for this in Russian with the formidable female Party member in charge of the factory group to which the blonde girl belonged.

Most importantly, the Russian I acquired at JSSL has enabled me to research in Eastern Europe and plunder Russian Internet sites, archives and publications for accounts of personal experiences while writing four books published by The History Press. *The Kremlin Conspiracy* (published 2010 by Ian Allen and 2014 by The History Press and also in Czech, Polish, Estonian, Brazilian Portuguese and Mongolian editions) is a history of 2,000 years of Russian expansionism, of which the first seed was sown all those years ago in the classroom of Nikolai Ivanovich Kravchenko at Crail. *The Other First World War* (The History Press, published 2014) is the relatively little-documented and often hard to believe history of the appalling suffering in the several Russian theatres of the First World War, misleadingly called in English 'the Eastern Front' – a war known even in Russia as '*zabytaya voina*' – the forgotten war. *Daughters of the KGB* (published by The History Press in 2015 and also in Czech and Brazilian Portuguese editions) is a history of the KGB clone secret police services imposed on the countries of Central and Eastern Europe by Stalin after 1945, to terrorise and control their populations and to spy on the Western democracies. And then there's this book …

So, thank you, Nikolai Ivanovich and my other teachers at JSSL! *Bolshoe spasibo vam i moyim drugim uchitelim*!

POSTSCRIPT

When the last National Service linguists left Gatow, they were replaced by regular servicemen, who tended to be older, having practised other, more airman-like, trades before undergoing language training. Many of them were married with wives and children. Although the British zone of Western Germany and sector of Berlin were regarded as a 'home posting' with no overseas allowance added to pay, this also meant that married quarters had to be at least as good as in the UK. These regular linguists claim to have had a more responsible attitude to their work than the National Servicemen, but one thing that did not change was the attitude of this new breed of linguists to service 'bull'. Using their shift work and the rigours of the job, they did not attend parades or perform other boring station duties. They managed not to even participate in the occasional all-hands-on-deck exercises when all other British troops in Berlin practised repelling an invasion by Russian and East German units based just across the border. As found after German reunification, the original Warsaw Pact plan for invading the Western sectors of Berlin was to occupy them all within 24 hours of H-hour. In 1988 the plan was changed to blocking all access to the western sectors and starving the occupants out.

The linguists' refusal to play soldiers' games created friction with the other servicemen in Gatow, who did have to run about with guns for twenty-four hours on such exercises and took their revenge by referring to the linguists as 'the fairies'. The term 'servicemen' is used because the regular Russian, Polish, Czech and German linguists included 'brown jobs', i.e. army linguists wearing Pay Corps insignia, perhaps as camouflage to deceive the enemy, and civilians wearing uniform who had been temporarily detached from GCHQ in Cheltenham.

At some time in 1962 this heterogeneous bunch was removed from its hated accommodation in an uncomfortable block designated 'Hanbury', whose location remains a mystery to the author, and they were accommodated more congenially in specially built offices inside Hangar 4, adjacent to the control tower and headquarters building on the airfield itself, where two 100ft towers topped by radomes to conceal and protect the aerials inside were built and still proclaim the activity carried on in the hangar. Since the border was only 200 metres distant, the NVA built a tower close to their side of the fence, from which to observe through binoculars the comings and goings of linguists at the start and end of their shifts in Hangar 4. To prove that Westerners could also handle bricks and mortar, a wall was hastily erected to prevent the East Germans photographing linguists, although one wonders why they did not simply use a door on the back of the Hangar, where they would have been invisible to watchers across the border.

Shortly after the move, the German, Czech and Polish linguists, plus some of the Russian interceptors moved again to a draughty, ill-heated temporary wooden hut on the top of the Teufelsberg, reached by a 30-minute bus ride. Despite the traditional military moving about, the regulars seem to have had a better grasp of where they fitted in the RAF and army scheme of things, which had never bothered their National Service predecessors. No National Serviceman can recall what unit we belonged to, but the regulars' accounts are larded with references to, e.g. 5 Signals Wing assimilating 29 Signals Unit', etc. By October 1972 all the linguists were working in custom-built accommodation on the Teufelsberg that provided air-conditioning, rest rooms and on-site catering. To the delight of the men working there, their new communications receivers had been purchased from American suppliers and were considerably more efficient than the equipment they had left behind in Gatow. Throughout the Seventies and early Eighties, this SIGINT base was improved and expanded – a process that ground to a halt after the fall of the Wall in October 1989.[1]

In 1968 linguist SIGINT in the British zone had ceased as RAF bases were handed over to the Bundesrepublik's Luftwaffe, but operations in Berlin continued right through until 1996. This was partly because the 'Two plus Four Agreement' established at the eponymous talks of May 1990 and attended by the four occupying powers, the GDR and the Bundesrepublik, provided for the Western Allies to keep garrisons in Berlin until the departure of Russian forces from Eastern Germany, which lasted for another four years.

FURTHER READING IN ENGLISH

Boyd, D., *The Kremlin Conspiracy* (Stroud: The History Press, 2010).

Boyd, D., *The Other First World War* (Stroud: The History Press, 2014).

Boyd, D., *Daughters of the KGB* (Stroud: The History Press, 2015).

Cash, T., and M. Gerrard, *The Coder Special Archive* (Surbiton: Hodgson, 2012).

Elliott, G., and H. Shukman, *Secret Classrooms* (London: St Ermin's Press, 2002).

Footit, H., and S. Tobia, *War Talk: Foreign Languages and the British War Effort in Europe 1940–47.* (London: Palgrave Macmillan, 2013)

Funder, A., *Stasiland* (London: Granta, 2003).

Glees, A., *The Stasi Files* (London: Free Press, 2003).

Hooper, D., *Official Secrets* (London: Coronet, 1987).

Hunt, R.C., G.L. Russell & K.G.A. Scott, *Mandarin Blue – RAF Chinese Linguists in the Cold War* (Oxford: Hurusco Books, 2008).

Johnson, B.S., *All Bull* (London: Quartet, 1973).

McKay, S., *The Secret Listeners* (London: Aurum, 2012).

Macrakis, K., *Seduced by Secrets* (Cambridge University Press, 2008).

Thorne, T., *Brasso, Blanco and Bull* (London: Constable and Robinson, 2000).

Woodhead, L., *My Life as a Spy* (London: Pan, 2006).

PLACES TO VISIT

(Check days/times of visiting and admission prices.)

Bautzen II (infamous former Stasi prison for convicted prisoners, now a memorial), Bautzen, Saxony.

Crail Visitor Centre, Crail, Fife, Scotland.

DDR Museum, Karl-Liebknechtstrasse No. 1, Berlin 10178.

Gedenkstätte Hohenschönhausen, Berlin (formerly the main Stasi interrogation prison, now a memorial to the prisoners incarcerated there), Genslerstrasse 66, Berlin 13055.

Gedenkstätte Lindenstrasse, Potsdam (formerly the Nazi/NKVD/Stasi interrogation prison where the author was detained, now a memorial to the prisoners incarcerated there).

Luftwaffe Museum, Gatow (formerly RAF Gatow).

Stasi Museum (formerly Normannenstrasse HQ of the GDR Ministerium für Staatssicherheit), entrance round the corner at Ruschstrasse 103, Berlin 10365.

NOTES AND SOURCES

Foreword
1 Reported in *Private Eye*, May 2016, in the parliamentary feature 'Called to Ordure' on p.9.

Chapter 1
1 For a comprehensive history of Russian expansionism, see D. Boyd, *The Kremlin Conspiracy – 1,000 Years of Russian Expansionism* (Stroud: The History Press, 2014), also available in Polish, Czech, Estonian and Mongolian editions.
2 Quoted in W. Bedell Smith, *Moscow Mission* (London: Heinemann, 1950), p.305.
3 Author's italics.
4 For the full text of the speech, see http://www.historyguide.org/europe/churchill.html.
5 T. Cash & M. Gerrard, *The Coder Special Archive* (Surbiton: Hodgson Press, 2012), p.16.
6 Personal communication to the author.
7 See also Boyd, *Kremlin*, pp.265–8.

Chapter 2
1 Boyd, *Kremlin*, pp.227–34.
2 A more detailed history of the political and military run-up to JSSL may be found in G. Elliott and H. Shukman *Secret Classrooms* (London: St Ermin's Press, 2002), pp.22–38.
3 Two years after leaving the RAF, the author had an operation in St Thomas' Hospital, London. Told by the anaesthetist to count down from ten, he was surprised on regaining consciousness, to be told by the surgeon that when going under, after saying 'six' he switched to Russian: *pyat, chetyrye, tri, dva, odyin.*
4 The title being borrowed from Connie Francis' eponymous 1959 hit.
5 Described in N. Bethell, *The Last Secret* (London: Penguin 1995).
6 Ibid. p.39.

Chapter 3
1 Bethell, p.90.
2 Ibid. p.67.
3 Ibid. p.71.

4 Ibid. p.88.
5 Ibid. pp.74–5.
6 Ibid. p.97.
7 It is now a much-visited tourist attraction, with road signs incongruously indicating the way to 'Scotland's Secret Bunker'.

Chapter 4

1 Thought to be derived from a recruit's confusion of 'sprocket' and 'cog'.
2 From 1921, the Navy, Army & Air Force Institutes (NAAFI) ran canteens and shops for servicemen to buy food, supplementing the free food in the canteen, and sold everything from shoelaces to cigarettes to the men and their dependants. A 'Naafi break' was a fifteen-minute break in normal duties – time for a cigarette and cup of tea.
3 The pull-through is a lead weight on a cord, which drops through the barrel, pulling an oiled cleaning rag after it.

Chapter 5

1 L. Woodhead, *My Life as a Spy* (London: Pan, 2006), p.41.
2 Name changed.
3 Quoted in Elliott and Shukman, p.70.
4 Personal communication with the author.
5 Quoted in Cash and Gerrard, p.106.
6 Ibid. pp.91, 103.
7 Ibid. p.92.
8 Published by The History Press, 2013.

Chapter 6

1 J. Drummond, *Tainted by Experience* (London: Faber & Faber, 2000), p.60.
2 Cash & Gerrard, p.77.
3 Ibid. pp.141–2.

Chapter 7

1 Official Secrets Act of 1911, amended by the Official Secrets Act of 1920.
2 Quoted in Elliott and Shukman, p.16.
3 Ibid. p.152.

Chapter 8

1 Elliott & Shukman, p.189, quoting US espionage expert James Bamford.

Chapter 9

1 Elliott & Shukman, p.173.
2 The East Prussian campaign is covered in Boyd, *The Other First World War* (Stroud: The History Press, 1914), pp.73–82.
3 Elliott & Shukman, p.174.
4 See Boyd, *Voices from the Dark Years*, pp.253–7.
5 For a detailed exposé of this phase of Soviet expansionism, see Boyd, *Daughters of the KGB*.

6 There was no provision at Yalta for a French zone of occupation or a French sector of Berlin. These were carved out of the British zone and sector.

7 Apparently named, but for reasons unknown, after Dame Felicity Hanbury, the first Director of the WAAF and later WRAF.

8 Article by Dave Haysom on RAFling site.

Chapter 10

1 Elliott & Shukman, p.176.

2 Woodhead, p.98.

3 Extract from C.G. Grey, *The Luftwaffe* (London: 1944), quoted in P. Best & A. Gerloff, *Gatow Airfield* (Berlin: Kai Homilius Verlag, 1998).

4 Named for the nationwide British carrier of that name.

Chapter 11

1 Now renamed Theodor-Heuss-Platz after the first Bundespräsident.

2 More on NSA in Berlin in Boyd, *Daughters of the KGB*, pp.82–90.

3 E. Taylor, *The Berlin Wall* (London: Bloomsbury, 2007), p.129.

4 D.E. Murphy, S.A. Kondrashev and G. Bailey, *Battleground Berlin* (New Haven and London: Yale University Press, 1997), p.163.

5 For more detail see Boyd, *Daughters of the KGB*, pp.33–42.

6 Ibid.

Chapter 12

1 Elliott & Shukman, p.181.

Chapter 13

1 Name changed, just in case.

2 It is now sixty years.

3 Quoted with permission from John Fuller's unpublished memoir.

Chapter 15

1 An example is displayed in the Normannenstrasse Museum. The modus operandi was shown in the film *Das Leben der Anderen* (*Other People's Lives*).

Chapter 16

1 A direct translation of the usual way of referring to the Second World War in Russian.

2 For obvious reasons, I always put some money into a Red Cross collecting tin.

Chapter 18

1 Name changed.

2 Stasi file ref: Allg/P 11626/62.

3 Bearden & Risen, pp.395–6.

4 Figures checked against statistics in G. Schnell, *'Das Lindenhotel': Berichte aus dem Potsdamer Geheimdienstgefängnis* (Berlin: Links Verlag, 2007), pp.148–9.

Chapter 19

1 Schnell, *'Das Lindenhotel'*, pp.10–16.
2 *Gefangen in Hohenschönhausen*, ed. H. Knabe (Berlin: List, 2012), pp.147–53.
3 Ibid. pp.166–73.
4 Schnell, *'Das Lindenhotel'*, pp.30–3.
5 W. Janka in Knabe, pp.174–91 (author's italics).
6 Schnell, *'Das Lindenhotel'*, pp.34–9.
7 W. Krüger in Knabe, pp.303–7.
8 Ibid.
9 Schnell, *'Das Lindenhotel'*, pp.83–91.
10 G. Schnell, *Jugend im Visier der Stasi* (Brandenburg: Brandenburgische Landeszentrale für Politische Bildung, 2001), pp.21–2.
11 S. Paul in Knabe, pp.236–47.
12 Ibid.
13 Ibid. pp.23–9.
14 Schnell, *Jugend*, pp.47–50.
15 Ibid. pp.51–7.

Chapter 20

1 A 'reel' conventionally lasts ten minutes.
2 Elliott & Shukman, p.151.
3 The producer is responsible for content and budget control. The director directs the 'talent' and camera operators. In ITV companies, producers and directors belonged to different unions, but in the BBC there was no obligation to be a union member, so the two jobs could be done by the same person.

Postscript

1 Article by Dave Haysom on RAFling site.

INDEX